Beginning Game Development with Python and Pygame

From Novice to Professional

Will McGugan

Apress®

Beginning Game Development with Python and Pygame: From Novice to Professional

Copyright © 2007 by Will McGugan

ISBN-13 (pbk): 978-1-59059-872-6

ISBN-10 (pbk): 1-59059-872-5

Printed and bound in the United States of America 9 8 7 6 5 4 3 2 1

Trademarked names may appear in this book. Rather than use a trademark symbol with every occurrence of a trademarked name, we use the names only in an editorial fashion and to the benefit of the trademark owner, with no intention of infringement of the trademark.

Lead Editor: Jason Gilmore
Technical Reviewer: Richard Jones
Editorial Board: Steve Anglin, Ewan Buckingham, Tony Campbell, Gary Cornell, Jonathan Gennick, Jason Gilmore, Kevin Goff, Jonathan Hassell, Matthew Moodie, Joseph Ottinger, Jeffrey Pepper, Ben Renow-Clarke, Dominic Shakeshaft, Matt Wade, Tom Welsh
Project Manager: Kylie Johnston
Copy Editor: Liz Welch
Assistant Production Director: Kari Brooks-Copony
Production Editor: Kelly Winquist
Compositor: Pat Christenson
Proofreader: Erin Poe
Indexer: Becky Hornyak
Cover Designer: Kurt Krames
Manufacturing Director: Tom Debolski

Distributed to the book trade worldwide by Springer-Verlag New York, Inc., 233 Spring Street, 6th Floor, New York, NY 10013. Phone 1-800-SPRINGER, fax 201-348-4505, e-mail orders-ny@springer-sbm.com, or visit http://www.springeronline.com.

For information on translations, please contact Apress directly at 2855 Telegraph Avenue, Suite 600, Berkeley, CA 94705. Phone 510-549-5930, fax 510-549-5939, e-mail info@apress.com, or visit http://www.apress.com.

The information in this book is distributed on an "as is" basis, without warranty. Although every precaution has been taken in the preparation of this work, neither the author(s) nor Apress shall have any liability to any person or entity with respect to any loss or damage caused or alleged to be caused directly or indirectly by the information contained in this work.

The source code for this book is available to readers at http://www.apress.com in the Source Code/ Download section.

For Maria

Contents at a Glance

Contents

About the Author

WILL McGUGAN is a Scottish software developer who lives and works in North West England. Will has worked on a number of game projects, from self-published shareware games to triple A titles, most recently on MotorStorm, one of the first games released for Sony's PlayStation 3. He has been an enthusiastic user of Python for many years, having written a script to automate source code backup as well as several popular desktop applications and a web site in Python. Will is currently working from home as a contractor and developing a Web 2.0 site with the TurboGears framework in his spare time. When not programming, Will enjoys photography, cycling, and juggling—although not at the same time. For more information on Will's current projects and various musings, visit his web site at www.willmcgugan.com.

About the Technical Reviewer

 **RICHARD JONES** organizes the biannual Python Programming Game Challenge (PyWeek http://www.pyweek.org/) challenge and develops OpenGL applications in Python for a living.

Acknowledgments

I thank the Apress team for giving me the wonderful opportunity to write a book—something that has been my dream for many years. Many thanks to Jason Gilmore, whose enthusiastic response to my proposal and guidance as my editor was much appreciated. I also thank Kylie Johnston for her diligence and hard work. Liz Welch's eagle eye kept this book free from spelling and grammar mistakes. Richard Jones did an excellent job as my technical reviewer and kept this book technically correct—the best kind of correct.

I can't go without thanking my parents, Bill and Audrey, and my sisters, Ruth and Jen, for their unwavering support and encouragement throughout the months of writing. Thanks, Mum and Dad, for buying me the Spectrum 48K computer that put me on this path and for always being there for me.

If I have omitted any names, it is because there are too many people to thank. My claim to be a self-taught engineer is a little dubious because I have learned much from the talented people I have had the good fortune to work with over the years.

Introduction

I have accumulated a large collection of game development books over the years, virtually all of which are an inch or two thicker than this book—even though they cover similar subjects and techniques. The disparity is not because my writing is terse or I use a smaller font—it is because traditional game development tools tend to require a large amount of technical knowledge that the reader must first absorb before building even the simplest of games. Even seasoned game developers find the technical requirements of starting a game to be enough of a barrier that they are less likely to work on game ideas that are unproven or potentially not commercial-worthy. Game development may have become easier over the years, with simplified programming interfaces and more programmers wishing to share their knowledge, but writing a game is still a significant undertaking.

When I discovered Python, it lowered a number of barriers to writing software, because I could work faster and accomplish more with less effort, and when combined with Pygame I could experiment with game ideas and build a complete game from scratch in record time. The beauty of Pygame is that it makes the various tasks in creating a game (setting up a display, drawing to the screen, playing sound, etc.) only as complicated as they need to be—and it turns out that's not particularly complicated at all! Many one-liners in Pygame would take dozens of lines in C++, the traditional tool of game developers.

Although Python and Pygame are superb tools for rapid game development, there is little in the way of books or web tutorials for Python game programmers, who often have no choice but to mentally translate from another language to Python when researching a new topic in game development. This book was conceived to fill that gap and allow the beginner game programmer to get up to speed with Python and learn the fundamentals of game programming without having to first learn C++, C#, Java, or another language first. It was also my opportunity to explain 3D game programming in a way that is accessible to nonmathematicians—something that is not easy to find in other books.

In short, this is the book I would have wanted to have when I started out in game development!

Who This Book Is For

This book is for anyone who has thought about creating a computer game, or wants to learn about the technology behind game development. Although Python is the tool of choice for this book, many of the techniques covered are equally applicable to other languages.

How This Book Is Structured

Beginning Game Development with Python and Pygame is divided into 12 chapters, each of which builds on the previous chapter—with a few notable exceptions. I've structured it so that you can get results quickly and see something on screen, which you may appreciate if you are as impatient as I am. Virtually all the listings are self-contained, and hopefully entertaining, little projects that run independently. Since experimentation is the best way to learn, you are encouraged to play with the sample code and modify it to produce different effects. You can also use any of the code in your own projects—with my blessing!

The first two chapters introduce the Python language in a fairly conversational manner. If you read them with a Python prompt in front of you, you should find you can quickly pick up the language. These two chapters don't make a complete language tutorial, but will cover enough for you to be able to understand the Python code in the book and write some of your own. Occasionally, new syntaxes and language features are introduced in the rest of the book, but I explain them where they are first used. If you are proficient in Python, you can skip straight to Chapter 3.

Chapter 3 is your first introduction to Pygame and covers its history and capabilities. It also explains the basics of setting up a graphical display and handling events, skills that are essential for any game. You will become intimately familiar with the code introduced in this chapter, as it is used in all the sample code for the rest of the book.

Chapter 4 dives straight into creating visuals and the various ways in which you can draw to the screen with Pygame. Chapter 5 explores the techniques that game programmers use to make those images move. You should find the discussion on *time-based movement* to be particularly valuable, as it is essential for any kind of animation in a game.

Chapter 6 tells you all you need to know to interface your game with virtually any gaming device. The sample code in this chapter will have you moving a character around with the keyboard, mouse, and joystick.

Chapter 7 is a little unusual in that it is more self-contained than the others and doesn't depend as much on previous chapters. It covers the subject of artificial intelligence and includes a fully working simulation of an ant's nest, but the techniques I explain in this chapter can be used to add seemingly intelligent characters to any game.

Chapters 8 and 9 are a gentle introduction to working with three-dimensional graphics in Pygame, which is an essential topic since most games have 3D elements these days—even if they are not full 3D games. I explain the math in visual terms that make it easier to grasp, and you should find that it is not as an intimidating a subject as it first appears.

Chapter 10 takes a break from 3D graphics to discuss how to use Pygame to add sound effects and music, and even includes a fully working jukebox application.

The final two chapters build on Chapters 8 and 9 to advance your knowledge of 3D graphics, and explain how to take advantage of the dedicated game hardware on your graphics card. By the end of Chapter 11 you will have enough knowledge to render and manipulate a three-dimensional object on the screen. Chapter 12 explores several techniques you can use to create even more impressive 3D visuals and generate special effects.

In addition to the 12 chapters, there are two appendixes: Appendix A is a reference to the Game Objects library that is used throughout this book, and Appendix B explains how you can package your game and send it to others.

Prerequisites

To run the code in this book, you will need at least version 2.4 of Python and version 1.7.1 of Pygame, which you can download from www.python.org and www.pygame.org, respectively. If you want to run the 3D sample code, you will also need PyOpenGL, which you can download from pyopengl.sourceforge.net. All are free software, and this book contains instructions on how to install them and get started.

Downloading the Code

The source code for this book is available to readers at www.apress.com in the Source Code section of this book's home page. Please feel free to visit the book's home page on the Apress web site and download all the code there. You can also check for errata and find related titles from Apress.

Contacting the Author

I am happy to respond to any questions regarding this book's content and source code. Feel free to e-mail me at will@willmcgugan.com, or alternatively post a comment on my blog: www.willmcgugan.com.

I hope you find this book informative and that you enjoy reading it! If it inspires you to write a game, I would be more than happy to be one of your play-testers.

Introducing Python

The language we are going to use to make games is Python, so called because the original author of the language was a fan of the UK television series *Monty Python*. Python is popular in game development, but it is also used to create everything from applications to web sites. Even NASA and Google rely heavily on Python.

There are plenty of alternative languages that can be used to create games, but I have chosen Python because it has the tendency to take care of the details and leave you—the programmer—to concentrate on solving problems. For our purposes, *solving problems* means displaying game characters on the screen, making them look great, and having them interact with a virtual environment.

This chapter is a friendly introduction to Python; it will get you up to speed with the language so that you can read the sample code and start writing code of your own. If you are familiar with Python, then feel free to skip the first two chapters. Read on if you are completely new to Python or if you would like a refresher course.

To start working with Python, you will first need to install a Python *interpreter* for your computer. There are versions for PC, Linux, and Mac. We will be using version 2.4 of Python, which is not quite the most recent version but is supported by all the code libraries we will be using.

Note By the time this book is published, it is likely that all the libraries used in this book will support a more recent version of Python. You don't have to get the latest version, but if you do want to try out the new features then you can because new versions will run files created for older versions.

Your First Look at Python

The usual way of running Python code is to save it to a file and then *run* it. We will be doing this soon, but for now we are going to use Python in *interactive* mode, which lets us enter code a line at a time and receive immediate feedback. You will find this to be one of Python's strengths. It is an excellent aid to learning the language, but even experienced Python programmers often return to interactive mode to do the odd experiment.

Once you have installed Python on your system, you can run it like any other program. If you have Windows, it is simply a matter of double-clicking the icon or selecting it in the Start menu. For other systems with a command line, just type `python` to launch Python in interactive mode.

When you first run the Python interpreter, you will see something like the following:

```
ActivePython 2.4.3 Build 12 (ActiveState Software Inc.) based on
Python 2.4.3 (#69, Apr 11 2006, 15:32:42) [MSC v.1310 32 bit (Intel)] on win32
Type "help", "copyright", "credits" or "license" for more information.
>>> _
```

The text may vary depending on the version of Python you are running and the platform (Windows, Mac, Linux, etc.) you are running it on. But the important part is the three chevrons (>>>), which is the Python *prompt*—it is your invitation to type in some code, which Python will then attempt to run.

A long-standing tradition in computer language tutorials is that the first program you write displays the text "Hello, World!" on the screen—and who am I to break with tradition! So take a deep breath and type `print 'Hello, World!'` after the prompt. The Python window will now display this on the prompt line:

```
>>> print 'Hello, World!'
```

If you hit the Enter key, Python will run the line of code you just entered, and if all goes well you will see this on the screen:

```
>>> print 'Hello, World!'
Hello, World!
>>> _
```

Python has *executed* your line of code, displayed the result, and given you a new prompt to enter more code. So how exactly does our line of code work? The word `print` is a *statement* that tells Python to print what follows to the screen. Following the `print` statement is a *string*, which is simply a collection of letters and/or digits. Python treats anything between quotes (') as a string. Try entering your own text between the quote marks and you should find that Python will print it to the screen just as before.

Numbers

We will come back to strings later, but for now let's start with the most simple piece of information that Python can work with: numbers. Python is so good at working with numbers that you can use it almost like a calculator. To see it in action, type the following into Python (you don't need to type the prompt, since Python displays it for you):

```
>>> 2+2
```

Take a guess at what Python will make of this line and hit Enter. If you guessed 4, help yourself to a cookie—that is exactly what it does. Python has *evaluated* 2+2, which in Python terms is known as an *expression*, and displayed the result. You can also use – for subtract, * for multiply, and / for divide. These symbols are known as *operators*. You will probably use +, –, *, and / the most. Here are some examples:

```
>>> 10-5
5
>>> 2*4
8
>>> 6/2+1
4
>>> -2+7
5
```

In the real world there is only one kind of number, but computers—and consequently Python—have several ways of representing numbers. The two most commonly used types of number are the *integer* and the *float*. Integers are whole numbers with no decimal point, whereas floats do have a decimal point and can store fractional values. Often it is obvious which one you should use—for instance, if your game has the concept of *lives*, you would use an integer to store them because you are not likely to have half a life or 3.673 lives. Float values are more often used for real-world values that need precision—for example, in a racing game your car may have a speed of 92.4302 miles per hour, which you would store in a float.

So far the numbers you have entered have been integers. To tell Python a number is a float, simply include a decimal point. For example, 5 and 10 are integers, but 5. and 10.0 are floats. Something to watch out for is that if you do math with integers, the result is always an integer and the fractional part is discarded. To see this in action, type the following:

```
>> 3/2
1
```

Relax, Python has not gone crazy—it does understand numbers. The reason you get the result 1 and not 1.5 is because 3 and 2 are integers and the result is also an integer, so Python discards the fractional part of the result. To get the result you would expect, simply make one or both of the numbers a float:

```
>>> 3./2
1.5
>>> 3/2.
1.5
>>> 3./2.
1.5
```

In addition to the basic math there are a number of other things you can do with numbers. Parentheses are used to ensure that something is calculated first; here is an example:

```
>>> 3./2.+1.
2.5
>>> 3./(2.+1.)
1.0
```

The first line calculates 3 divided by 2 first and then adds 1, giving the result 2.5. The second line calculates 2 plus 1 first, and so the result works out as 3 divided by 3, which is 1.

Another operator at your disposal is the *power* operator, which raises a value to a power. For instance, 2 to the power of 3 is the same as 2*2*2. The power operator is ** and works on integers and floats. Here are two examples of the power operator in action:

```
>>> 2**3
8
>>> 3.**4
81.0
```

This would be an opportune time to introduce you to *longs*, which is another type of number Python knows about. Because of the way integers are stored, they have a maximum value and a minimum value. The value varies depending on the computer you are using, but my computer can store integers in the range –2,147,483,648 to 2,147,483,647—which is a little over 4 thousand million possible values!

So integers have a very large range, and you may not even need to store any numbers larger than the maximum or smaller than the minimum, but if you do, Python will automatically replace them with long numbers. A long can store numbers of any size, as long as they can fit in memory! This may not sound like much, but most languages make long numbers very difficult to use. You can recognize long numbers by the L at the end; for example, 8589934592L is a long. Let's create a long by calculating 2 to the power of 100, which is 2*2*2*2…*2 repeated 100 times.

```
>>> 2**100
1267650600228229401496703205376L
```

Now that is a big number! If you are feeling brave, try calculating 2**1000 or even 2**10000 and watch your screen fill up with massive numbers.

Let's introduce you to one more operator before the next section. The *modulus* (%) operator calculates the remainder of a division. For example, 15 modulus 6 is 3, because 6 goes into 15 two times with 3 left over. Let's ask Python to do this for us:

```
>>> 15%6
3
```

With this handful of operators, you now have the ability to calculate anything that can be calculated, whether it is a 15 percent tip on two plates of *fugu-sashi* or the damage done by an orc hitting armor with a +1 axe.

I don't know much about orcs, but let's calculate that tip on two plates of fugu-sashi (raw blowfish, a delicacy in Japan that I hope to try one day). Fugu is quite expensive, anything up to $200, because if it isn't prepared by specially trained chefs, eating it can be fatal! Let's say we find a restaurant in Tokyo that serves a tempting plate of fugu for $100. We can use Python to calculate the tip for us:

```
>>> (100.*2.)*15./100.
30.0
```

This calculates 15 percent of the price of two $100 plates—a $30 tip. Good enough for this restaurant but the numbers will change depending on where we buy our fugu and the quality of the service. We can make this clearer and more flexible by using *variables*. A variable is a label for a value, and when you create a variable you can use it in place of the number itself. In our tip calculation we could have three variables: the price of the fugu, the number of plates, and the tip percentage. To create a variable, type its name followed by an equal sign (=), then the value you want to give it:

```
>>> price = 100.
>>> plates = 2.
>>> tip = 15.
```

Caution Python variables are *case sensitive*, which means that if the variable names are capitalized differently, Python will treat them as being completely unique—which means `Apples`, `APPLES`, and `ApPlEs` are treated as three different variables.

We can now use these three variables in place of numbers. Let's calculate our tip again:

```
>>> (price*plates)*(tip/100.)
30.0
```

This calculates the same value, but now it is a little clearer because we can tell at a glance what the numbers represent. It's also a lot more flexible, because we can change the variables and redo the calculation. Let's say we have fugu for breakfast the following morning, but at a cheaper restaurant ($75 a plate), where the service is not quite as good and only worth a 5 percent tip:

```
>>> price = 75.
>>> tip = 5.
>>> (price*plates)*(tip/100.)
7.5
```

That's a $7.50 tip because the waiter was slow to bring the sake, and I hate to wait for my sake.

Strings

Another piece of information that Python can store is the *string*. A string is a collection of characters (a *character* is a letter, number, symbol, etc.) and can be used to store literally any kind of information. A string could contain an image, a sound file, or even a video, but the most common use for strings is to store text. To enter a string in Python, enclose it in either single quotes (') or double quotes ("). Here are two strings; both contain exactly the same information:

```
"Hello"
'Hello'
```

So why have more than one way of creating a string? Good question; let's say we want to store the sentence I said "hocus pocus" to the wizard in a string. If we put the entire sentence in a string with double quotes, Python has no way of knowing that you want to end the string after the word wizard, and will assume that the string ends at the space after said. Let's try it and see what happens:

```
>>> print "I said "hocus pocus" to the wizard."
Traceback (  File "<interactive input>", line 1
    print "I said "hocus pocus" to the wizard."
                          ^
SyntaxError: invalid syntax
```

Python has *thrown an exception*. More about exceptions later in the book, but for now if you see an exception like this Python is telling you that something is wrong with the code you entered. We can get around the problem of including quotes in strings by using the alternative quote symbol. Let's try the same sentence, but with single quotes (') this time:

```
>>> print 'I said "hocus pocus" to the wizard.'
I said "hocus pocus" to the wizard.
```

Python is quite happy with this, and does not throw an exception this time. This is probably the easiest way around the quote problem, but there are alternatives. If you type a backslash character (\) before a quote, it tells Python that you don't want to end the string here—you just want to include the quote symbol in the string. Here is an example:

```
>>> print "I said \"hocus pocus\" to the wizard."
I said "hocus pocus" to the wizard.
```

This solves the problem in a different way, but the result is the same. At the risk of burdening you with too much information, there is one more way of defining strings: if you begin a string with triple single (''') or triple double quotes ("""), Python knows not to end the string until it reaches another set of the same type of triple quotes. This is useful because text rarely contains three quotes in row. Here's our wizard string again using triple quotes:

```
>>> print """I said "hocus pocus" to the wizard."""
I said "hocus pocus" to the wizard.
```

Concatenating Strings

So now you have several ways of creating strings, but what can you do with them? Just like numbers, strings have operators that can be used to create new strings. If you add two strings together, you get a new string containing the first string with the second string appended to the end. You can add strings with the + operator just like you do with numbers; let's try it:

```
>>> "I love "+"Python!"
'I love Python!'
```

Python has added two strings together and displayed the result. Adding strings together like this is called string *concatenation*. You can concatenate any two strings together, but you can't concatenate a string with a number. Let's try it anyway to see what happens:

```
>>> "high "+5
Traceback (most recent call last):
  File "<interactive input>", line 1, in ?
TypeError: cannot concatenate 'str' and 'int' objects
```

Here we have tried to produce the string 'high 5' by adding the number 5 to a string. This doesn't make sense to Python, and it lets you know by throwing another exception. If you do want to add a number to a string, you have to first convert the number to a string. You can easily create strings from numbers by *constructing* a new string from that number. Here's how you would create our high 5 string.

```
>>> "high "+str(5)
'high 5'
```

This works because str(5) constructs a string from the number 5, which Python will happily concatenate with another string.

You can also use the multiply (*) operator with strings, but you can only multiply strings by integers. Take a guess at what the following line of Python code will do:

```
>>> 'eek! '*10
```

You can see that Python can be quite intuitive; if you multiply a string by 10 it will repeat it 10 times. Strings do not support all mathematical operators such as / and -, because it's not intuitive what they would do. What could "apples"-"oranges" possibly mean?

Parsing Strings

Since a string can be thought of as a collection of characters, it is often useful to be able to refer to parts of it rather than as a whole. Python does this with the index operator, which consists of square brackets [ ], containing the *offset* of the character. The first character is [0], the second is [1], the third is [2], and so forth. Starting at 0 rather than 1 may seem a little odd, but it is a tradition among computer languages, and you will find it actually simplifies things when you write more Python code. Let's see string indexing in action. First we will create a variable containing a string, which we do just like numbers:

```
>>> my_string = 'fugu-sashi'
>>> print my_string
'fugu-sashi'
```

Normally you would give strings a better name, but for this little example we will just call it my_string (the underscore character between my and string is used in place of a space because

Python does not allow spaces in variable names). We can pick out individual letters from the string with the index operator:

```
>>> my_string[0]
'f'
>>> my_string[3]
'u'
```

my_string[0] gives you a string with the first character in fugu-sashi, which is f. The second line gives you the *fourth* character, since the first character is offset 0 and not 1. Try to think of the offset not as the number of the character itself, but as the spaces *between* characters (see Figure 1-1); this will make the indexing a little more intuitive.

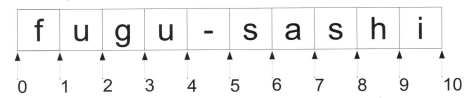

Figure 1-1. *String indexing*

Let's say we want to find the last character in a string. You can see from Figure 1-1 that the last character is "i" at offset 9, but what if we don't know the string ahead of time? We could have extracted the string from a file, or the player may have typed it in a high score table. To find the last offset, we first need to find the length of the string, which we can do with the len *function*. Think of a function as stored Python code; you pass the function some information, which it uses to carry out an action and then return, possibly with new information. This is exactly what len does; we give it a string and it returns the length of that string. Let's try the len function on my_string:

```
>>> len(my_string)
10
```

There are 10 characters in my_string, but we can't use 10 as an offset because it is right at the end of the string. To get the end character, we need the offset before 10, which is simply 9, so we subtract 1. Here's how to use len to find the last character in a string:

```
>>> my_string[len(my_string)-1]
'i'
```

Easy enough, I hope you will agree! But Python can make it even easier for us by using *negative indexing*. If you index with a negative number, Python treats it as an offset from the end of the string, so [-1] is the last character, [-2] is the second-to-last character, and so forth (see Figure 1-2).

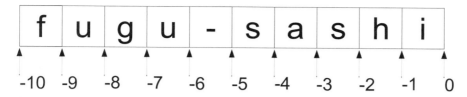

Figure 1-2. *Negative indexing*

We can now find the last character with a little less code:

```
>>> my_string[-1]
'i'
```

Slicing Strings

In addition to extracting individual characters in a string, you can pick out groups of characters by *slicing* strings. Slicing works a lot like indexing, but you use two offsets separated by a colon (:) character. The first offset is where Python should start slicing from; the second offset is where it should stop slicing. Again, think of the offsets as the spaces between the characters, not as the characters themselves.

```
>>> my_string[2:4]
'gu'
>>> my_string[5:10]
'sashi'
```

The first line tells Python to slice between offset 2 and 4. You can see from the diagram that there are two characters between these offsets: g and u. Python returns them as a single string, 'gu'. The second line slices the string between offsets 5 and 10 and returns the string 'sashi'. If you leave out the first offset, Python uses the start of the string; if you leave out the second, it uses the end of the string.

```
>>> my_string[:4]
'fugu'
>>> my_string[5:]
'sashi'
```

Slicing can take one more value that is used as the *step* value. If the step value is 1 or you don't supply it, Python will simply return the slice between the first two offsets. If you slice with a step value of 2, then a string with every second character of the original will be returned. A step of 3 will return every third character, and so on. Here are some examples of this kind of slicing:

```
>>> my_string[::2]
'fg-ah'
>>> my_string[1::3]
'u-s'
```

The first line slices from the beginning to the end of the string (because the first two offsets are omitted), but since the step value is 2, it takes every second character. The second line starts from offset 1 (at u) and slices to the end, taking every third character. The step value in a slice can also be negative, which has an interesting effect. When Python sees a negative step, it reverses the order of the slicing so that it goes down from the second offset to the first. You can use this feature to easily reverse a string:

```
>>> my_string[::-1]
'ihsas-uguf'
>>> my_string[::-2]
'issuu'
```

The first line simply returns a string with the characters in reverse order. Because the step value is negative, it goes from the end of the string to the beginning.

String Methods

Along with these operators, strings have a number of *methods*, which are functions contained *within* Python objects and that carry out some action on them. Python strings contain a number of useful methods to help you work with strings. Here are a just few of them, applied to our fugu string:

```
>>> my_string.upper()
'FUGU-SASHI'
>>> my_string.capitalize()
'Fugu-sashi'
>>> my_string.title()
'Fugu-Sashi'
```

Here we are applying various methods to a string. Each one returns a new string modified in some way. We can see that upper returns a string with all letters converted to uppercase, capitalize returns a new string with the first character converted to a capital, and title returns a new string with the first character of each word converted to a capital. These methods don't require any other information, but the parentheses are still necessary to tell Python to call the function.

■**Note** Python strings are *immutable*, which means that you can't modify a string once created, but you can create new strings from it. In practice you will rarely notice this, because creating new strings is so easy.

Lists and Tuples

Like most languages, Python has ways of storing groups of objects, which is fortunate because a game with only one alien, one bullet, or one weapon would be quite dull! Python objects that store other objects are known as *collections*, and one of the simplest and most often used collection is the list. Let's start by creating an empty list:

```
>>> my_list=[]
```

The square brackets create an empty list, which is then assigned to the variable my_list. To add something to a list you can use the append method, which tacks any Python object you give it onto the end. Let's pretend our list is going to hold our shopping for the week, and add a couple of items:

```
>>> my_list.append('chopsticks')
>>> my_list.append('soy sauce')
```

Here we have added two strings to my_list, but we could just as easily have added any other of Python's objects, including other lists. If you now type my_list at the Python prompt, it will display the contents of it for you:

```
>>> my_list
['chopsticks', 'soy sauce']
```

Here we can see that the two strings are now stored inside the list. We cannot live on chopsticks and soy sauce alone, so let's add a few more items to our shopping list:

```
>>> my_list.append('wasabi')
>>> my_list.append('fugu')
>>> my_list.append('sake')
>>> my_list.append('apple pie')
>>> my_list
['chopsticks', 'soy sauce', 'wasabi', 'fugu', 'sake', 'apple pie']
```

Modifying List Items

Python lists are *mutable*, which means you can change them after they have been created. So as well as retrieving the contents of a list with the index operator, you can change the item at any index by assigning a new item to it. Let's say we specifically want to get *dark* soy sauce; we can change the second item by assigning it a new value with the assignment operator (=):

```
>>> my_list[1]='dark soy sauce'
>>> my_list
['chopsticks', 'dark soy sauce', 'wasabi', 'fugu', 'sake', 'apple pie']
```

Removing List Items

Along with changing items in a list, you can remove items from it. Let's say we want to remove apple pie because it just doesn't seem to fit with the rest of our shopping list. We can do this with the del operator, which will remove any item from our list—in this case, it is the last item, so we will use negative indexing:

```
>>> del my_list[-1]
>>> my_list
['chopsticks', 'dark soy sauce', 'wasabi', 'fugu', 'sake']
```

Lists support a number of operators that work in a similar way to strings. Let's look at slicing and indexing, which you should find very familiar:

```
>>> my_list[2]
'wasabi'
>>> my_list[-1]
'sake'
```

The first line returns the string at offset 2, which is the *third* slot in our shopping list. Just like strings, the first item in a list is always 0. The second line uses negative indexing, and just like strings [-1] returns the last item.

Slicing lists works similar to slicing strings, with the exception that they return a new list rather than a string. Let's slice our shopping list into two portions:

```
>>> my_list[:2]
['chopsticks', 'dark soy sauce']
>>> my_list[2:]
['wasabi', 'fugu', 'sake']
>>>
```

In the first slice we have asked Python to give us all the items from the beginning of the list to offset 2; in the second slice we have asked for everything from offset 2 to the end of the list. List offsets work just like string offsets, so try to think of them as the spaces between objects in the list and not the objects themselves. Therefore, offset 0 is before the first item and offset 1 is after the first item and before the second.

You can also add lists together with the + operator. When you add lists together, it creates a single list containing the items from both lists. Let's create a new list and add it to our shopping list:

```
>>> my_list2 = ['ramen', 'shiitake mushrooms']
>>> my_list += my_list2
>>> my_list
['chopsticks', 'dark soy sauce', 'wasabi', 'fugu', 'sake', 'ramen', ➥
'shiitake mushrooms']
```

The first line creates a new list of strings called my_list2. We have created this second list slightly differently from the first; instead of creating a blank list and adding items to it one at a time, we have created a list with two items already in there. The second line uses the += operator, which is useful shorthand: my_list+=my_list2 is the same as my_list=my_list+my_list2, which has the effect of adding the two lists together and storing the result back in my_list.

List Methods

Along with these operators, lists support a number of methods. Let's use the sort method to sort our shopping list into alphabetical order:

```
>>> my_list.sort()
>>> my_list
['chopsticks', 'dark soy sauce', 'fugu', 'ramen', 'sake', ➡
'shiitake mushrooms', 'wasabi']
```

The sort method sorts the contents of the list. The order depends on the contents of the list, but for a list of strings the sort is in alphabetical order.

You will notice that Python doesn't print anything after the call to sort; this is because the sort does not return a sorted list but just sorts the list it was called on. The second line is necessary to ask Python to display the contents of our list.

Let's say we are going shopping and we want to take an item off the list and go looking for it in the supermarket. We can do this with the pop method, which removes an item from the list and returns it:

```
>>> my_list.pop(0)
'chopsticks'
```

We have asked my_list to "pop" the item at offset 0, which is chopsticks. If we now display the contents of the shopping list, we should see that the first item has indeed been removed:

```
>>> my_list
['fugu', 'ramen', 'sake', 'shiitake mushrooms', 'soy sauce', 'wasabi']
```

There are more list methods than we have covered here; see Table 1-1 for more.

Table 1-1. *Methods in Pythons Lists*

Method	Description
append	Appends items to the list
count	Counts the number of times an item occurs in a list
extend	Adds items from another collection
index	Finds the offset of a string
insert	Inserts an item into the list
pop	Removes an item at an offset from the list and returns it
remove	Removes a particular item from a list
reverse	Reverses the list
sort	Sorts the list

Tuples

Another collection we are going to introduce in this section is the *tuple*. Tuples are similar to lists with the exception that they are *immutable*; that is, like strings, once they have been created the contents cannot be changed. Tuples are generally used in preference to lists when the information they contain is tied together in some way—for example, a tuple could represent a phone number and area code because both parts are required to dial. They are created in a similar way to lists, but use parentheses, (), rather than square brackets. Let's create a tuple that stores the phone number of our favorite sushi takeaway:

```
>>> my_tuple=('555', 'EATFUGU')
>>> my_tuple
('555', 'EATFUGU')
```

Here we have created a tuple with two strings containing the area code and number of our fugu takeaway. To prove a tuple is immutable, let's try appending an item to it:

```
>>> my_tuple.append('ramen')
Traceback (most recent call last):
  File "<interactive input>", line 1, in ?
AttributeError: 'tuple' object has no attribute 'append'
```

Python has thrown an AttributeError exception, letting you know that tuples do not support append. You will get similar results if you try to do anything that modifies the tuple. Tuples do support all the indexing and slicing operators, however, because these operators don't modify the tuple.

```
>>> my_tuple[0]
'555'
>>> my_tuple[1]
'EATFUGU'
```

Unpacking

Since tuples are often used to pass around group values, Python gives you a simple way of extracting them called *unpacking*. Let's unpack our tuple into two variables: one for the area code and one for the number.

```
>>> my_tuple=('555', 'EATFUGU')
>>> area_code, number = my_tuple
>>> area_code
'555'
>>> number
'EATFUGU'
```

Here you can see that in a single line, Python has unpacked the two parts of our tuple into two separate values. Unpacking actually works for lists and other Python objects, but you will most often use it with tuples.

Another way to extract the values in a tuple is to convert it into a list. You can do this by constructing a list with the tuple as a parameter—for example, list(my_tuple) will return the list equivalent, which is `['555', 'EATFUGU']`. You can also do the reverse and create a tuple by calling `tuple` on a list— for example, `tuple(['555', 'EATFUGU'])` returns our original tuple.

You will learn the best places to use tuples over lists in the following chapters; for now use the rule of thumb that you should use a tuple if you never need to modify the contents.

■Note Creating a tuple with one or zero items is a little different from lists. This is because Python also uses parentheses to define the priority in mathlike expressions. To define a tuple with just one item, add a comma after the item; to define an empty tuple, just include the comma by itself in parentheses. For example, `('ramen',)` is a tuple with one item, and `(,)` is an empty tuple.

Dictionaries

The final collection type we are going to look at is the *dictionary*. The previous collections we looked at have all been *sequence* collections, because the values are in a sequence from first to last and you access them by their position within the list. Dictionaries are *mapping* collections because they map one piece of information to another. We could use a dictionary to store the prices of our shopping list by mapping the name of the food item to its price. Let's say that fugu costs $100 and ramen costs $5; we can create a dictionary that holds this information as follows:

```
>>> my_dictionary={'ramen': 5.0, 'fugu': 100.0}
```

The curly braces create a dictionary. Inside the braces we have the string `'ramen'` followed by a colon, then the number `5.0` (price in dollars). This tells Python that the string maps to the number; in other words, we can look up the price if we have the name of the food item. Multiple items in a dictionary are separated with a comma; in this example we have a second item that maps `'fugu'` to the value `100.0`.

To retrieve that information, we use the square brackets (`[]`) operator again, passing in the *key* we want to search for (in this case the key is either `fugu` or `ramen`). The dictionary returns the *value* associated with the key—the price of the item. Let's look up our two keys:

```
>>> my_dictionary['fugu']
100.0
>>> my_dictionary['ramen']
5.0
```

You can also add new items to the dictionary by assigning new values to it:

```
>>> my_dictionary['chopsticks']=7.50
>>> my_dictionary['sake']=19.95
>>> my_dictionary
{'sake': 19.0, 'ramen': 5.0, 'chopsticks': 7.5, 'fugu': 100.0}
```

Here we have added two new items to the dictionary. You may have noticed that when Python displays the list for us, the items are in a different order than the way we originally created it. This is because dictionaries don't have any notion of order for keys in a dictionary and what you see displayed is in no particular order. The important thing is that Python remembers what key maps to what value—which it does very well!

Loops

A *loop* is a way of running through a piece of code more than once. Loops are pretty fundamental in programming languages, and you will find that almost every line of code you write in a game is inside some kind of loop. Like many other programming languages, Python has two types of loop to handle all your looping needs: the *while* loop and the *for* loop.

While Loops

A while loop is used when you repeat a piece of code only when a condition is true. Let's use a simple while loop to display the numbers from 1 to 5. We'll start by entering the following lines in the interpreter:

```
>>> count=1
>>> while count<=5:
...
```

When you hit Enter after the second line, you will notice that instead of the usual Python prompt you now see three periods (...). This is because the colon at the end of the line indicates that there is more code to follow. In the case of a while loop, it is the code that we want to be repeated.

All languages need some way to mark the beginning and end of code blocks. Some use symbols like curly braces ({ }), and others use words like do and end. Python does things slightly differently and uses *indentation* to define blocks. To tell Python that a line of code is part of the block and not the rest of the code, insert a tab before the line (by pressing the Tab key):

```
...     print count
...     count+=1
```

Note On some systems you may find that a tab is automatically inserted on the first line of a block. This can be convenient if there is a lot of code in a block. Delete the tab and press Enter as normal to end the block.

Hit Enter twice after the last line; the blank line tells the interpreter that you have finished entering the code block. The while loop will now run and display the numbers 1 through 5. So how does this work? Well, after the while statement is a *condition* (count<=5), which can be read as "Is count *less than or equal* to 5?" The first time Python encounters the while loop, count is 1, which satisfies our condition of being less than or equal to 5—so Python runs the code block. The two lines in the code block first print the value of count, then add one to it. The second time around, count is 2, which also satisfies the condition and we go around the loop again. Eventually count becomes 6, which is definitely *not* less than or equal to 5, and this time Python skips the code block.

Less than or equal to (<=) is just one comparison operator. See Table 1-2 for others you can use.

Table 1-2. *Comparison Operators*

Operator	Description
<	Less than
<=	Less than or equal to
>	Greater than
>=	Greater than or equal to
==	Equal to
!=	Not equal to

■**Caution** Be careful with your loops! If you use a condition that is always true, such as 2>1, Python will keep going round the loop forever. If you do end up in this pickle, hit Ctrl+Z (Ctrl+C for Linux and Mac OS X) to stop Python in its tracks. Every programmer has been stuck in an infinite loop at least once!

For Loops

While loops have their uses and it is important you know how to use them, but often the for loop is a better choice. A for loop runs through an *iterable* Python object, giving you a new value until there are no more items remaining. You have met iterables before: lists, tuples, dictionaries, and even strings are all iterable objects. Let's rewrite the while loop example as a for loop:

```
>>> for count in range(1,6):
...     print count
```

Here we are iterating over the result of the range function, which creates a list of values from the first parameter up to—but not including—the second parameter. The interpreter can tell us exactly what the call to range produces:

```
>>> range(1,6)
[1, 2, 3, 4, 5]
```

As you can see, the call to range has created a list containing the numbers 1 through 5, which is exactly what we want to display inside our loop. When Python first goes through the for loop, it picks the first value from the list and assigns it to the variable count; it then runs the code in the loop, which simply prints the current value of count to the screen. The loop finishes after five passes, when it reaches the end of the list.

■**Tip** You can use the range method like this, but a better choice is probably xrange, which works identically to range but doesn't create the entire list in memory. This is important if you want to use a for loop to iterate over very large ranges.

Python in Practice

Before we move on to the next chapter, let's put what we have learned to some practical use. Mental arithmetic has never been one of my strong points, so I'd like to write a small piece of Python code to run through our shopping list and find the total price. We'll start by creating a list containing our groceries for the week and a dictionary that maps the name of each item on to its price:

```
>>> shopping=['fugu', 'ramen', 'sake', 'shiitake mushrooms', 'soy sauce', 'wasabi']
>>> prices={'fugu':100.0, 'ramen':5.0, 'sake':45.0, 'shiitake mushrooms':3.5,➡
'soy sauce':7.50, 'wasabi':10.0}
>>> total=0.00
```

OK, great. We now have two Python collections that store all the information regarding our groceries, and a variable to store the total. What we need to do now is loop through shopping, look up each price in prices, and add it to total:

```
>>> for item in shopping:
...     total+= prices[item]
>>> total
171.0
```

That's all it takes! The variable total now holds the sum of every item in our shopping list, and we can see the grand total is a very reasonable $171. Don't worry, the sample code in the following chapters will be much more entertaining than a grocery list!

Summary

We have explored some of the basic Python constructs in this first chapter, most of which you will use regularly when writing new code. You can think of what you have learned so far as the most basic tools of the trade when it comes to writing games and other Python programs. The data (numbers and strings) and collections (tuples, list, and dictionaries) are particularly fundamental because you can store every aspect of a game within them.

In the following chapter you will learn how to fit together what you have learned to create more sophisticated programs. You will discover how to use logic, create functions, and leverage the power of object-oriented programming.

CHAPTER 2

■■■

Exploring Python

In the previous chapter we entered our Python code a line at a time, but now we are going to put the interactive interpreter to the side and start creating Python files. In this chapter we will cover more of the building blocks of Python code, and show you how to use classes to help with creating games. We will also explain how to use the code libraries that come with all installations of Python.

Creating Scripts

A file containing Python code is called a *script*. All you need to create scripts is a simple text editor, but it's best to use a Python-aware editor such as SciTE (see Figure 2-1) or IDLE (which comes with the standard distribution of Python).

Just save your script with a `.py` extension, so that your operating system knows that it contains Python. To run a script, you typically just double-click it, or if you prefer the command line, type `python` followed by a space and the name of your script. Most Python editors will have a shortcut key to run the script you have been editing.

■**Note** Python allows both spaces and tabs for indentation, but it is better to use four spaces. Most Python editors will be set this way, but you may have to check it in the Options dialog of your editor.

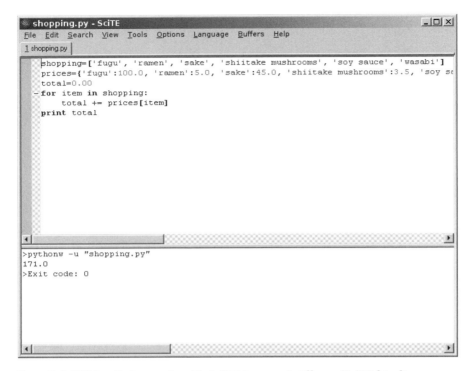

Figure 2-1. *Editing Python code with SciTE (www.scintilla.org/SciTE.html)*

Working with Logic

Not just for green-blooded Vulcans, logic is an important part of any software—and that includes games. Any game needs to make decisions based on information it either has been given or has calculated. If a laser blast hits the player's hover tank, the game has to decide if enough damage has been done to destroy it—and display an explosion animation if it has. This is just an example of a whole host of decisions a computer game has to make in order to convince us that it is more than just a dumb machine. So please put on your Spock ears and we will cover logic.

Understanding Booleans

The logic that computers use is *boolean* logic, so called because it was invented by George Boole way back in the 1800s—a few years before PlayStation hit the street.

You have already seen logic used in the previous chapter as part of a while loop; count<=5 is a *logical expression*, and like all logical expressions it results in either True or False. These *truth values*, as they are called, are used when making decisions. In the case of a while loop, a value of True tells Python to carry on around the loop one more time, but a value of False causes Python to skip past the code block. (See Listing 2-1 for a few examples of logical expressions.) The important thing to remember with boolean logic is that there are no in-between values: you can't have 25 percent true and 75 percent false—it's always one or the other!

Listing 2-1. *Simple Logic*

```
score = 100
health = 60
damage = 50
fugu = "tasty"
print score != 100
print health - damage > 0
print fugu == "tasty"
```

Running this simple script produces the following output:

```
False
True
True
```

Boolean values can be treated just like any other Python type, so you could have a variable that refers to a boolean. For example, if we were to add the line is_fugu_tasty = (fugu == "tasty"), then is_fugu_tasty would refer to the value True.

If Statement

Logical expressions come into their own when using if statements. You use if statements to run code only when a condition is true. If the condition is false, then Python jumps past the end of your code block. Here is a simple example of the if statement:

```
if fugu == "tasty":
    print "Eat the fugu!"
```

The condition uses the comparison operator (==) to compare a variable with a string. Assuming we are using the value of fugu from Listing 2-1, this comparison will result in True, which gives Python the green light to run the indented code block.

And Operator

Often you have several conditions you want to check for. Let's say we want to eat fugu if it is tasty *and* under $100 a plate. We can combine these two conditions with the and operator:

```
price = 50.0
if fugu == "tasty" and price < 100.0:
    print "Eat the fugu!"
```

Here we will only eat the fugu if `fugu` is set to `"tasty"` *and* the `price` has a value less than `100.0`. Table 2-1 lists how the and operator combines values, but I hope it is self-explanatory. You can find this operator at work in real life; for example, my car will start only if the battery is not dead *and* I have gas.

Table 2-1. *Truth Table for the And Operator*

Logic	Result
False and False	False
True and False	False
False and True	False
True and True	True

Or Operator

To complement the and operator, we have the or operator, which results in `True` if either the first or second value is `True`. Let's say we want to eat fugu if it is tasty *or* it is very cheap (after all, who can turn down cheap fugu?):

```
if fugu == "tasty" or price < 20.0:
    print "Eat the fugu!"
```

Just like the and operator, the or operator has plenty of applications in real life. My car will stop if I run out of gas *or* the battery goes dead. See Table 2-2 for the or truth table.

Table 2-2. *Truth Table for the Or Operator*

Logic	Result
False or False	False
True or False	True
False or True	True
True or True	True

Not Operator

The final logic operator we will look at is the `not` operator, which swaps the state of a boolean value, so `True` becomes `False` and `False` becomes `True` (see Table 2-3). You can use this to reverse any condition:

```
if not (fugu == "tasty" and price < 100.0):
    print "Don't eat the fugu!"
```

Here we have reversed the `fugu == "tasty"` and `price < 100.0` condition so that Python runs the code block only if the condition is *not* true (that is, false).

Table 2-3. *Truth Table for the Not Operator*

Logic	Result
not True	False
not False	True

Else Statement

You may have noticed that the previous snippet is the opposite of our first fugu logic statement. We have an action that occurs when a condition is true and another that runs when that same condition is not true. This is such a common situation that Python has a way of tacking on the alternative action to an if statement. The else statement follows an if statement and introduces a new code block that will run only if the condition is false. Let's see an example of how else is used:

```
if fugu == "tasty":
    print "Eat the fugu!"
else:
    print "Don't eat the fugu!"
```

When Python runs this code, it will run the first print statement if the condition is true; else it will run the second condition.

Elif Statement

Often another if statement will follow an else statement. Python combines an else followed by an if into a single statement: the elif statement. Let's say we want to classify the fugu into three categories based on the price. For sake of argument, we will classify $20–$100 as reasonably priced fugu, anything above that range as expensive fugu, and anything below that as cheap fugu. Python can do this for us using elif:

```
if price < 20:
    print "Cheap fugu!"
elif price < 100:
    print "Reasonably priced fugu."
else:
    print "Expensive fugu!"
```

Here we have three code blocks, but only one of them runs. If price is less than 20, then the first block will run; if price is less than 100, then the second block will run; and any other value of price will cause the third block to run. You can have as many elif statements as you want after an if, but if you have an else statement it must come at the end.

Understanding Functions

A *function* is a stored piece of Python code that you can pass information to and potentially get information back from. Python provides a large number of useful functions (see Table 2-4 for some examples), but you can also create your own.

Table 2-4. *Some Built-in Python Functions*

Function	Description	Example
abs	Finds the absolute value of a number	abs(-3)
help	Displays usage information for any Python object	help([])
len	Returns the length of a string or collection	len("hello")
max	Returns the largest value	max(3, 5)
min	Returns the smallest value	min(3, 4)
range	Returns a list containing a range of numbers	range(1,6)
round	Rounds a float to a given precision	round(10.2756, 2)

* For a more comprehensive list of Python's built-in functions, see the Python documenta-tion, or visit http://doc.python.org.

Defining Functions

To define a function in Python, you use the def statement followed by the name you want to give to your function. You can use any name you want, but it is a good idea to give it a name that describes what it actually does! Function names are typically in lowercase and may use underscores to divide words. Listing 2-2 is a simple Python function for calculating the tip on a meal of fugu.

Listing 2-2. *Calculating the Tip on Fugu*

```
def fugu_tip(price, num_plates, tip):
    total = price * num_plates
    tip = total * (tip / 100.)
    return tip

print fugu_tip(100.0, 2, 15.0)
print fugu_tip(50.0, 1, 5.0)
```

This script produces the following output:

```
30.0
2.5
```

When Python first encounters a def statement, it knows to expect a function *definition*, which consists of the name of the function followed by a list of *parameters* in parentheses. Just as with for, while, and if statements, a colon is used to introduce a block of code (known as the function *body*). In the aforementioned statements, the block of code doesn't run immediately—it's just stored away until it is needed. Calling the function causes Python to jump to the beginning of the function body and assign information given in the call to each of the parameters. So in Listing 2-2, the first call to fugu_tip runs with price set to 100, num_plates set to 2, and tip set to 15.

The only thing you haven't already encountered in fugu_tip is the return statement, which tells Python to jump back from the function, potentially with some new information. In the case of fugu_tip we return with the value of our tip, but a function can return any Python object.

■**Note** You don't need a return statement in the function. Without a return statement, a function will return when it gets to the end of the code block with the value None—which is a special Python value indicating "nothing here."

You may have noticed that inside fugu_tip two variables are created; these are called *local* variables, because they only exist inside the function. When the function returns, total and tip will no longer exist in Python's memory—although it is possible to have variables with the same name outside of the function.

Default Values

Parameters can have a *default* value, which is used if you don't supply a value in the function call. Without default values Python will throw an exception if you forget a parameter. Let's give default values to fugu_tip. I am a generous tipper, so we'll set the default of tip to be 15 (which represents a percentage of the meal cost), and since I don't like to eat alone we will assign num_plates a default of 2.

To set default values in Python, append the parameter name with a = symbol followed by the value you want to give it. See Listing 2-3 for a modified fugu_tip function with these default values. fugu_tip can now be called with just one value; the other two values are filled in automatically if you omit them. There can be as many default values in a function definition as you want, but parameters with defaults must come at the end of the parameter list.

Listing 2-3. *Calculating the Tip on Fugu*

```
def fugu_tip(price, num_plates=2, tip=15.):
    total = price * num_plates
    tip = total * (tip / 100.)
    return tip

print fugu_tip(100.0)
print fugu_tip(50.0, 1, 5.0)
print fugu_tip(50.0, tip=10.0)
```

Running this code gives us the following values for tips:

```
30.0
2.5
10.0
```

You may have noticed that there is something unusual about Listing 2-3. The third call to fugu_tip omits a value for num_plates and sets the value of tip by name. When you set parameters explicitly like this, they are called *keyword* arguments. They are useful if you have a function with many parameters, but you only need to set a few of them. Without defaults, parameters must be given in the same order as the parameter list.

Introducing Object-Oriented Programming

You may have heard the term object-oriented programming (OOP) before. But don't worry if you are unfamiliar with it, because the concept is remarkably simple.

So what exactly is an object in OOP terms? Well, it can literally be *anything*. In a game we may have an object for a particle—say, a burning ember emitted from an explosion, or the hover tank that caused the explosion. In fact, the entire game world could be an object. The purpose of an object is to contain information and to give the programmer the ability to do things with that information.

When constructing an object, it is usually best to start by working out what information, or *properties*, it contains. Let's think about what would be found in an object designed to represent a futuristic hover tank. It should contain a bare minimum of the following properties:

- Position: Where is the tank?

- Direction: In what direction is it facing?

- Speed: How fast is it going?

- Armor: How much armor does it have?

- Ammo: How many shells does it have?

Now that we have the information to describe a tank and what it is doing, we need to give it the ability to perform all the actions that a tank needs to do in a game. In OOP-speak, these actions are called *methods*. I can think of the following methods that a tank will definitely require, but there will likely be far more:

- Move: Move the tank forward.

- Turn: Rotate the tank left/right.

- Fire: Launch a shell.

- Hit: This is the action when an enemy shell hits the tank.

- Explode: Replace the tank with an explosion animation.

You can see that the methods typically change the properties of an object. When the Move method is used, it will update the tank's Position. Similarly, when the Fire method is used, the value of Ammo will be updated (unless of course there is no Ammo left; then Fire would not do anything!).

Using Classes

A *class* is Python's way of defining objects. You have actually used classes before; lists, dictionaries, and even strings are all classes, but you can also create your own. Think of a class as a kind of a *template* for an object, because you define the class once and use it to create as many objects as you need. Let's write a simple Tank class (Listing 2-4); we will use it later to create a simple game.

Listing 2-4. *An Example Tank Class Definition*

```
class Tank(object):

    def __init__(self, name):
        self.name = name
        self.alive = True
        self.ammo = 5
        self.armor = 60
```

When Python encounters class Tank(object):, it creates a class called Tank, which is *derived* from the *base* class called object. Deriving from a class means building on what it does. We *could* first create a class called Vehicle, which could handle moving and turning, and then create a tank by *deriving* from it and adding the ability to fire weapons. The advantage of this approach is that Vehicle could be reused to give other game entities the ability to rotate and move. For this example, we don't have another class to build on, so our base class will be object, which is a simple class built into Python itself.

■**Note** I may have given you the impression that object doesn't do much, but actually it does a lot of useful things behind the scenes when working with classes—you just don't use it directly.

Everything in the indented code block after the class statement is the *class definition*. This is where we set up the properties used to describe the object and supply all the methods that it will need. In Python, properties are simply variables stored within the object, and methods are functions that work with the object. In our Tank class, there is an oddly named method called __init__, which has special meaning to Python. When you create an object, Python calls this method automatically. It is typically used by Python programmers to assign properties to the object, but you can do anything else that may be needed when the object is first created.

This __init__ method takes two parameters: self and name. Because methods are potentially used for many objects, we need some way to know which object we are using. This is where self comes in—it is a reference to the current object that Python supplies automatically to all method calls. The second parameter (name) is a string we will use to tell one tank from another, because there will be more than one.

The code in __init__ first copies the name parameter to a property so we can retrieve it later; it then assigns a few other properties we will need. We don't require a great deal of information for the tank in the game I have planned; we just need to know if the tank is alive (self.alive), how much ammo it has (self.ammo), and how much armor it has remaining (self.armor).

■**Note** You don't have to call the first parameter self. You could name it anything you want, but it is a good idea to stick to self so you will know exactly what it is for when you read over your code. Python programmers tend to stick to this convention, so there is no confusion when exchanging code.

Now that we have a tank definition, we can create a new tank by calling Tank, which we supply with a string. Let's see an example:

```
my_tank = Tank("Bob")
```

This creates a new tank called Bob and calls __init__ to initialize it. Bob the tank is then assigned to the variable my_tank, which is called an *instance* of the Tank class. We can now treat my_tank as an individual object—passing it into functions, storing it in lists, and so forth, or we can access the properties individually. For instance, print my_tank.name would display Bob.

With just one method, the Tank class can't do anything interesting. Let's flesh it out with a few more methods in Listing 2-5.

Listing 2-5. *Extended Tank Class*

```
def __str__(self):

    if self.alive:
        return "%s (%i armor, %i shells)" % (self.name, self.armor, self.ammo)
    else:
        return "%s (DEAD)" % self.name

def fire_at(self, enemy):

    if self.ammo >= 1:
        self.ammo -= 1
        print self.name, "fires on", enemy.name
        enemy.hit()
    else:
        print self.name, "has no shells!"
```

```
def hit(self):

    self.armor -= 20
    print self.name, "is hit!"
    if self.armor <= 0:
        self.explode()

def explode(self):

    self.alive = False
    print self.name, "explodes!"
```

The first method in Listing 2-5 is another special method. Any name with two underscores at the front and end has a special meaning to Python. The purpose of __str__ is to return a string that describes the object; it is called when you try to convert the object to a string with str, which will happen when you print it. So if we were to do print my_tank, it should display a string with some useful information about Bob the tank. The __str__ in Listing 2-5 returns a different string depending on whether the tank is alive or dead. If the tank is alive, then this line will run:

```
return "%s (%i armor, %i shells)" % (self.name, self.armor, self.ammo)
```

This does something you may not have seen before. The string "%s (%i armor, %i shells)" is combined with a tuple (self.name, self.armor, self.ammo), using the % operator. This is known as string *formatting*, which is a great way of creating complex strings without much fuss. The first two characters in the string are %s, this tells Python to replace them with the first item in the tuple, which is a string containing the name of the tank. Later in the string Python reaches %i, which is replaced by the second item in the tuple (an integer) and so on until there are no more items in the tuple. String interpolation is often simpler to use than adding many small strings together. This line does the same thing, but uses simple string concatenation:

```
return self.name+"  ("+str(self.armor)+" armor, "+str(self.ammo)+" shells)"
```

This is a little more complex, as I'm sure you will agree! String formatting can format integers, floats, and strings in a variety of ways. See the Python documentation for more information (http://docs.python.org/lib/typesseq-strings.html).

The second method in the Tank class, fire_at, is where things get interesting. It takes the parameter enemy, which is the tank object we want to fire at. First it checks how much ammo is remaining. If there is at least one shell, it reduces self.ammo by 1 (because we just fired a shell) and calls the enemy tank's hit method. Inside the enemy tank's hit method it reduces self.armor by 20. If there is no armor remaining, then the enemy is dead, so we call its explode method to mark the tank as deceased.

If this were a graphical game we were working on, these methods would create some visual effects. fire_at would create a shell image or 3D model and set its trajectory, and explode would likely display some kind of impressive explosion animation. But for this small test game we will just use a few print statements to describe what is currently happening.

Listing 2-6 shows the Tank class in its entirety; save it as tank.py. If you run this script it will do nothing, because it just defines the Tank class. We will create another Python script with the rest of the game code.

Listing 2-6. *tank.py*

```python
class Tank(object):

    def __init__(self, name):

        self.name = name
        self.alive = True
        self.ammo = 5
        self.armor = 60

    def __str__(self):

        if self.alive:
            return "%s (%i armor, %i shells)" % (self.name, self.armor, self.ammo)
        else:
            return "%s (DEAD)" % self.name

    def fire_at(self, enemy):

        if self.ammo >= 1:
            self.ammo -= 1
            print self.name, "fires on", enemy.name
            enemy.hit()
        else:
            print self.name, "has no shells!"

    def hit(self):

        self.armor -= 20
        print self.name, "is hit!"
        if self.armor <= 0:
            self.explode()

    def explode(self):

        self.alive = False
        print self.name, "explodes!"
```

Python in Practice

The game we are going to create is more of a simulation than a game, but it should be enough to introduce a few important game concepts. We will create a number of tanks and let them take shots at each other. The winner is simply the last tank left in the game. Listing 2-7 shows the code that completes the tank game.

Listing 2-7. *tankgame.py*

```python
from tank import Tank

tanks = { "a":Tank("Alice"), "b":Tank("Bob"), "c":Tank("Carol") }
alive_tanks = len(tanks)

while alive_tanks > 1:

    print
    for tank_name in sorted( tanks.keys() ):
        print tank_name, tanks[tank_name]

    first = raw_input("Who fires? ").lower()
    second = raw_input("Who at? " ).lower()

    try:
        first_tank = tanks[first]
        second_tank = tanks[second]
    except KeyError, name:
        print "No such tank!", name
        continue

    if not first_tank.alive or not second_tank.alive:
        print "One of those tanks is dead!"
        continue

    print
    print "*" * 30

    first_tank.fire_at(second_tank)
    if not second_tank.alive:
        alive_tanks -= 1

    print "*" * 30

for tank in tanks.values():
    if tank.alive:
        print tank.name, "is the winner!"
        break
```

When you see any piece of code for the first time (in any language), it can be a little intimidating. But once you break it down you should find that it consists of familiar things. So let's dissect Listing 2-7 like a trained chef preparing fugu!

The first thing `tankgame.py` needs to do is *import* our tank module, which contains the `Tank` class. When a new script runs, it only has access to the built-in classes, such as strings and lists. If you want to use another class that isn't defined directly, you first have to import it from another Python file. The line `from tank import Tank` tells Python to look for the module called `tank` (`.py` is assumed) and read in the `Tank` class. An alternative would be to do a simple `import tank`, which would let us access everything inside `tank.py`.

■**Note** When you do `from tank import Tank`, it imports the `Tank` class (capital T) to the current *namespace*—which means you can now use `Tank` as if you had just cut and pasted it into your script. However, if you just do `import tank`, you have imported the `tank` namespace, which means you would have to refer to the `Tank` class as `tank.Tank`, as in `my_tank = tank.Tank("Bob")`. See the section "Introducing import" later in this chapter for more details on the `import` statement.

Next we create a dictionary called `tanks`, which will be used to store all our tank objects. We will work with three, but feel free to add more tanks if you like.

```
tanks = { "a":Tank("Alice"), "b":Tank("Bob"), "c":Tank("Carol") }
alive_tanks = len(tanks)
```

The three tanks have the strings `"a"`, `"b"`, and `"c"` as keys, so we can look them up easily. Once we create our tanks, we store the number of tanks in `alive_tanks` so we can keep count of tanks still in the game:

```
while alive_tanks > 1:
```

This starts off a while loop that keeps going while there is more than one surviving tank. Games always have a big loop at their core. For a visual game the *main loop* runs once per frame to update and display visuals, but here the loop represents a single round in the simulation.

Inside the while loop we first print a blank line to make the text for each round a little easier to separate. Then we have another loop that displays a little information on each of the tanks:

```
print
for tank_name in sorted( tanks.keys() ):
    print tank_name, tanks[tank_name]
```

The keys method of dictionaries returns a list of the keys that it contains, but because of the nature of dictionaries the keys won't necessarily be in the order that they were added. So when we get the list of keys for `tanks` we immediately pass it to `sorted`, which is a built-in function that returns a sorted copy of a list.

The `print` statement inside the for loop looks up the key in the `tanks` dictionary and prints the tank object it finds. Remember, printing an object calls its `__str__` function to get some useful information.

Next we ask the user for two tanks: the tank that fires (first) and the tank that it hits (second):

```
first = raw_input("Who fires? ").lower()
second = raw_input("Who at? " ).lower()
```

The built-in function raw_input displays a prompt and waits until the user has entered some text, which it returns as a string. In the preceding code we call the lower method of the returned string to convert it to lowercase because we need a lowercase string to look up the appropriate tank, but we don't mind if the user enters a name using uppercase letters.

With the two tank keys in hand, we can use them to look up the actual tank object. This is simple enough: we can just do tanks[first] to retrieve the tank:

```
try:
    first_tank = tanks[first]
    second_tank = tanks[second]
except KeyError, name:
    print "No such tank!", name
    continue
```

But because the user could type anything at the prompt, we need some way of handling a situation where the user makes an error or deliberately tries to break our game!

Whenever Python is unable to do something it is asked to do, it will *throw an exception*. If you don't do anything to handle these exceptions, the Python script will exit—which would be disastrous in a real game. Fortunately it is possible to predict potential exceptions and handle them if they occur. If either first or second is *not* a key in the tanks dictionary, then Python will throw a KeyError exception when we try to look either of them up. This won't make the script exit because we look up the keys inside a try: block, which says to Python that the code block *may* throw an exception. If a KeyError does occur, Python jumps to the code under except KeyError: (which is ignored if no exception occurs).

Inside our KeyError exception handler we first display a brief message to inform the user that they did something wrong, and then move on to a continue statement, which tells Python to ignore the rest of the code in this loop and jump back to the top of the innermost loop.

```
if not first_tank.alive or not second_tank.alive:
    print "One of those tanks is dead!"
    continue
```

This piece of code handles the situation if one or both of the tanks is dead—since there is no point in firing on a dead tank, and tanks that are dead can't fire anyway! It simply displays a message and does another continue.

If we have managed to get to this point in the code, we have two valid tank objects: first_tank and second_tank:

```
first_tank.fire_at(second_tank)
if not second_tank.alive:
    alive_tanks -= 1
```

The first tank does the firing, so we call its fire_at method and pass in the second tank as the enemy. If the second tank is killed by the first (armor reaches 0), its alive property will be set to False. When this happens, the alive_tanks count is reduced by 1.

Eventually, after a few rounds of the game the value of alive_tanks will reach 1. And when that happens, the main game loop will end, as it only loops when alive_tanks is greater than 1.

The purpose of the last section of code is to display which tank won the game:

```
for tank in tanks.values():
    if tank.alive:
        print tank.name, "is the winner!"
        break
```

It is another loop that goes through each value in tanks.values(), which is the complement to keys()—it gives us a list of all our tank objects. We know that there is only one tank that has alive set to True, so we test it with a simple if statement. Once we find that last remaining tank, we print a little message and then execute the break statement. The break statement is the partner to continue, but rather than jumping to the beginning of the loop, it jumps to the end and stops looping.

So that's our little game. Now I'd be the first to admit that it is not the most exciting of games. It's no Quake beater, but even Quake will do similar things. All 3D shooters must keep track of health/armor and ammunition, as well as who is still alive. By the end of this book, though, our game objects will be rendered in stunning 3D rather than a line of text. The following is the output from tankgame.py:

```
a Alice (60 armor, 5 shells)
b Bob (60 armor, 5 shells)
c Carol (60 armor, 5 shells)
Who fires? a
Who at? b

*****************************
Alice fires on Bob
Bob is hit!
*****************************

a Alice (60 armor, 4 shells)
b Bob (40 armor, 5 shells)
c Carol (60 armor, 5 shells)
Who fires?
```

Using the Standard Library

Python is packaged with a huge collection of classes and functions known as the *standard library*. This is why Python is often described as having *batteries included*, because you can take advantage of code written by Python experts to do everything from trigonometry to downloading web pages and sending e-mails. Libraries are organized into *modules*, or packages, with each having a specific purpose. You make use of these modules by importing them in the same way that the tank game (Listing 2-7) imported the Tank class.

When you import something in Python, it will first look in the current directory for a corresponding Python file. If it doesn't find it, Python will look for a module in the standard library.

Let's go over just a few of the modules in the standard library. We can't cover them all—that would take a book in itself—but if you need more information on any module, take a look at the docs that came with your Python distribution or browse them online at http://docs.python.org/lib/lib.html.

Introducing import

There are few ways in which you can import things from your own code, or from the standard library. Which method you use depends on how you want to access the classes and functions contained in the module. Modules can be imported with the import keyword, followed by the name of a module. For example, the following line would import a module called mymodule:

```
import mymodule
```

Importing a module this way creates a new namespace, which means that you will need to type the name of the module and a dot before any of the classes or functions that you use. For instance, if there were a function in mymodule called myfunction, you would call it like this:

```
 mymodule.myfunction()
```

This is the usual way of importing modules from the standard library, because it keeps things in each module separate; if you had another function called myfunction in a different module, there would be no confusion as to which function is being called.

It is also possible to import specific classes or functions from a module, using the from statement. The following line imports myclass from mymodule to the current namespace:

```
from mymodule import myclass
```

Use this method if you just want a few things from the module and you know that their names won't conflict with anything else in your script. You can import several classes, functions, and so forth by adding a comma between each one. So from mymodule import myclass, myfunction would import two things from the mymodule class.

You can use a * symbol to indicate that you want to import everything from a module into the current namespace. For example, the following line would import everything from `mymodule` to the current namespace:

```
from mymodule import *
```

This import method saves on typing, because you don't need the name of the module to refer to it—but only use this method if the module contains a small number of things and you know the names won't conflict with other classes or functions in your script. The `math` module is a good candidate for this kind of import.

Useful Modules for Games

The standard library contains a large number of modules, but you will only use a few of them in game. Let's go over some of the more commonly used modules.

Math Module

People are often surprised when I tell them I'm not very good at math. "But you are a computer programmer!" they exclaim. "Exactly," I tell them. "I get the computer to do the math for me." Basic math is built into Python; you can add, subtract, and multiply without importing a special module. But you do need the `math` module for more advanced functions—the kind of thing you would find on a scientific calculator. See Table 2-5 for a few of them.

Table 2-5. *Some Functions in the math Module*

Function	Description	Example
sin	Returns the sine of a number, in radians	sin(angle)
cos	Returns the cosine of a number, in radians	cos(angle)
tan	Returns the tangent of a number, in radians	tan(angle)
ceil	Returns the largest integer greater than or equal to a number	ceil(3.4323)
fabs	Returns the absolute value (without the sign) of number	fabs(-2.65)
floor	Returns the largest integer less than or equal to a number	floor(7.234)
pi	The value of pi	pi*radius**2

Let's use the math module to calculate the area of a circle, given its radius. If you remember from school, the formula for this is pi times the radius squared, where pi is a magic number that equals 3.14 something. Fortunately Python has a better memory for numbers than me, and you can rely on it having a more accurate representation of pi. It's such a simple function we will use the interactive interpreter:

```
>>> from math import *
>>> def area_of_circle(radius):
...     return pi*radius**2
...
>>> area_of_circle(5)
78.539816339744831
```

Because the math module has just a few small functions, we are lazy and import everything to the current module, just to use pi. We then define a very trivial function that takes the radius and returns the area of the circle. To test it, we calculate the area of a circle with a radius of 5 units, which turns out to be a little over 78.5 units squared.

Datetime Module

The datetime module has a number of functions and classes that deal with date and time. You can use it to query the time of your PC's internal clock and to calculate time differences between dates. It may sound like a simple task, because we often do mental calculations about dates, but it can get a little complicated when you think about leap years and time zones! Fortunately we can rely on the work of some smart programmers and have Python do this effortlessly. In the datetime module is a class of the same name. Let's use it to find the current time:

```
>>> from datetime import datetime
>>> the_time = datetime.now()
>>> the_time.ctime()
'Thu Dec 28 15:35:26 2006'
```

After importing the datetime class from the datetime module, we call the function now to return a datetime object with the current time. The function now is what is called a *static* method because you use it on a class rather than an object created with that class. Once we have the current date and time stored in the_time, we call the ctime method, which returns a friendly representation of the time as a string. Obviously it will return a different result when you run it.

So what use is finding the time in a game? Well, you may want to store a time stamp with saved games and high scores. You could also link the game with the current time of day, so it is bright and sunny at midday but dark and gloomy if you play it in the evening. Have a look at Table 2-6 for some of the things you can find in the datetime module.

Table 2-6. *Some Classes in the datetime Module*

Class	Description
timedelta	Stores a difference between two times
date	Stores a date value
datetime	Stores date and time values
time	Stores a time value

Random Module

You won't be surprised to learn that the random module is used to generate random numbers, although you may be surprised to learn that the numbers it generates aren't truly random. That's because computers aren't actually capable of selecting something at random; they will do the same thing again given identical conditions. The numbers that random generates are *pseudorandom*, which means they are pulled from a very long sequence of numbers that appear random but will eventually repeat if you generate enough of them. Fortunately you can use them in a game because nobody will notice if they repeat after a few billion times!

Random (or pseudorandom) numbers are very useful in games to stop them from getting predictable. If a game has no random elements, players will eventually memorize all the sequences of actions, making it less fun (for most people).

Let's write a short script to simulate ten throws of a standard six-sided die (Listing 2-8).

Listing 2-8. *Dice Simulator*

```
import random
for roll in xrange(10):
    print random.randint(1,6)
```

Wow, just three lines. All this does is import the random module, then call random.randint ten times and prints the results. The function randint takes two parameters, a and b, and returns a pseudorandom number in the range of a to b (possibly including the end values). So randint(1, 6) returns 1, 2, 3, 4, 5, or 6—as a die would.

▇**Note** You may have noticed in Listing 2-8 that the value of roll is never actually used inside the loop. The call to xrange(10) generates numbers from 0 to 9, but we ignore them because all we are interested in is repeating the loop ten times. Rather than thinking of a name for a value that is never used, it is common to use a single underscore in its place. So the loop in Listing 2-8 may be rewritten as for _ in xrange(10):.

Although the numbers that Listing 2-8 produces appear random, they are actually *pseudo-random*, which means they are chosen from a large mathematically generated sequence. Occasionally you may need to repeat a sequence of pseudorandom numbers—when playing back a demo, for instance. You can tell the random module to start generating numbers from a particular point in the sequence by calling the random.seed function. If you call it twice with the same value, it will cause the random module to reproduce the same sequence of numbers. Listing 2-9 demonstrates how the seed function can be used to create predictable sequences.

Listing 2-9. *A Better Dice Simulator*

```
import random
random.seed(100)
for roll in xrange(10):
    print random.randint(1, 6)
print "Re-seeded"
random.seed(100)
for roll in xrange(10):
    print random.randint(1, 6)
```

If you run this small script, you will see the same sequence of numbers, repeated twice. Have a look at Table 2-7 for a few of the capabilities of the random module.

Table 2-7. *Some Functions in the random Module*

Function	Description
seed	Seeds the random number generator
randint	Returns a random integer between two values
choice	Selects a random element from a collection
random	Return a float between 0 and 1

Summary

We've seen that you can use boolean logic to make decisions in Python code. The if statement takes a boolean expression, such as a > 3, and runs a code block only if that condition results in True. You can append an if statement with one or more else statements, which run their code block only if the condition is False. Logic can be combined using the and and or operators, and can be reversed using the not operator.

Functions are stored Python code, created with the def statement. When you define functions, you specify a list of parameters, which is a list of the information that the function needs to run and optionally return a value. A number of built-in functions are available for you to use.

Object-oriented programming is a fancy term for a simple concept. It simply means storing the information needed to describe something together with a number of actions that work with that information. In a game, just about everything will be defined as an object. Python classes are defined with the `class` statement, which you can think of as a template for creating new objects. Functions created within a `class` statement are called *methods*, which are similar to other functions with the exception that the very first parameter is the object that the method applies to. The `__init__` function is a special method that is called when an object is first created; you use it to initialize the information, or *properties*, contained in the object.

Python has a large standard library that can do a variety of useful things. The library is organized into a number of modules, which can contain classes, functions, or other Python objects.

In the next chapter, we cover how to use the Pygame module to open a window and display graphics.

CHAPTER 3

■■■

Introducing Pygame

Have you ever opened up your computer and had a look inside the case? No need to do it now, but you will find that it is built from a number of parts necessary to deliver your computing experience. The video card generates an image and sends a signal to your monitor. The sound card mixes sound together and sends audio to your speakers. Then there are the input devices, such as the keyboard, mouse, and joystick(s), and a variety of other electronic gizmos—all of which are essential in making a game.

In the early days of home computers, programmers with bad haircuts and thick-rimmed glasses had to come to grips with each of the computer's components. The game programmer had to read the technical manual for each device in order to write the computer code to communicate with it—all before working on the actual game. The situation only got worse when the manufacturers brought out different devices and versions of existing devices with new capabilities. Programmers wanted to support as many devices as possible so there was a bigger market for their games, but they found themselves bogged down in the details of working with these new graphics and sound cards. It was also a pain for the game-buying public, who had to carefully check the box to see if they had the right combination of devices to make the game work.

Things got a little easier with the introduction of graphical operating systems like Microsoft Windows. They gave the game programmer a single way of communicating with the devices. It meant that the programmer could throw away the technical manuals because the manufacturers supplied *drivers*, small programs that handle the communication between the operating system and the hardware.

Fast-forward to more recent times, when programmers still have bad haircuts but thinner rims on their glasses. The life of a game programmer is still not an easy one. Even though there is a common way of communicating with graphics, audio, and input, it can still be tricky to write games because of the variety of hardware on the market. The cheap family PC that Mom bought at the local superstore is vastly different from the top-of-the-range machine purchased by a company executive. It's this variety that makes it such an effort to initialize the hardware and ready it for use in the game. Fortunately, now that Pygame is here we have a way of creating games without having to worry about these details (and game programmers have time to go out and get decent haircuts).

In this chapter we will introduce you to Pygame and explain how to use it to create a graphical display and read the state of input devices.

History of Pygame

Pygame is built on another game creation library called Simple DirectMedia Layer (SDL). SDL was written by Sam Lantinga while he was working for Loki Software (a now-defunct game company) to simplify the task of porting games from one platform to another. It provided a common way to create a display on multiple platforms as well as work with graphics and input devices. Because it was so simple to work with, it became very popular with game developers when it was released in 1998, and has since been used for many hobby and commercial games.

SDL was written in C, a language commonly used for games because of its speed and ability to work with the hardware at a low level. But developing in C, or its successor C++, can be slow and error prone. So programmers produced *bindings* to their favorite languages, and SDL can now be used from just about any language out there. One such binding is Pygame, which lets Python programmers use the powerful SDL library.

Pygame and SDL have been in active development for many years, and because they are both open source, a large number of programmers have worked to refine and enhance this superb tool for creating games.

Installing Pygame

You can download Pygame for your operating system from `www.pygame.org/`. Click the Downloads link and it will take you to a page listing the installers for a variety of systems, including Windows, Linux, and Mac. Many Unix/Linux distribution repositories already include Pygame; on this page you can learn more about these distributions.

Once you have installed an appropriate package, you can test it by opening the Python interpreter and entering the following two lines:

```
>>> import pygame
>>> print pygame.ver
```

If Pygame was installed successfully, then you should see the version displayed:

```
1.7.1release
```

At the time of this writing version 1.7.1 is the most recent, but you may find that a later version is available when this book is released. The example code will still work, since newer versions of Pygame tend to be backward compatible.

Using Pygame

The Pygame package contains a number of modules that can be used independently. There is a module for each of the devices that you might use in a game, and many others to make game creation a breeze. See Table 3-1 for all the Pygame modules. You access these modules through the `pygame` namespace; for instance, `pygame.display` refers to the `display` module.

Some of the modules you will use in every game. You will always have some sort of display, so the display module is essential, and you will definitely need some kind of input, whether it is keyboard, joystick, or mouse. Other modules are less commonly used, but in combination they give you one of the most powerful game creation tools around.

Table 3-1. *Modules in the Pygame Package*

Module Name	Purpose
pygame.cdrom	Accesses and controls CD drives
pygame.cursors	Loads cursor images
pygame.display	Accesses the display
pygame.draw	Draws shapes, lines, and points
pygame.event	Manages external events
pygame.font	Uses system fonts
pygame.image	Loads and saves an image
pygame.joystick	Uses joysticks and similar devices
pygame.key	Reads key presses from the keyboard
pygame.mixer	Loads and plays sounds
pygame.mouse	Manages the mouse
pygame.movie	Plays movie files
pygame.music	Works with music and streaming audio
pygame.overlay	Accesses advanced video overlays
pygame	Contains high-level Pygame functions
pygame.rect	Manages rectangular areas
pygame.sndarray	Manipulates sound data
pygame.sprite	Manages moving images
pygame.surface	Manages images and the screen
pygame.surfarray	Manipulates image pixel data
pygame.time	Manages timing and frame rate
pygame.transform	Resizes and moves images

* *For complete documentation on the Pygame modules, see* www.pygame.org/docs/.

Not all of the modules in Table 3-1 are guaranteed to be present on every platform. It is possible that the hardware the game is running on does not have certain capabilities, or that required drivers are not installed. If this is the case, Pygame will set the module to None, which makes it easy to test for. The following snippet will detect whether the `pygame.font` module is available and exit if it isn't:

```
if pygame.font is None:
    print "The font module is not available!"
    exit()
```

Hello World Revisited

As I mentioned in Chapter 1, there is a tradition when learning new languages that the first code you write displays the text "Hello, World!" on the screen. Technically we have already done this with a `print 'Hello, World!'` statement—but it is a little disappointing because as game programmers we are interested in creating appealing visuals and a line of text just does not cut it! We are going to create a Hello World script with Pygame that opens a graphical window on your desktop and draws an image under the standard mouse cursor. When run, you'll see a window similar to what's shown in Figure 3-1.

Figure 3-1. *Hello World in Pygame*

See Listing 3-1 for the code. Run it now if you like; we will go through it step by step in this chapter.

Listing 3-1. *Hello World Redux (helloworld.py)*

```python
#!/usr/bin/env python

background_image_filename = 'sushiplate.jpg'
mouse_image_filename = 'fugu.png'

import pygame
from pygame.locals import *
from sys import exit

pygame.init()

screen = pygame.display.set_mode((640, 480), 0, 32)
pygame.display.set_caption("Hello, World!")

background = pygame.image.load(background_image_filename).convert()
mouse_cursor = pygame.image.load(mouse_image_filename).convert_alpha()

while True:

    for event in pygame.event.get():
        if event.type == QUIT:
            exit()

    screen.blit(background, (0,0))

    x, y = pygame.mouse.get_pos()
    x-= mouse_cursor.get_width() / 2
    y-= mouse_cursor.get_height() / 2
    screen.blit(mouse_cursor, (x, y))

    pygame.display.update()
```

We need two images for Listing 3-1: one to use as a background and another to draw as our mouse cursor. You can download the files for this and the other samples from the Source Code/ Download section at the Apress web site. If you don't have Internet access at the moment, you can use image files you have on your hard drive, or make them with any graphics- or photo-editing software. Any image is fine for the background, as long as it is at least 640 by 480 in size (any larger and the excess will be clipped). For the mouse cursor, you will need a smaller image that fits comfortably inside the background; a good size is 80 by 80. To continue with the fugu theme of the first chapter, the official background will be a picture of bowls and chopsticks, and a picture of a *very* raw fugu for the mouse cursor. The first two lines set the file names of the images; if you are using different images, you should replace the file names with the location of your images. Let's break this script into bite-sized chunks. At the top of the script we import the external modules, classes, functions, and so forth we will need when running the example:

```
import pygame
from pygame.locals import *
from sys import exit
```

The first line imports the pygame package, which gives us access to all of its submodules, such as pygame.image and pygame.sound. The second line imports a number of functions and constants (values that don't change) into the top-level namespace. It isn't essential to do this in order to use Pygame, but it is convenient because we don't have to precede frequently used values with the pygame namespace. The last import statement imports a single function from sys (a module in the standard library). As you may have guessed, the purpose of exit is to immediately finish with the script. Calling it will cause the Pygame window to disappear and Python to close. The script will call exit when the user clicks the close button; otherwise, the user would have no way of closing the window!

■**Tip** If you get into a situation where you can't close the Pygame window, you may be able to stop Python in its tracks by pressing Ctrl+C.

This rather simple line of Python code actually does a lot of work:

```
pygame.init()
```

It initializes each of the submodules in the pygame package, which may load drivers and query hardware so that Pygame is ready to use all the devices on your computer. You can initialize only the modules you intend to use by calling the init function in each submodule individually; for example, pygame.sound.init() will initialize the sound module. This can make the script start a little quicker because only the modules you actually use will be initialized. For games you will require most, if not all, of the modules—so we will stick with this catchall initialize function. After we call it, we have the full power of Pygame at our disposal!

After initializing Pygame we need to create a display surface:

```
screen = pygame.display.set_mode((640, 480), 0, 32)
pygame.display.set_caption("Hello, World!")
```

The display could be a window on your desktop or it could be the entire screen, but you always access it via a Pygame Surface object. The call to pygame.display.set_mode in our script returns the Surface object representing the window on your desktop. It takes three parameters; only the first is required, which should be a tuple containing the width and height of the display we want to create. Our window will be 640 ×480 pixels, which is large enough so we can see what is happening, but not so large that it obscures too much of the desktop. The next parameter we give to set_mode is a value containing flags used in the display creation. A *flag* is a feature that can be switched on or off; you can combine several flags together with the *bitwise OR* operator (|). For instance, to create a double-buffered hardware surface, set the flags parameter to DOUBLEBUF|HWSURFACE. See Table 3-2 for the flags you can use. I will cover them in more detail in the "Opening a Display" section later in this chapter. We won't be enabling any of these flags for this first Pygame script, so the value we give for flags is just 0, which is also the default.

Table 3-2. *Flags for pygame.display.set_mode*

Flag	Purpose
FULLSCREEN	Creates a display that fills the entire screen.
DOUBLEBUF	Creates a "double-buffered" display. Recommended for HWSURFACE or OPENGL.
HWSURFACE	Creates a hardware-accelerated display (must be combined with the FULLSCREEN flag).
OPENGL	Creates an OpenGL renderable display.
RESIZABLE	Creates a resizable display.
NOFRAME	Removes the border and title bar from the display.

The next parameter specifies the *depth* of the display surface, which is the amount of *bits* used to store colors in the display. A bit, or *binary digit*, is the most fundamental unit of storage in a computer. Bits have exactly two potential values, 1 or 0, and are arranged in memory as groups of 8. A group of 8 bits is called a byte. Don't worry if this sounds like techno-babble to you; Python tends to hide this kind of thing from the programmer. We will use the value 32 for our bit depth because it gives us the most colors; see Table 3-3 for other potential bit-depth values. If you don't supply a value for the depth or set it to 0, Pygame will use the depth of your desktop.

Table 3-3. *Bit-Depth Values*

Bit Depth	Number of Colors
8 bits	256 colors, chosen from a larger *palette* of colors
15 bits	32,768 colors, with a spare bit
16 bits	65,536 colors
24 bits	16.7 million colors
32 bits	16.7 million colors, with a spare 8 bits

* It is possible to have other bit depths, but these are the most common.

Note Sometimes Pygame is unable to give us the exact display we ask for. It may be that the graphics card doesn't support the features we are requesting. Fortunately, Pygame will choose a display that is compatible with the hardware and emulates the display we actually asked for. Thank you, Pygame!

If all goes well, the call to set_mode will display a Pygame window on your desktop and return a Surface object, which is then stored in the variable screen. The first thing we do with our newly created surface is call set_caption in the display module to set the title bar of the Pygame window. We set the title to "Hello, World!"—just to make it a valid Hello World script!

Next up we use the load function in pygame.image to load the two images for the background and mouse cursor. We pass in the file names of the images stored at the start of the script:

```
background = pygame.image.load(background_image_filename).convert()
mouse_cursor = pygame.image.load(mouse_image_filename).convert_alpha()
```

The load function reads a file from your hard drive and returns a surface containing the image data. These are the same type of objects as our display, but they represent images stored in memory and aren't visible until we draw them to the main display. The first call to pygame.image.load reads in the background image and then immediately calls convert, which is a member function for Surface objects. This function converts the image to the same format as our display, because it is faster to draw images if the display is of the same depth. The mouse cursor is loaded in a similar way, but we call convert_alpha rather than convert. This is because our mouse cursor image contains *alpha* information, which means that portions of the image could be translucent or completely invisible. Without alpha information in our mouse image, we are limited to an unsightly square or rectangle as our mouse cursor! The next chapter will cover alpha and image formats in more detail.

The next line in the script jumps straight into the *main game loop*:

```
while True:
```

This while loop has True as the condition, which means it will loop continually until we break out of it, or force it to exit in some other way. All games will have a loop similar to this, which typically repeats once per screen refresh.

Inside the main game loop we have another loop—the *event* loop, which most games will also have in one form or another:

```
for event in pygame.event.get():
    if event.type == QUIT:
        exit()
```

An event is how Pygame informs you that something has happened outside your code. Events are created for many things, from key presses to receiving information from the Internet, and are queued up for you until you handle them. The function get in the pygame.event module returns any events waiting for us, which we then loop through in a for loop. For this script, we are only interested in the QUIT event, which is generated by Pygame when the user clicks the close button in the Pygame window. So if the event type is QUIT we call exit to shut down, and all other events are ignored. In a game, of course, we would have to handle a greater number of events.

The next line *blits* the background image to the screen (*blitting* means copying from one image to another):

```
screen.blit(background, (0,0))
```

This line uses the blit member function of the screen Surface object, which takes a source image—in this case, our 640 ×480 background—and a tuple containing the destination position. The background will never move; we just want it to cover the entire Pygame window, so we blit to the coordinate (0, 0), which is the top left of the screen.

■**Tip** It is important that you blit to every portion of the screen. If you don't, strange visual effects may occur when you animate things, and your game may look different on each computer it is run on. Try commenting out the call to screen.blit to see what happens.

After we draw the background, we want to draw mouse_cursor underneath the usual mouse pointer:

```
x, y = pygame.mouse.get_pos()
x -= mouse_cursor.get_width()/2
y -= mouse_cursor.get_height()/2
screen.blit(mouse_cursor, (x, y))
```

Getting the position of the mouse is nice and simple; the pygame.mouse module contains all we need to work with the mouse, including get_pos, which returns a tuple containing the mouse coordinates. The first line unpacks this tuple into two values for convenience: x and y. We could use these two values as coordinates when we blit the mouse cursor, but that would place the top-left corner of the image under the mouse, and we want the center of the image to be under the mouse. So we do a little math (fear not!) to adjust x and y so that the mouse image is moved up by half its height and left by half its width. Using these coordinates places the center of the image right under the mouse pointer, which looks better. At least it does for an image of a fish—if you want to use a more typical pointer image, adjust the coordinates so that the tip lies underneath the real mouse coordinates.

Blitting the mouse image is done in the same way as blitting the background, but we use the coordinates we calculated rather than (0, 0). This is enough to create the effect we are looking for, but there is one more thing we have to do before we can see anything:

```
pygame.display.update()
```

When you build an image through blits to the screen surface, you won't see them right away. This is because Pygame first builds up an image to a *back buffer*, which is an invisible display in memory, before it is displayed. If we didn't have this step, the user would see individual blits as they happen, which would flicker most unpleasantly. For games programmers, flicker is the enemy! We want to see silky-smooth, convincing animation. Fortunately a call to pygame.display.update() is all we need to ensure that the image we have created in memory is shown to the user without flicker.

When you run this script, you should see something like Figure 3-1. If you are using the "official" images, then an odd-looking fish will dutifully follow the mouse cursor.

Understanding Events

In Hello World we only handled the QUIT event, which is essential unless you want to have immortal Pygame windows! Pygame creates other events to inform you of things such as mouse movement and key presses.

Events can be generated at any time, no matter what your program is currently doing. For example, your code could be drawing a tank on the screen when the user presses the fire button on the joypad. Because you can't react to events the instant they happen, Pygame stores them in a queue until you are ready to handle them (typically at the beginning of the main game loop). You can think of the event queue as a line of people waiting to get into a building, each carrying specific information about an event. When the player presses the fire button, the joystick event arrives, carrying information about which key was pressed. Similarly, when the player releases the fire button, a clone of the same joystick event arrives with information about the button that was released. They could be followed by a mouse event and key event.

Retrieving Events

In the earlier example, we called pygame.event.get() to retrieve all the events and remove them from the queue, which is like opening the door and letting everyone in. This is probably the best way to deal with events, as it ensures we have handled everything before we go on to draw something to the screen—but there are other ways to work with the event queue. If you call pygame.event.wait(), Pygame will wait for an event to occur before it returns, which is like waiting by the door until someone arrives. This function isn't often used for games because it suspends the script until something happens, but it can be useful for Pygame applications that cooperate more with other programs on your system, such as media players. An alternative is pygame.event.poll(), which returns a single event if there is one waiting, or a dummy event of type NOEVENT if there are no events in the queue. Whatever method you use, it is important to not allow them to build up, because the event queue is limited in size and events will be lost if the queue overflows.

It is necessary to call at least one of the event-handling functions at regular intervals so that Pygame can process events internally. If you don't use any of the event-handling functions, you can call pygame.event.pump() in place of an event loop.

Event objects contain a few member variables that describe the event that occurred. The information they contain varies depending on the event. The only thing common to all event objects is type, which is a value that indicates the type of the event. It is this value that you first query so you can decide what to do with it. Table 3-4 lists the standard events that you may receive; we will go over a few of them in this chapter.

Table 3-4. *Standard Events*

Event	Purpose	Parameters
QUIT	User has clicked the close button.	none
ACTIVEEVENT	Pygame has been activated or hidden.	gain, state
KEYDOWN	Key has been pressed.	unicode, key, mod
KEYUP	Key has been released.	key, mod
MOUSEMOTION	Mouse has been moved.	pos, rel, buttons
MOUSEBUTTONDOWN	Mouse button was pressed.	pos, button
MOUSEBUTTONUP	Mouse button was released.	pos, button
JOYAXISMOTION	Joystick or pad was moved.	joy, axis, value
JOYBALLMOTION	Joy ball was moved.	joy, ball, rel
JOYHATMOTION	Joystick hat was moved.	joy, hat, value
JOYBUTTONDOWN	Joystick or pad button was pressed.	joy, button
JOYBUTTONUP	Joystick or pad button was released.	joy, button
VIDEORESIZE	Pygame window was resized.	size, w, h
VIDEOEXPOSE	Part or all of the Pygame window was exposed.	none
USEREVENT	A user event has occurred.	code

Let's write a simple Pygame script to display all the events that are generated. Listing 3-2 uses pygame.event.wait() to wait for a single event. As soon as it gets one, it turns it into a string with str and adds it to a list. The rest of the code displays the new event along with as many previous events as it can fit on the screen. It uses the font module to display text (which we will discuss later).

■**Tip** If you change the fill color in Listing 3-2 to (0,0,0) and the color of the font to (0, 255, 0), it will look a little like *Matrix*-style code. You may have to use your imagination a little!

Listing 3-2. *Displaying the Message Queue*

```
import pygame
from pygame.locals import *
from sys import exit

pygame.init()
SCREEN_SIZE = (800, 600)
screen = pygame.display.set_mode(SCREEN_SIZE, 0, 32)

font = pygame.font.SysFont("arial", 16);
font_height = font.get_linesize()
event_text = []

while True:

    event = pygame.event.wait()
    event_text.append(str(event))
    event_text = event_text[-SCREEN_SIZE[1]/font_height:]

    if event.type == QUIT:
        exit()

    screen.fill((255, 255, 255))

    y = SCREEN_SIZE[1]-font_height
    for text in reversed(event_text):
        screen.blit( font.render(text, True, (0, 0, 0)), (0, y) )
        y-=font_height

    pygame.display.update()
```

If you run Listing 3-2, you will see a simple white window. Move the mouse over it and it will start to stream MOUSEMOTION events, which are created whenever the mouse changes position (see Figure 3-2). These events specify the current position of the mouse, how far the mouse has moved since the last motion event, and which buttons are currently pressed. You *can* get the current position of the mouse with the pygame.mouse module, as we did in the Hello World example, but you risk losing information about what the player has been doing. This is a particular problem on desktop computers that do a lot of work in the background, and may occasionally pause your game for a brief amount of time. For a mouse cursor, you only need to know where the mouse is at the beginning of every frame, so it is reasonable to use pygame.mouse.get_pos(). If you were using mouse movement to drive a tank and the buttons to fire, it would be better to work with events so that the game can more closely monitor what the player has been doing.

```
pygame window                                                    _ □ ✕
<Event(4-MouseMotion {'buttons': (0, 0, 0), 'pos': (228, 183), 'rel': (-2, 0)})>
<Event(2-KeyDown {'key': 304, 'unicode': u'', 'mod': 4096})>
<Event(2-KeyDown {'key': 104, 'unicode': u'H', 'mod': 4097})>
<Event(3-KeyUp {'key': 304, 'mod': 4096})>
<Event(3-KeyUp {'key': 104, 'mod': 4096})>
<Event(2-KeyDown {'key': 101, 'unicode': u'e', 'mod': 4096})>
<Event(3-KeyUp {'key': 101, 'mod': 4096})>
<Event(2-KeyDown {'key': 108, 'unicode': u'l', 'mod': 4096})>
<Event(3-KeyUp {'key': 108, 'mod': 4096})>
<Event(2-KeyDown {'key': 108, 'unicode': u'l', 'mod': 4096})>
<Event(3-KeyUp {'key': 108, 'mod': 4096})>
<Event(2-KeyDown {'key': 111, 'unicode': u'o', 'mod': 4096})>
<Event(3-KeyUp {'key': 111, 'mod': 4096})>
<Event(2-KeyDown {'key': 303, 'unicode': u'', 'mod': 4096})>
<Event(2-KeyDown {'key': 49, 'unicode': u'!', 'mod': 4098})>
<Event(3-KeyUp {'key': 49, 'mod': 4098})>
<Event(3-KeyUp {'key': 303, 'mod': 4096})>
<Event(5-MouseButtonDown {'button': 1, 'pos': (228, 183)})>
<Event(6-MouseButtonUp {'button': 1, 'pos': (228, 183)})>
<Event(4-MouseMotion {'buttons': (0, 0, 0), 'pos': (228, 183), 'rel': (0, 0)})>
<Event(5-MouseButtonDown {'button': 3, 'pos': (228, 183)})>
<Event(6-MouseButtonUp {'button': 3, 'pos': (228, 183)})>
<Event(4-MouseMotion {'buttons': (0, 0, 0), 'pos': (228, 183), 'rel': (0, 0)})>
<Event(4-MouseMotion {'buttons': (0, 0, 0), 'pos': (232, 183), 'rel': (4, 0)})>
<Event(4-MouseMotion {'buttons': (0, 0, 0), 'pos': (248, 171), 'rel': (16, -12)})>
<Event(4-MouseMotion {'buttons': (0, 0, 0), 'pos': (250, 169), 'rel': (2, -2)})>
<Event(4-MouseMotion {'buttons': (0, 0, 0), 'pos': (258, 155), 'rel': (8, -14)})>
<Event(4-MouseMotion {'buttons': (0, 0, 0), 'pos': (268, 145), 'rel': (10, -10)})>
<Event(4-MouseMotion {'buttons': (0, 0, 0), 'pos': (278, 133), 'rel': (10, -12)})>
<Event(2-KeyDown {'key': 308, 'unicode': u'', 'mod': 4096})>
```

Figure 3-2. *Output from the events script*

Handling Mouse Motion Events

As you have seen, MOUSEMOTION events are issued whenever you move the mouse over the Pygame window. They contain these three values:

- buttons—A tuple of three numbers that correspond to the buttons on the mouse. So buttons[0] is the left mouse button, buttons[1] is the middle button, and buttons[2] is the right button. If the button is pressed, then its value is set to 1; if it is not pressed, the value will be 0. Multiple buttons can be pressed at once.

- pos—A tuple containing the position of the mouse when the event was generated.

- rel—A tuple containing the distance the mouse has moved since the last mouse motion event (sometimes called the mouse *mickies*).

Handling Mouse Button Events

In addition to motion events, the mouse generates MOUSEBUTTONDOWN and MOUSEBUTTONUP events. If you click the mouse on the message queue script, you will first see the *down* event, followed by an *up* event when you take your finger off the button. So why have the two events? If you are using the mouse button as a trigger to fire a rocket, you would only need one of the events, but you may have a different type of weapon, such as a chain gun that fires continuously while the button is held down. In this case you would start the chain gun speeding up on the *down* event and have it fire until you get the corresponding *up* event. Both types of mouse button events contain the following two values:

- button—The number of the button that was pressed. A value of 1 indicates that the left mouse button was pressed, 2 indicates that the middle button was pressed, and 3 indicates that the right button was pressed.

- pos—A tuple containing the position of the mouse when the event was generated.

Handling Keyboard Events

The keyboard and joystick have similar up and down events; KEYDOWN is issued when a key is pressed, and KEYUP is issued when the key is released. Listing 3-3 demonstrates how you might respond to KEYUP and KEYDOWN events to move something on screen with the cursor keys. If you run this listing, you will see a window containing a simple background image. Press up, down, left, or right and the background will slide in that direction. Take your finger off the cursor key and the background will stop moving.

Listing 3-3. *Using Keyboard Events to Move a Background*

```
background_image_filename = 'sushiplate.jpg'

import pygame
from pygame.locals import *
from sys import exit

pygame.init()
screen = pygame.display.set_mode((640, 480), 0, 32)
background = pygame.image.load(background_image_filename).convert()

x, y = 0, 0
move_x, move_y = 0, 0

while True:

    for event in pygame.event.get():
        if event.type == QUIT:
            exit()
        if event.type == KEYDOWN:
            if event.key == K_LEFT:
                move_x = -1
            elif event.key == K_RIGHT:
                move_x = +1
            elif event.key == K_UP:
                move_y = -1
            elif event.key == K_DOWN:
                move_y = +1
```

```
        elif event.type == KEYUP:
            if event.key == K_LEFT:
                move_x = 0
            elif event.key == K_RIGHT:
                move_x = 0
            elif event.key == K_UP:
                move_y = 0
            elif event.key == K_DOWN:
                move_y = 0

    x+= move_x
    y+= move_y

    screen.fill((0, 0, 0))
    screen.blit(background, (x, y))

    pygame.display.update()
```

Listing 3-3 begins just like Hello World; it imports and initializes Pygame, then loads a background image. The event loop in this script is different, because it handles KEYDOWN and KEYUP. These key events both contain the same three values:

- key—This is a number representing the key that was pressed or released. Each physical key on the keyboard has a constant that begins with K_. The alphabet keys are K_a through K_z, but there are also constants for all the other keys, such as K_SPACE and K_RETURN. For a complete list of the key constants you can use, see www.pygame.org/docs/ ref/key.html.

- mod—This value represents keys that are used in combination with other keys, such as Shift, Alt, and Ctrl. Each of these modifier keys are represented by a constant that begins with KMOD_, such as KMOD_SHIFT, KMOD_ALT, and KMOD_CTRL. Check for these values by using the *bitwise AND* operator. For example, mod & KMOD_CTRL will evaluate to True if the Ctrl key is pressed. www.pygame.org/docs/ref/key.html provides a full list of the modifier keys.

- unicode—This is the *Unicode* value of the key that was pressed. It is produced by combining the pressed key with any of the modifier keys that was pressed. There is a Unicode value for every symbol in the English alphabet and other languages. You won't often use this value in a game because keys tend to be used more like switches than for entering text. An exception would be for entering a high score table, where you would want the player to be able to type non-English letters as well as mix upper- and lowercase.

Inside the handler for KEYDOWN we check for the four key constants that correspond to the cursor keys. If K_LEFT is pressed, then the value of move_x is set to –1; if K_RIGHT is pressed, it is set to +1. This value is later added to the x coordinate of the background in order to move it left or right. There is also a move_y value, which is set if K_UP or K_DOWN is pressed, which will move the background vertically.

We also handle the KEYUP event, because we want the background to stop moving when the user releases the cursor key. The code inside the handler for KEYUP events is similar to the down event, but it sets move_x or move_y back to zero to stop the background from moving.

After the event loop, all we have to do is add the values `move_x` and `move_y` to x and y, then draw the background at (x, y). The only thing you haven't seen before is `screen.fill((0, 0, 0))`, which is used to clear the display to black (colors are explained in Chapter 4). This line is necessary because if we move the background image it no longer covers the whole display— which I guess would technically mean it is no longer a background!

Filtering Events

Not all events need to be handled in every game, and there are often alternative ways of getting the information that events might give you. For example, if you are using `pygame.mouse.get_pos()` you will not need to respond to the `MOUSEMOTION` event.

Occasionally you also need to suspend the handling of certain events. If you were to play a cut scene movie between levels, you would probably want to ignore input events until it is finished. The Pygame event module has a number of functions to help you just do that.

You can block events from the event queue with the `set_block` function. For example, the following line will disable mouse movement:

```
pygame.event.set_blocked(MOUSEMOTION)
```

If you pass in a list of event types, all those events will be blocked. For example, the following line will disable all keyboard input by blocking both `KEYDOWN` and `KEYUP` events:

```
pygame.event.set_blocked([KEYDOWN, KEYUP])
```

If you want to unblock all events, pass the value of `None` to `set_blocked`. This line will allow all events to occur in the event queue:

```
pygame.event.set_blocked(None)
```

The opposite of `set_blocked` is `set_allowed`, which selects the events that should be allowed (unblocked). It also takes a single event type, or a list of event types. But if you pass in the value of `None`, it effectively blocks *all* events. You can ask Pygame if an event is currently blocked with `pygame.event.get_block`, which takes a single event type.

Posting Events

Generally it is Pygame that creates all the events for you, but you can create your own. You could use this ability to play back demos (by replicating the player's input), or simulate the effects of a cat walking across the keyboard (I like to make my games cat proof).

To send an event, you first construct an event object with `pygame.event.Event` and then post it with `pygame.event.post`. The event will be placed on the end of the queue, ready for retrieval in the event loop. Here's how to simulate the player pressing the spacebar:

```
my_event = pygame.event.Event(KEYDOWN, key=K_SPACE, mod=0, unicode=u' ')
pgame.event.post(my_event)
```

The `Event` constructor takes the type of the event, such as one of the events in Table 3-4, followed by the values the event should contain. Since we are simulating the `KEYDOWN` event, we need to supply all the values that the event handler would expect to be there. If you prefer, you can supply these values as a dictionary. This line will create the same event object:

```
my_event = pygame.event.Event(KEYDOWN, {"key":K_SPACE, "mod":0, "unicode":u' '})
```

In addition to simulating Pygame-generated events, you can create completely new events. All you have to do is use a value for the event that is above `USEREVENT`, which is the maximum value that Pygame will use for its own event IDs. This can sometimes be useful if you want to do something in the event loop before you go on to draw to the screen. Here's an example of a user event to respond to a cat walking over the keyboard:

```
CATONKEYBOARD = USEREVENT+1
my_event = pygame.event.Event(CATONKEYBOARD, message="Bad cat!")
pgame.event.post(my_event)
```

Handling user events is done in the same way as the usual events that Pygame generates—just check the event type to see if it matches your custom event. Here's how you might handle a `CATONKEYBOARD` event:

```
for event in pygame.event.get():
    if event.type == CATONKEYBOARD:
        print event.message
```

Opening a Display

I deliberately glossed over opening a display in the Hello World example because we only needed a simple display, but Pygame has a variety of options for displays. The type of display you create depends on the game. It is generally easier to used fixed resolution (display size) because it can simplify your code. Your decision also depends on how much action you will have in the game—the more things you have moving on screen at one time, the slower the game will run. You may have to compensate by selecting a lower resolution (which will speed things up again).

The best solution is usually to let the player decide what resolution they want to run in so that they can adjust the display until they have a good compromise between visual quality and how smoothly the game runs. If you go this route, you will have to make sure that your game looks OK in all potential resolutions!

Don't worry about this until it comes time to write your game. Just select a resolution that works for you while you are experimenting with Pygame scripts, but feel free to experiment a little.

Full-Screen Displays

In Hello World we used the following line to create a Pygame window:

```
screen = pygame.display.set_mode((640, 480), 0, 32)
```

The first parameter is the size of the window we want to create. A size of (640, 480) creates a small window that will fit comfortably on most desktops, but you can select a different size if you wish. Running in a window is great for debugging, but most games fill the entire screen with the action and don't have the usual borders and title bar. *Full-screen* mode is usually faster because your Pygame script doesn't have to cooperate with other windows on your desktop. To set full-screen mode, use the FULLSCREEN flag for the second parameter of set_mode:

```
screen = pygame.display.set_mode((640, 480), FULLSCREEN, 32)
```

■**Caution** If something goes wrong with your script in full-screen mode, it can sometimes be difficult to get back to your desktop. Therefore, it's best to test it in windowed mode first. You should also provide an alternative way to exit the script because the close button is not visible in full-screen mode.

When you go full screen, your video card will probably switch to a different video mode, which will change the width and height of the display, and potentially how many colors it can show at one time. Video cards only support a few combinations of size and number of colors, but Pygame will help you if you try to select a video mode that the card does not support directly. If the size of display you ask for isn't supported, Pygame will select the next size up and copy your display to the center of it, which may lead to black borders at the top and bottom of your display. To avoid these borders, select one of the standard resolutions that virtually all video cards support: (640, 480), (800, 600), or (1024, 768). To see exactly what resolutions your display supports, you can use pygame.display.list_modes(), which returns a list of tuples containing supported resolutions. Let's try this from the interactive interpreter:

```
>>> import pygame
>>> pygame.init()
>>> pygame.display.list_modes()
```

```
[(800, 600), (1280, 1024), (1280, 960), (1280, 800), (1280, 768), (1280, 720),
(1152, 864), (1088, 612), (1024, 768), (960, 600), (848, 480), (800, 600),
(720, 576), (720, 480), (640, 480), (640, 400), (512, 384), (480, 360), (400, 300),
(320, 240), (320, 200), (640, 480)]
```

If the video card can't give you the number of colors you asked for, Pygame will convert colors in the display surface automatically to fit (which may result in a slight drop in image quality).

Listing 3-4 is a short script that demonstrates going from windowed mode to full-screen mode. If you press the F key, the display will fill the entire screen (there may be a delay of a few seconds while this happens). Press F a second time, and the display will return to a window.

Listing 3-4. *Full-Screen Example*

```python
background_image_filename = 'sushiplate.jpg'

import pygame
from pygame.locals import *
from sys import exit

pygame.init()
screen = pygame.display.set_mode((640, 480), 0, 32)
background = pygame.image.load(background_image_filename).convert()

Fullscreen = False

while True:

    for event in pygame.event.get():
        if event.type == QUIT:
            exit()
    if event.type == KEYDOWN:
        if event.key == K_f:
            Fullscreen = not Fullscreen
            if Fullscreen:
                screen = pygame.display.set_mode((640, 480), FULLSCREEN, 32)
            else:
                screen = pygame.display.set_mode((640, 480), 0, 32)

    screen.blit(background, (0,0))
    pygame.display.update()
```

Resizable Pygame Windows

Occasionally you may want the user to be able to resize a Pygame window, which you typically do by clicking on the corner of the window and dragging with the mouse. It's easy enough to do this by using the RESIZABLE flag when you call set_mode. Pygame informs your code if the user has changed the window size by sending a VIDEORESIZE event that contains the new width and height of the window. When you get one of these events, you should call pygame.display.set_mode again to set the display to the new dimensions. Listing 3-5 demonstrates how to respond to VIDEORESIZE events.

Listing 3-5. *Using a Resizable Window*

```python
background_image_filename = 'sushiplate.jpg'

import pygame
from pygame.locals import *
from sys import exit
```

```
SCREEN_SIZE = (640, 480)

pygame.init()
screen = pygame.display.set_mode(SCREEN_SIZE, RESIZABLE, 32)

background = pygame.image.load(background_image_filename).convert()

while True:

    event = pygame.event.wait()
    if event.type == QUIT:
        exit()
    if event.type == VIDEORESIZE:
        SCREEN_SIZE = event.size
        screen = pygame.display.set_mode(SCREEN_SIZE, RESIZABLE, 32)
        pygame.display.set_caption("Window resized to "+str(event.size))

    screen_width, screen_height = SCREEN_SIZE
    for y in range(0, screen_height, background.get_height()):
        for x in range(0, screen_width, background.get_width()):
            screen.blit(background, (x, y))

    pygame.display.update()
```

When you run this script, it will display a simple Pygame window with a background image. If you click on the corner or edge of the window and drag with the mouse, the script will get a VIDEORESIZE event. In the handler to that message is another call to set_mode, which creates a new screen surface that matches the new dimensions. The resize message contains the following values:

- size—This is a tuple containing the new dimensions of the window; size[0] is the width and size[1] is the height.

- w—This value contains the new width of the window. It is the same value as size[0], but may be more convenient.

- h—This value contains the new height of the window. It is the same value as size[1], but may be more convenient.

Because the display size can vary with this script, we draw the background slightly differently by blitting the background image as many times as necessary to cover the display. The two calls to range produce the coordinates needed to place these multiple background images.

Most games run in full screen so resizable displays are perhaps not a feature you will use very often. But it is there in your toolbox if you need it!

Windows with No Borders

Generally when you create a Pygame window you will want a standard window with title bars and border. It is possible, though, to create a window that doesn't have these features so that the user will not be able to move or resize the window, or close it via the close button. One instance of such a use is the window used for splash screens. Some games can take a while to load because they contain many image and sound files. If there is nothing visible on the screen while this is happening, the player may feel that the game is not working and try to launch it again. To set a display with no borders, use the NOFRAME flag when calling set_mode. For example, the following line will create a "naked" window:

```
screen = pygame.display.set_mode(SCREEN_SIZE, RESIZABLE, 32)
```

Additional Display Flags

There are a few more flags you can use in a call to set_mode. I consider them advanced, because they can hurt performance if used incorrectly or cause compatibility problems on some platforms. It is usually best to use the value 0 for windowed displays and FULLSCREEN for full-screen displays to ensure your game will work well on all platforms. That said, if you know what you are doing you can set a few advanced flags for extra performance. There is also no harm in experimenting (it won't hurt your computer).

If you set the HWSURFACE flag, it will create what is called a *hardware surface*. This is a special kind of display surface that is stored in the memory of your graphics card. It can only be used in combination with the FULLSCREEN flag, like this:

```
screen = pygame.display.set_mode(SCREEN_SIZE, HWSURFACE | FULLSCREEN, 32)
```

Hardware surfaces can be faster than surfaces created in system (regular) memory, because they can take advantage of more features of your graphics card to speed up blitting. The disadvantage of hardware surfaces is that they are not that well supported on all platforms. They tend to work on Windows platforms but not so well on others. Hardware surfaces will also benefit from the DOUBLEBUF flag. This effectively creates two hardware surfaces, but only one is visible at any one time. The following line will create a double-buffered hardware surface:

```
screen = pygame.display.set_mode(SCREEN_SIZE, DOUBLEBUF | HWSURFACE | FULLSCREEN, ➡
32)
```

Normally when you call pygame.display.update() an entire screen is copied from memory to the display—which takes a little time. Double-buffered surfaces allow you to switch to the new screen instantly and thus makes your game run a little faster.

The last display flag you can use is OPENGL. OpenGL (www.opengl.org/) is a graphics library that uses the 3D graphics accelerator found on just about every graphics card. The downside of using this flag is that you will no longer be able to use Pygame's 2D graphics functions. We will cover using OpenGL to create 3D in Chapter 9.

■**Note** If you use a double-buffered display, you should call `pygame.display.flip()` rather than `pygame.display.update()`. This does the instant display switch rather than copying screen data.

Using the Font Module

I promised to cover the font module that we used in the event queue script. The ability to draw text on the screen can really help with testing scripts; you may also need it to display game instructions, menu options, and so forth. The font module uses TrueType fonts (TTFs), which are used on most systems to render high-quality, smooth text. There will be many such fonts installed on your computer that can be used by the font module.

To use a font, you must first create a `Font` object. The easiest way to do this is with `pygame.font.SysFont`, which uses one of the fonts you have installed on your computer. The following line creates a `Font` object for the Arial font (a common font that is easy to read):

```
my_font = pygame.font.SysFont("arial", 16)
```

The first parameter is the name of font you want to create, and the next parameter specifies the font size in pixels. Pygame will look for a font with the name "arial" in your installed fonts; if it doesn't find it, a default font will be returned. You can get a list of the fonts installed on your system by calling `pygame.font.get_fonts()`. Fonts can also be created directly from `.ttf` files by calling `pygame.font.Font`, which takes a file name. The following line loads the file `my_font.ttf` and returns a `Font` object:

```
my_font = pygame.font.Font("my_font.ttf", 16)
```

Once you have created a `Font` object, you can use it to *render* text to a new surface. To render text, use the `render` member function of `Font` objects. It creates a new surface containing the text, which you can then blit to the display. The following line renders a piece of text and returns a new surface:

```
text_surface = my_font.render("Pygame is cool!", True, (0,0,0), (255, 255, 255))
```

The first parameter of `render` is the text you want to render. It has to be a single line; if you want multiple lines, you will have to break the string and use multiple render calls. The second parameter is a boolean (`True` or `False`), used to enable *antialiased* text. If it is set to `True`, the text will have a modern, smooth look; otherwise, it will appear more pixelated. The next two parameters of `render` are the text color, followed by the background color. The background is optional, if you leave it out (or set it to `None`), the background will be transparent.

To finish this introduction to the font module, let's write a small script to render my name to a surface and save it as an image. Feel free to change the name that is drawn to your own. If you modify the first line of Listing 3-6, it will do just that.

Listing 3-6. *Writing Your Name to an Image File*

```
my_name = "Will McGugan"
import pygame
pygame.init()
my_font = pygame.font.SysFont("arial", 64)
name_surface = my_font.render(my_name, True, (0, 0, 0), (255, 255, 255))
pygame.image.save(name_surface, "name.png")
```

This script is so simple that we don't even need to create a display! When you run Listing 3-6, you won't see much happen on the screen, but the code will have created an image file called name.png in the same location as the script. You can open the file with any image viewer software. Saving the surface to a file is done with the pygame.image module, which we will cover in the next chapter.

The font module provides other functions as well as Font objects, which you may occasionally need to use. They are mostly informational, designed to retrieve various pieces of information regarding the fonts. There are functions that will simulate bold and italic text, but it is better to use a dedicated bold or italic font. For complete details on the font module, see the documentation at www.pygame.org/docs/ref/font.html.

■**Caution** Installed fonts vary from computer to computer, and you cannot always rely on a particular font being present. If Pygame doesn't find the font you are asking for, it will use a default font that may not look the same. The solution is to distribute the .ttf files with your game, but make sure you have permission from the font author to do this! For a free-to-distribute font, you could use something from the BitStream Vera family (http://en.wikipedia.org/wiki/Bitstream_Vera).

When Pygame Goes Wrong

Sometimes even with Pygame's best efforts it will be unable to give you what you ask for. For example, if you have run out of memory you will not be able to load any more images and pygame.image.load will have no space to read an image to. In this case, Pygame will throw a pygame.error exception. Other situations will also produce errors. Here's what happens if you try to set a display mode with a height of 0 pixels:

```
>>> import pygame
>>> screen = pygame.display.set_mode((640, 0))
```

```
Traceback (most recent call last):
  File "<interactive input>", line 1, in ?
pygame.error: Cannot set 0 sized display mode
```

Generally speaking, there is not a great deal you can do when you get `pygame.error` exceptions that aren't programming errors. If you can't set the desired video mode, the game simply can't run. Similarly, if you can only load half the image you will not be able to properly display the visuals in the game. Often the best you can do is apologize to the player and perhaps direct them somewhere for help.

I have omitted catching Pygame exceptions in the samples to simplify the code a little, but if you ever produce a game that you would like to distribute, it is good practice to check for errors. The following snippet will display a message and exit if `set_mode` throws an exception:

```
try:
    screen = pygame.display.set_mode(SCREEN_SIZE)
except pygame.error, e:
    print "Can't create the display :-("
    print e
    exit()
```

If you have chosen sensible values for the display, you are unlikely to get these exceptions. A more likely place they will occur is when reading images. If you try to load an image that you don't have on your hard drive, or there is a typo in the file name, you will also get a `pygame.error` exception. It is good practice to catch all exceptions that could potentially occur when your game is distributed. Nobody likes games or applications that fail unexpectedly without any information! Some exceptions indicate a *bug* (programmer error) in the code. It is reasonable to leave these uncaught, so that you can find problems—and hopefully fix them before the game is released.

Pygame in Action

Back when I was a youngling, the "scrolly message" was a very popular effect among hobbyist graphics programmers. A scrolly message, or *marquee* as it is now known, is simply text sliding across the screen from right to left. Listing 3-7 is a Pygame implementation of a scrolly message. It's not without its faults, the most major of which is that it will move at an inconsistent speed, and may be faster or slower on different computers. This is a problem that you will learn how to solve in the next chapter.

Most of this script should be familiar by now, so I won't break it down. Try tweaking the code to produce different results. You may also want to insert text of your own choice, which you can do by modifying the `message` string at the start of the script.

Listing 3-7. *Scrolly Message Script*

```
background_image_filename = 'sushiplate.jpg'
SCREEN_SIZE = (640, 480)
message="   This is a demonstration of the scrolly message script.    "
```

```
import pygame
from pygame.locals import *
from sys import exit

pygame.init()
screen = pygame.display.set_mode(SCREEN_SIZE)

font = pygame.font.SysFont("arial", 80);
text_surface = font.render(message, True, (0, 0, 255))

x = 0
y = ( SCREEN_SIZE[1] - text_surface.get_height() ) / 2

background = pygame.image.load(background_image_filename).convert()

while True:

    for event in pygame.event.get():
        if event.type == QUIT:
            exit()

    screen.blit(background, (0,0))

    x-= 2
    if x < -text_surface.get_width():
        x = 0

    screen.blit(text_surface, (x, y))
    screen.blit(text_surface, (x+text_surface.get_width(), y))
    pygame.display.update()
```

Summary

Pygame is a powerful platform for building games. It consists of many submodules for a variety of game-related tasks. Pygame works equally well on a large number of platforms. Ports are available for all the major desktop systems and even some consoles—so you can develop a game on your favorite platform and play it on another.

We've produced a Hello World script that demonstrates the basics of starting Pygame, creating a display, receiving events, and then drawing to the screen—steps that you will use when creating more sophisticated games and demos. If you have done any game programming in C or C++, you will appreciate the simplicity of the code, especially the one-liner to create a display.

We explored the flags you can use when creating a display, which can improve performance or add capabilities. It is probably best to leave most of these flags disabled, at least until you are more familiar with Pygame and computer graphics in general. You should find that the default settings still give you excellent performance.

You also learned how to manage the event queue to handle the various events that Pygame can send you, and you even learned how to create custom events. Listing 2-3 lets you see exactly what events are generated and the information they contain. You will find this listing to be a handy tool when you experiment with your own script.

This chapter covered all the boilerplate code you need to get up and running with Pygame. The next chapter examines graphics, movement, and animation.

CHAPTER 4

■ ■ ■

Creating Visuals

Computer games tend to be very visual in nature, and game developers will spend a lot of time working on manipulating graphics and refining the visuals to create the most entertaining experience for the player. This chapter will give you a strong foundation in generating visuals for computer games.

Using Pixel Power

If you peer closely at your computer screen, you should be able to make out that it is composed of rows and columns of colored dots. These dots are packed so tightly together that when you view the screen at a comfortable distance they merge to form a single image. An individual dot in the display is called a picture element, or *pixel*. Because computer games are primarily visual in nature, pixels are very much the tools of the trade for game programmers.

I recently treated myself to a brand-new LCD monitor that has a *resolution* of 1280 ×1024, which means there are 1,280 pixels along the width of the screen and 1,024 pixels along the height of the screen. You can find the total number of pixels by multiplying the figures for width and height together, so my screen contains a total of 1,310,720 pixels. That's 1.3 million pixels, or 1.3 megapixels, enough to create a high-quality image. As a general rule, the more pixels there are on a screen, the higher quality the image. Computer displays can also vary in the amount of colors they can generate. The highest number of colors the typical home computer can display is 16.7 million, which is currently the most common setting for displays. Each color also has a range of brightness, from full intensity to virtually black. To put it into perspective, if you wanted to display every possible color on a monitor you would need a screen that is 4096 by 4096 pixels in size.

Let's write a small Python script to generate an image containing every possible color. Listing 4-1 uses Pygame to create a large image with every possible color value. The script will take a couple of minutes to run, but when it is finished it will have saved an image file called allcolors.bmp, which you can open in an image viewer or web browser. Don't worry about the details of Listing 4-1; we will cover the unfamiliar code in this chapter.

■**Caution** The image in Listing 4-1 is 48MB in size—make sure you have enough space on your hard drive!

Listing 4-1. *Generating an Image Containing Every Color*

```
import pygame
pygame.init()

screen = pygame.display.set_mode((640, 480))

all_colors = pygame.Surface((4096,4096), depth=24)

for r in xrange(256):
    print r+1, "out of 256"
    x = (r&15)*256
    y = (r>>4)*256
    for g in xrange(256):
        for b in xrange(256):
            all_colors.set_at((x+g, y+b), (r, g, b))

pygame.image.save(all_colors, "allcolors.bmp")
```

Listing 4-1 is unusual for a Pygame script because it is not interactive. When it runs you will see it count from 1 to 256 and then exit after saving the bitmap file in the same location as the script. Don't worry that it is slow; generating bitmaps one pixel at a time is something you should never need to do in a game!

Working with Color

You are probably familiar with how colors are created with paint. If you have a pot of blue paint and a pot of yellow paint, then you can create shades of green by mixing the two together. In fact, you can produce any color of paint by mixing the primary colors red, yellow, and blue in various proportions. Computer color works in a similar way, but the "primary" colors are red, green, and blue. To understand the difference we need to cover the science behind color— don't worry, it's not complicated.

To see a color, light from the sun or a bulb has to bounce off something and pass through the lens in your eye. Sunlight or artificial light from a bulb may appear white, but it actually contains all the colors of the rainbow mixed together. When light hits a surface, some of the colors in it are absorbed and the remainder is reflected. It's this reflected light that enters your eye and is perceived as color. When colors are created in this way, it is called *color subtraction*. Computer screens work differently. Instead of reflecting light, they generate their own and create color by adding together red, green, and blue light (a process known as *color addition*).

That's enough science for the moment. For now we need to know how to represent color in a Python program, because it is impractical to think of names for all 16.7 million of them!

Representing Color in Pygame

When Pygame requires a color, you pass it in as a tuple of three integers, one for each color component in red, green, and blue order. The value of each component should be in the range 0 to 255, where 255 is full intensity and 0 means that the component doesn't contribute anything to the final color. Table 4-1 lists the colors you can create by using components set to either off or full intensity.

Some early computers were limited to just these gaudy colors; fortunately you can create more subtle hues nowadays!

Table 4-1. *Color Table*

Color	Red	Green	Blue	Tuple
Black	0	0	0	(0, 0, 0)
Blue	0	0	255	(0, 0, 255)
Green	0	255	0	(0, 255, 0)
Cyan	0	255	255	(0, 255, 255)
Red	255	0	0	(255, 0, 0)
Magenta	255	0	255	(255, 0, 255)
Yellow	255	255	0	(255, 255, 0)
White	255	255	255	(255, 255, 255)

It's well worth experimenting with different values so that you have an intuitive feel for computer-generated color. With a little practice you should find that you can look at the three color values and make an educated guess at what the color looks like. Let's write a script to help us to do this. When you run Listing 4-2, you will see a screen split into two halves. At the top of the screen are three scales—one for each of the red, green, and blue components—and a circle to represent the currently selected value. If you click anywhere on one of the scales, it will modify the component and change the resulting color, which is displayed on the lower half of the screen.

Try adjusting the sliders to (96, 130, 51), which gives a convincing shade of zombie green, or (221, 99, 20) for a pleasing fireball orange.

Listing 4-2. *Script for Tweaking Colors*

```python
import pygame
from pygame.locals import *
from sys import exit

pygame.init()
```

```python
screen = pygame.display.set_mode((640, 480), 0, 32)

# Creates images with smooth gradients
def create_scales(height):
    red_scale_surface = pygame.surface.Surface((640, height))
    green_scale_surface = pygame.surface.Surface((640, height))
    blue_scale_surface = pygame.surface.Surface((640, height))
    for x in range(640):
        c = int((x/639.)*255.)
        red = (c, 0, 0)
        green = (0, c, 0)
        blue = (0, 0, c)
        line_rect = Rect(x, 0, 1, height)
        pygame.draw.rect(red_scale_surface, red, line_rect)
        pygame.draw.rect(green_scale_surface, green, line_rect)
        pygame.draw.rect(blue_scale_surface, blue, line_rect)
    return red_scale_surface, green_scale_surface, blue_scale_surface

red_scale, green_scale, blue_scale = create_scales(80)

color = [127, 127, 127]

while True:

    for event in pygame.event.get():
        if event.type == QUIT:
            exit()

    screen.fill((0, 0, 0))

    # Draw the scales to the screen
    screen.blit(red_scale, (0, 00))
    screen.blit(green_scale, (0, 80))
    screen.blit(blue_scale, (0, 160))

    x, y = pygame.mouse.get_pos()

    # If the mouse was pressed on one of the sliders, adjust the color component
    if pygame.mouse.get_pressed()[0]:
        for component in range(3):
            if y > component*80 and y < (component+1)*80:
                color[component] = int((x/639.)*255.)
        pygame.display.set_caption("PyGame Color Test - "+str(tuple(color)))
```

```
# Draw a circle for each slider to represent the current setting
for component in range(3):
    pos = ( int((color[component]/255.)*639), component*80+40 )
    pygame.draw.circle(screen, (255, 255, 255), pos, 20)

pygame.draw.rect(screen, tuple(color), (0, 240, 640, 240))

pygame.display.update()
```

Listing 4-2 introduces the pygame.draw module, which is used to draw lines, rectangles, circles, and other shapes on the screen. We will cover this module in more detail later in this chapter.

Once you have a color, there are a number of things you may want to do to it. Let's say we have a soldier in a space game that has the misfortune to be caught in a meteor shower without an umbrella. We could use "fireball orange" for the meteors as they streak through the atmosphere, but when they hit the ground they would gradually fade to black. How do we find the darker colors?

Scaling Colors

To make a color darker, you simply multiply each of the components by a value between 0 and 1. If you take fireball orange (221, 99, 20) and multiply each component by 0.5 (in other words, decrease them by one-half), then you get (110.5, 49.5, 10). But because color components are integers we need to drop the fractional part to get (110, 49, 10). If you use Listing 4-2 to create this color, you should see that it is indeed a darker shade of fireball orange. We don't want to have to do the math in our head every time, so let's write a function to do it for us. Listing 4-3 is a function that takes a color tuple, multiplies each number by a float value, and returns a new tuple.

Listing 4-3. *Function for Scaling a Color*

```
def scale_color(color, scale):
    red, green, blue = color
    red = int(red*scale)
    green = int(green*scale)
    blue = int(blue*scale)
    return red, green, blue

fireball_orange = (221, 99, 20)
print fireball_orange
print scale_color(fireball_orange, .5)
```

If you run Listing 4-3, it will display the color tuple for fireball orange and the darker version:

```
(221, 99, 20)
(110, 49, 10)
```

Multiplying each of the components by a value between 0 to 1 makes a color darker, but what if you multiply by a value that is greater than 1? It will make the color brighter, but there is something you have to watch out for. Let's use a scale value of 2 to make a really bright fireball orange. Add the following line to Listing 4-3 to see what happens to the color:

```
print scale_color(fireball_orange, 2.)
```

This adds an additional color tuple to the output:

```
(442, 198, 40)
```

The first (red) component is 442—which is a problem because color components must be a value between 0 and 255! If you use this color tuple in Pygame it will throw a TypeError exception, so it is important that we "fix" it before using it to draw anything. All we can do is check each component and if it goes over 255, set it back to 255—a process known as *saturating* the color. Listing 4-4 is a function that performs color saturation.

Listing 4-4. *Function for Saturating a Color*

```
def saturate_color(color):
    red, green, blue = color
    red = min(red, 255)
    green = min(green, 255)
    blue = min(blue, 255)
    return red, green, blue
```

Listing 4-4 uses the built-in function min, which returns the lower of the two values. If the component is in the correct range, it is returned unchanged. But if it is greater than 255, it returns 255 (which is exactly the effect we need).

If we saturate the extra bright fireball orange after scaling it, we get the following output, which Pygame will happily accept:

```
(255, 198, 40)
```

With color components saturated at 255, the color will be brighter but may not be exactly the same hue. And if you keep scaling a color, it may eventually change to (255, 255, 255), which is bright white. So it is usually better to select the brightest shade of the color you want and scale it downward (using a factor less than 1).

So we now know what scaling does when using a value that is greater than zero. But what if it is less than zero—that is, negative? Using negative values when scaling a color produces negative color components, which don't make sense because you can't have less than zero red, green, or blue in a color. So avoid scaling colors by a negative value!

Blending Colors

Something else you may want to do with colors is blend one color gradually into another. Let's say we have a zombie in a horror game that is normally a sickly shade of zombie green but has recently emerged from a lava pit and is currently glowing a bright shade of fireball orange. Over time the zombie will cool down and return to its usual color. But how do we calculate the intermediate colors to make the transition look smooth?

We can use something called *linear interpolation*, which is a fancy term for moving from one value to another in a straight line. It is such a mouthful that game programmers prefer to use the acronym *lerp*. To lerp between two values, you find the difference between the second and the first value, multiply it by a *factor* between 0 and 1, and then add that to the first value. A factor of 0 or 1 will result in the first or second values, but a factor of .5 gives a value that is halfway between the first and second. Any other factors will result in a proportional value between the two end points. Let's see an example in Python code to make it clearer. Listing 4-5 defines a function lerp that takes two values and a factor and returns a blended value.

Listing 4-5. *Simple Lerping Example*

```
def lerp(value1, value2, factor):
    return value1+(value2-value1)*factor

print lerp(100, 200, 0.)
print lerp(100, 200, 1.)
print lerp(100, 200, .5)
print lerp(100, 200, .25)
```

This results in the following output. Try to predict what the result of lerp(100, 200, .75) will be.

```
100.0
200.0
150.0
125.0
```

To lerp between colors, you simply lerp between each of the components to produce a new color. If you vary the factor over time, it will result in a smooth color transition. Listing 4-6 contains the function blend_color, which does color lerping.

Listing 4-6. *Blending Colors by Lerping*

```
import pygame
from pygame.locals import *
from sys import exit

pygame.init()
```

```python
screen = pygame.display.set_mode((640, 480), 0, 32)

color1 = (221, 99, 20)
color2 = (96, 130, 51)
factor = 0.

def blend_color(color1, color2, blend_factor):
    red1, green1, blue1 = color1
    red2, green2, blue2 = color2
    red = red1+(red2-red1)*blend_factor
    green = green1+(green2-green1)*blend_factor
    blue = blue1+(blue2-blue1)*blend_factor
    return int(red), int(green), int(blue)

while True:

    for event in pygame.event.get():
        if event.type == QUIT:
            exit()

    screen.fill((255, 255, 255))

    tri = [ (0,120), (639,100), (639, 140) ]
    pygame.draw.polygon(screen, (0,255,0), tri)
    pygame.draw.circle(screen, (0,0,0), (int(factor*639.), 120), 10)

    x, y = pygame.mouse.get_pos()
    if pygame.mouse.get_pressed()[0]:
        factor = x / 639.
        pygame.display.set_caption("PyGame Color Blend Test - %.3f"%factor)

    color = blend_color(color1, color2, factor)
    pygame.draw.rect(screen, color, (0, 240, 640, 240))

    pygame.display.update()
```

If you run Listing 4-6, you will see a slider at the top of the screen. Initially it will be at the far left, representing a factor of 0 (fireball orange). If you click and drag toward the right of the screen, you can smoothly change the blending factor toward 1 (zombie green). The resulting color is displayed in the lower half of the screen.

You can experiment with blending between other colors by changing the values of `color1` and `color2` at the top of the script. Try blending between completely contrasting colors and shades of similar colors.

Using Images

Images are an essential part of most games. The display is typically assembled from a collection of images stored on the hard drive (or CD, DVD, or other media device). In a 2D game, the images may represent background, text, player characters, or artificial intelligence (AI) opponents. In a 3D game, images are typically used as textures to create 3D scenes.

Computers store images as a grid of colors. The way these colors are stored varies depending on how many are needed to reproduce the image. Photographs require the full range of colors, but diagrams or black and white images may be stored differently. Some images also store extra information for each pixel. In addition to the usual red, green, and blue components, there may be an *alpha* component (sometimes known as the *attribute* component). The alpha value of a color is most often used to represent *translucency* so that when drawn on top of another image, parts of the background can show through. We used an image with an alpha channel in Hello World Redux (Listing 3-1). Without an alpha channel, the image of a fish would be drawn inside an ugly rectangle.

CREATING IMAGES WITH AN ALPHA CHANNEL

If you have taken a photo with a digital camera or drawn it with some graphics software, then it probably won't have an alpha channel. Adding an alpha channel to an image usually involves a little work with graphics software. To add an alpha channel to the image of a fish, I used Photoshop, but you can also use other software such as GIMP (`www.gimp.org`) to do this. For an introduction to GIMP, see Akkana Peck's *Beginning GIMP: From Novice to Professional* (Apress, 2006).

An alternative to adding an alpha channel to an existing image is to create an image with a 3D rendering package such as Autodesk's 3ds Max or the free alternative, Blender (`www.blender.org`). With this kind of software you can directly output an image with an invisible background (you can also create several frames of animation or views from different angles). This may produce the best results for a slick-looking game, but you can do a lot with the manual alpha channel technique. Try taking a picture of your cat, dog, or goldfish and making a game out of it!

Storing Images

There are a variety of ways to store an image on your hard drive. Over the years, many formats for image files have been developed, each with pros and cons. Fortunately a small number have emerged as being the most useful, two in particular: JPEG and PNG. Both are well supported in image-editing software and you will probably not have to use other formats for storing images in a game.

- *JPEG (Joint Photographic Expert Group)*—JPEG image files typically have the extension `.jpg` or sometimes `.jpeg`. If you use a digital camera, the files it produces will probably be JPEGs, because they were specifically designed for storing photographs. They use a process known as *lossy* compression, which is very good at shrinking the file size. The downside of lossy compression is that it can reduce the quality of the image, but usually it is so subtle that you will not notice the difference. The amount of compression can also be adjusted to compromise between visual quality and compression. They may be great for photos, but JPEGs are bad for anything with hard edges, such as fonts or diagrams, because the lossy compression tends to distort these kinds of images. If you have any of these kinds of images, PNG is probably a better choice.

- *PNG (Portable Network Graphics)*—PNG files are probably the most versatile of images formats because they can store a wide variety of image types and still compress very well. They also support alpha channels, which is a real boon for game developers. The compression that PNGs use is lossless, which means that images stored as PNG files will be exactly the same as the originals. The downside is that even with good compression they will probably be larger than JPEGs.

In addition to JPEG and PNG, Pygame supports reading the following formats:

- GIF (non animated)

- BMP

- PCX

- TGA (uncompressed only)

- TIF

- LBM (and PBM)

- PBM (and PGM, PPM)

- XPM

As a rule of thumb, use JPEG only for large images with lots of color variation; otherwise, use PNGs.

Working with Surface Objects

Loading images into Pygame is done with a simple one-liner; `pygame.image.load` takes the file name of the image you want to load and returns a surface object, which is a container for an image. Surfaces can represent many types of image, but Pygame hides most of these details from us so we can treat them in much the same way. Once you have a surface in memory, you can draw on it, transform it, or copy it to another surface to build up an image. Even the screen is represented as a surface object. The initial call to pygame.display.set_mode returns a surface object that represents the display.

Creating Surfaces

A call to pygame.image.load is one way to create a surface. It will create a surface that matches the colors and dimensions of the image file, but you can also create blank surfaces of any size that you need (assuming there is enough memory to store it). To create a blank surface, call the pygame.Surface constructor with a tuple containing the required dimensions. The following line creates a surface that is 256 by 256 pixels:

```
blank_surface = pygame.Surface((256, 256))
```

Without any other parameters, this will create a surface with the same number of colors as the display. This is usually what you want, because it is faster to copy images when they have the same number of colors.

There are also a few optional parameters that affect how the images are created. You can set the flags parameter to one or both of the following parameters:

- HWSURFACE—Creates a *hardware* surface, which may be faster than nonhardware surfaces. It is usually better not to set this flag and leave the choice of whether to use hardware surfaces up to Pygame.

- SRCALPHA—Creates a surface with alpha information. Set this if you want parts of the surface to be transparent, for images with irregular edges such as sprites and fonts. This flag also requires that you to set the depth parameter to 32.

There is also a depth parameter for pygame.Surface that defines the color depth for the surface. This is similar to the depth parameter in pygame.display.set_mode and defines the maximum number of colors in the surface. Generally it is best not to set this parameter (or set it to 0), because Pygame will select a depth that matches the display—although if you want alpha information in the surface, you should set depth to 32. The following line creates a surface with alpha information:

```
blank_alpha_surface = pygame.Surface((256, 256), flags=SRCALPHA, depth=32)
```

Converting Surfaces

When you use surface objects, you don't have to worry about how the image information is stored in memory because Pygame will hide this detail from you. So most of the time the image format is something you don't need to worry about, since your code will work regardless of what type of images you use. The only downside of this automatic conversion is that Pygame will have to do more work if you are using images with different formats, and that can potentially decrease game performance. The solution is to convert all your images to be the same format. Surface objects have a convert method for this purpose.

If you call convert without any parameters, the surface will be converted to the format of the display surface. This is useful because it is usually fastest to copy surfaces when the source and destination are the same type—and most images will be copied to the display eventually.

It is a good idea to tack on .convert() to any calls to pygame.image.load to ensure your images will be in the fastest format for the display. The exception is when your image has an alpha channel, because convert can discard it. Fortunately Pygame provides a convert_alpha method, which will convert the surface to a fast format but preserve any alpha information in the image. We have used both methods in the previous chapter; the following two lines are taken from Listing 3-1:

```
background = pygame.image.load(background_image_filename).convert()
mouse_cursor = pygame.image.load(mouse_image_filename).convert_alpha()
```

The background is just a solid rectangle so we use convert. However, the mouse cursor has irregular edges and needs alpha information, so we call convert_alpha.

Both convert and convert_alpha can take another surface as a parameter. If a surface is supplied, the surface will be converted to match the other surface.

Rectangle Objects

Pygame will often require you to give it a rectangle to define what part of the screen should be affected by a function call. For instance, you can restrict Pygame to drawing on a rectangular area of the screen by setting the clipping rectangle (covered in the next section). You can define a rectangle using a tuple that contains four values: the x and y coordinate of the top-left corner followed by the width and height of the rectangle. Alternatively, you can give the x and y coordinate as a single tuple followed by the width and height as another tuple. The following two lines define the rectangle with the same dimensions:

```
my_rect1 = (100, 100, 200, 150)
my_rect2 = ((100, 100), (200, 150))
```

You can use whichever method is most convenient at the time. For instance, you may already have the coordinate and size stored as a tuple, so it would be easier to use the second method.

In addition to defining rectangles, Pygame has a Rect class that stores the same information as a rectangle tuple but contains a number of convenient methods to work with them. Rect objects are used so often that they are included in pygame.locals—so if you have from pygame.locals import * at the top of your script, you don't need to precede them with a module name.

To construct a Rect object, you use the same parameters as a rectangle tuple. The following two lines construct the Rect objects equivalent to the two rectangle tuples:

```
my_rect3 = Rect(100, 100, 200, 150)
my_rect4 = Rect((100, 100), (200, 150))
```

Once you have a Rect object, you can do such things as adjusting its position or size, detect whether a point is inside or outside, or find where other rectangles intersect. See the Pygame documentation for more details (www.pygame.org/docs/ref/rect.html).

Clipping

Often when you are building a screen for a game, you will want to draw only to a portion of the display. For instance, in a strategy Command & Conquer–like game, you might have the top of the screen as a scrollable map, and below it a panel that displays troop information. But when you start to draw the troop images to the screen, you don't want to have them draw over the information panel. To solve this problem, surfaces have a *clipping area*, which is a rectangle that defines what part of the screen can be drawn to. To set the clipping area, call the set_clip method of a surface object with a Rect-style object. You can also retrieve the current clipping region by calling get_clip.

The following snippet shows how we might use clipping to construct the screen for a strategy game. The first call to clip sets the region so that the call to draw_map will only be able to draw onto the top half of the screen. The second call to set_clip sets the clipping area to the remaining portion of the screen:

```
screen.set_clip(0, 0, 640, 300)
draw_map()
screen.set_clip(0, 300, 640, 180)
draw_panel()
```

Subsurfaces

A subsurface is a surface *inside* another surface. When you draw onto a subsurface, it also draws onto its *parent* surface. One use of subsurfaces is to draw graphical fonts. The pygame.font module produces nice, crisp-looking text in a single color, but some games require more graphically rich lettering. You could save an image file for each letter, but it would probably be easier to create a single image with all the letters on it, and then create 26 subsurfaces when you load the image into Pygame.

To create a subsurface, you call the subsurface method of Surface objects, which takes a rectangle that defines what portion of the parent it should cover. It will return a new Surface object that has the same color format as the parent. Here's how we might load a font image and divide it into letter-sized portions:

```
my_font_image = Pygame.load("font.png")
letters = []
letters["a"] = my_font_image.subsurface((0,0), (80,80))
letters["b"] = my_font_image.subsurface((80,0), (80,80))
```

This creates two subsurfaces of my_font_image and stores them in a dictionary so that we can easily look up the subsurface for a given letter. Of course, we would need more than "a" and "b," so the call to subsurface would probably be in a loop that repeats 26 times.

When you work with subsurfaces, it is important to remember that they have their own coordinate system. In other words, the point (0, 0) in a subsurface is always the top-left corner no matter where it sits inside its parent.

Filling Surfaces

When you create an image on the display, you should cover the entire screen; otherwise, parts of the previous screen will show through. If you don't draw over every pixel, you will get an unpleasant strobing effect when you try to animate anything. The easiest way to avoid this is to clear the screen with a call to the `fill` method of surface objects, which takes a color. The following will clear the screen to black:

```
screen.fill((0, 0, 0))
```

The `fill` function also takes an optional rectangle that defines the area to clear, which is a convenient way to draw solid rectangles.

▪Note If you draw over the entire screen with other methods, you won't need to clear it with a call to `fill`.

Setting Pixels in a Surface

One of the most basic things you can do with a surface is set individual pixels, which has the effect of drawing a tiny dot. It is rarely necessary to draw pixels one at a time because there are more efficient ways of drawing images, but if you ever need to do any offline image manipulation it can be useful.

To draw a single pixel onto a surface, use the `set_at` method, which takes the coordinate of the pixel you want to set, followed by the color you want to set it to. We will test `set_at` by writing a script that draws random pixels. When you run Listing 4-7 you will see the screen *slowly* fill up with random-colored dots; each one is an individual pixel.

Listing 4-7. *Script That Draws Random Pixels (random.py)*

```
import pygame
from pygame.locals import *
from sys import exit
from random import randint

pygame.init()
screen = pygame.display.set_mode((640, 480), 0, 32)

while True:

    for event in pygame.event.get():
        if event.type == QUIT:
            exit()
```

```
rand_col = (randint(0, 255), randint(0, 255), randint(0, 255))
for _ in xrange(100):
    rand_pos = (randint(0, 639), randint(0, 479))
    screen.set_at(rand_pos, rand_col)

pygame.display.update()
```

Getting Pixels in a Surface

The complement of set_at is get_at, which returns the color of the pixel at a given coordinate. Getting pixels is occasionally necessary for collision detection so that the code can determine what the player character is standing on by looking at the color underneath it. If all platforms and obstacles are a certain color (or range of colors), this would work quite well. set_at takes just one parameter, which should be a tuple of the coordinates of the pixel you want to look at. The following line gets the pixel at coordinate (100, 100) in a surface called screen:

```
my_color = screen.get_at((100, 100))
```

■**Caution** The get_at method can be very slow when reading from hardware surfaces. The display can be a hardware surface, especially if you are running full screen—so you should probably avoid getting the pixels of the display.

Locking Surfaces

Whenever Pygame draws onto a surface, it first has to be *locked*. When a surface is locked, Pygame has full control over the surface and no other process on the computer can use it until it is unlocked. Locking and unlocking happens automatically whenever you draw onto a surface, but it can become inefficient if Pygame has to do many locks and unlocks.

In Listing 4-7 there is a loop that calls set_at 100 times, which will lead to Pygame locking and unlocking the screen surface 100 times. We can reduce the number of locks and unlocks and speed up the loop by doing the locking manually. Listing 4-8 is almost identical to the previous listing, but will run faster because there is a call to lock before drawing and a call to unlock after all the pixels have been drawn.

■**Caution** There should be the same number of calls to lock as there are to unlock. If you forget to unlock a surface, Pygame may become unresponsive.

Listing 4-8. *Random Pixels with Locking (randoml.py)*

```python
import pygame
from pygame.locals import *
from sys import exit
from random import randint

pygame.init()
screen = pygame.display.set_mode((640, 480), 0, 32)

while True:

    for event in pygame.event.get():
        if event.type == QUIT:
            exit()

    rand_col = (randint(0, 255), randint(0, 255), randint(0, 255))
    screen.lock()
    for _ in xrange(100):
        rand_pos = (randint(0, 639), randint(0, 479))
        screen.set_at(rand_pos, rand_col)
    screen.unlock()
    pygame.display.update()
```

Not all surfaces need to be locked. Hardware surfaces do (the screen is usually a hardware surface), but plain software surfaces do not. Pygame provides a mustlock method in surface objects that returns True if a surface requires locking. You could check the return value of mustlock before you do any locking or unlocking, but there is no problem in locking a surface that doesn't need it, so you may as well lock *any* surface that you plan on doing a lot of drawing to.

Blitting

The method of surface objects that you will probably use most often is blit, which is an acronym for *bit block transfer*. Blitting simply means copying image data from one surface to another. You will use it for drawing backgrounds, fonts, characters, and just about everything else in a game!

To blit a surface, you call blit from the destination surface object (often the display) and give it the source surface (your sprite, background, and so forth), followed by the coordinate you want to blit it to. You can also blit just a portion of the surface by adding a Rect-style object to the parameter that defines the source region. Here are two ways you use the blit method:

```python
screen.blit(background, (0,0))
```

which blits a surface called background to the top-left corner of screen. If background has the same dimensions as screen, we won't need to fill screen with a solid color.

The other way is

```python
screen.blit(ogre, (300, 200), (100*frame_no, 0, 100, 100))
```

If we have an image containing several frames of an ogre walking, we could use something like this to blit it to the screen. By changing the value of frame_no, we can blit from a different area of the source surface.

Drawing with Pygame

We have used a few functions from the pygame.draw module in the preceding examples. The purpose of this module is to draw lines, circles, and other geometric shapes to the screen. You could use it to create an entire game without loading any images. The classic Atari game Asteroids is an example of a great game that just uses shapes drawn with lines. Even if you don't use the pygame.draw module to create a complete game, you will find it useful for experimenting when you don't want to go to the trouble of creating images. You could also use it to draw a debug overlay on top of your game when you need to visualize what is happening in your code.

The first two parameters for functions in pygame.draw are the surface you want to render to—which could be the screen (display surface) or a plain surface—followed by the color you want to draw in. Each draw function will also take at least one point, and possibly a list of points. A point should be given as a tuple containing the x and y coordinates, where (0, 0) is the top left of the screen.

The return value for these draw functions is a Rect object that gives the area of the screen that has been drawn to, which can be useful if we only want to refresh parts of the screen that have been changed. Table 4-2 lists the functions in the pygame.draw module, which we will cover in this chapter.

Table 4-2. *The pygame.draw Module*

Function	Purpose
rect	Draws a rectangle
polygon	Draws a polygon (shape with three or more sides)
circle	Draws a circle
ellipse	Draws an ellipse
arc	Draws an arc
line	Draws a line
lines	Draws several lines
aaline	Draws an antialiased (smooth) line
aalines	Draws several antialiased lines

pygame.draw.rect

This function draws a rectangle onto a surface. In addition to the destination surface and color, pygame.rect takes the dimensions of the rectangle you want to draw and the width of the line. If you set width to 0 or omit it, the rectangle will be filled with solid color; otherwise, just the edges will be drawn.

Let's write a script to test Pygame's rectangle-drawing capabilities. Listing 4-9 draws ten randomly filled rectangles in random positions and colors. It produces a strangely pretty, modern art–like effect.

Listing 4-9. *Rectangle Test*

```
import pygame
from pygame.locals import *
from sys import exit

from random import *

pygame.init()
screen = pygame.display.set_mode((640, 480), 0, 32)

while True:

    for event in pygame.event.get():
        if event.type == QUIT:
            exit()

    screen.lock()
    for count in range(10):
        random_color = (randint(0,255), randint(0,255), randint(0,255))
        random_pos = (randint(0,639), randint(0,479))
        random_size = (639-randint(random_pos[0],639), 479-➥
                randint (random_pos[1],479))
        pygame.draw.rect(screen, random_color, Rect(random_pos, random_size))
    screen.unlock()

    pygame.display.update()
```

There is another way to draw *filled* rectangles on a surface. The `fill` method of `surface` objects takes a `Rect`-style object that defines what part of the surface to fill—and will draw a perfect filled rectangle! In fact, `fill` can be faster than `pygame.draw.rect`; it can potentially be hardware accelerated (in other words, performed by the graphics card and not the main processor).

pygame.draw.polygon

A polygon is a many-sided shape, that is, anything from a triangle to a myriagon (10,000 sides—I looked it up) and beyond. A call to `pygame.draw.polygon` takes a list of points and will draw the shape between them. Like `pygame.rect`, it also takes an optional `width` value. If `width` is omitted or set to 0, the polygon will be filled; otherwise, only the edges will be drawn.

We will test Pygame's polygon-drawing capabilities with a simple script. Listing 4-10 keeps a list of points. Every time it gets a `MOUSEBUTTONDOWN` event, it adds the position of the mouse to the list of points. When it has at least three points, it will draw a polygon.

Try adding a width parameter to the call to pygame.draw.polygon to use nonfilled polygons.

Listing 4-10. *Drawing Polygons with Pygame*

```
import pygame
from pygame.locals import *
from sys import exit

pygame.init()
screen = pygame.display.set_mode((640, 480), 0, 32)

points = []

while True:

    for event in pygame.event.get():
        if event.type == QUIT:
            exit()
        if event.type == MOUSEBUTTONDOWN:
            points.append(event.pos)

    screen.fill((255,255,255))

    if len(points) >= 3:
        pygame.draw.polygon(screen, (0,255,0), points)
    for point in points:
        pygame.draw.circle(screen, (0,0,255), point, 5)

    pygame.display.update()
```

pygame.draw.circle

The circle function draws a circle on a surface. It takes the center point and the radius of the circle (the radius is the distance from the center to the edge). Like the other draw functions, it also takes a value for the width of the line. If width is 0 or omitted, the circle will be drawn with a line; otherwise, it will be a solid circle. Listing 4.11 draws randomly filled circles on the screen, in a random color.

Listing 4-11. *Random Circles*

```
import pygame
from pygame.locals import *
from sys import exit

from random import *
```

```
pygame.init()
screen = pygame.display.set_mode((640, 480), 0, 32)

while True:

    for event in pygame.event.get():
        if event.type == QUIT:
            exit()

    random_color = (randint(0,255), randint(0,255), randint(0,255))
    random_pos = (randint(0,639), randint(0,479))
    random_radius = randint(1,200)
    pygame.draw.circle(screen, random_color, random_pos, random_radius)

    pygame.display.update()
```

pygame.draw.ellipse

You can think of an ellipse as being a *squashed* circle. If you were to take a circle and stretch it to fit it into a rectangle, it would become an ellipse. In addition to surface and color, the ellipse function takes a Rect-style object that the ellipse should fit in to. It also takes a width parameter, which is used just like rect and circle. Listing 4-12 draws an ellipse that fits in a rectangle stretching from the top-left corner of the screen to the current mouse position.

Listing 4-12. *Drawing an Ellipse*

```
import pygame
from pygame.locals import *
from sys import exit

from random import *

pygame.init()
screen = pygame.display.set_mode((640, 480), 0, 32)

while True:

    for event in pygame.event.get():
        if event.type == QUIT:
            exit()

    x, y = pygame.mouse.get_pos()
    screen.fill((255,255,255))
    pygame.draw.ellipse(screen, (0,255,0), (0,0,x,y))

    pygame.display.update()
```

pygame.draw.arc

The arc function draws just a section of an ellipse, but only the edge; there is no fill option for arc. Like the ellipse function, it takes a Rect-style object that the arc would fit into (if it covered the entire ellipse). It also takes two angles in radians. The first angle is where the arc should start drawing, and the second is where it should stop. It also takes a width parameter for the line, which defaults to 1, but you can set it to greater values for a thicker line. Listing 4-13 draws a single arc that fits into the entire screen. The end angle is taken from the x coordinate of the mouse, so if you move the mouse left and right it will change the length of the arc.

Listing 4-13. *Arc Test*

```
import pygame
from pygame.locals import *
from sys import exit

from random import *
from math import pi

pygame.init()
screen = pygame.display.set_mode((640, 480), 0, 32)

while True:

    for event in pygame.event.get():
        if event.type == QUIT:
            exit()

    x, y = pygame.mouse.get_pos()
    angle = (x/639.)*pi*2.
    screen.fill((255,255,255))
    pygame.draw.arc(screen, (0,0,0), (0,0,639,479), 0, angle)

    pygame.display.update()
```

pygame.draw.line

A call to pygame.draw.line will draw a line between two points. After the surface and color, it takes two points: the start point and the end point of the line you want to draw. There is also the optional width parameter, which works the same way as rect and circle. Listing 4-14 draws several lines from the edges of the screen to the current mouse position.

Listing 4-14. *Line Drawing (drawinglines.py)*

```
import pygame
from pygame.locals import *
from sys import exit
```

```
pygame.init()
screen = pygame.display.set_mode((640, 480), 0, 32)

while True:

    for event in pygame.event.get():
        if event.type == QUIT:
            exit()

    screen.fill((255, 255, 255))

    mouse_pos = pygame.mouse.get_pos()

    for x in xrange(0,640,20):
        pygame.draw.line(screen, (0, 0, 0), (x, 0), mouse_pos)
        pygame.draw.line(screen, (0, 0, 0), (x, 479), mouse_pos)

    for y in xrange(0,480,20):
        pygame.draw.line(screen, (0, 0, 0), (0, y), mouse_pos)
        pygame.draw.line(screen, (0, 0, 0), (639, y), mouse_pos)

    pygame.display.update()
```

pgame.draw.lines

Often lines are drawn in sequence, so that each line begins where the previous one left off. The first parameter to pygame.draw.lines is a boolean that indicates whether the line is closed. If set to True an additional line will be drawn between the last point in the list and the first; otherwise, it will be left open. Following this value is a list of points to draw lines between and the usual width parameter.

Listing 4-15 uses pygame.draw.lines to draw a line from a list of points, which it gets from the mouse position. When there are more than 100 points in the list, it deletes the first one, so the line miraculously starts to "undraw" itself! This might be a good starting point for a *worm* game.

Listing 4-15. *Drawing Multiple Lines (multiplelines.py)*

```
import pygame
from pygame.locals import *
from sys import exit

pygame.init()
screen = pygame.display.set_mode((640, 480), 0, 32)

points = []

while True:
```

```
    for event in pygame.event.get():
        if event.type == QUIT:
            exit()
        if event.type == MOUSEMOTION:
            points.append(event.pos)
            if len(points)>100:
                del points[0]

    screen.fill((255, 255, 255))

    if len(points)>1:
        pygame.draw.lines(screen, (0,255,0), False, points, 2)

    pygame.display.update()
```

pygame.draw.aaline

You may have noticed from the previous line drawing functions that the lines have a *jagged* appearance. This is because a pixel can only be drawn at a coordinate on a grid, which may not lie directly underneath a line if it is not horizontal or vertical. This effect is called *aliasing*, something which computer scientists have put a lot of work into avoiding. Any technique that attempts to avoid or reduce aliasing is called *antialiasing*.

Pygame can draw antialiased lines that appear significantly smoother than the lines drawn by pygame.draw.line. The function pygame.draw.aaline has the same parameters as pygame.draw.line but draws smooth lines. The downside of antialiased lines is that they are slower to draw than regular lines, but only marginally so. Use aaline whenever visual quality is important.

To see the difference, replace the call to pygame.draw.line in the previous example code with the aaline version.

pygame.draw.aalines

Just like pygame.draw.line, there is an antialiased version of pygame.draw.lines. A call to pygame.draw.aalines uses the same parameters as pygame.draw.lines but draws smooth lines, so it is easy to switch between the two in code.

Summary

Colors are the most fundamental things in creating computer graphics. All images in a game are ultimately created by manipulating colors in some form or another. We've seen how Pygame stores colors and how to make new colors by combining existing ones. In the process of learning about color manipulation, we introduced lerping (linear interpolation), which we will use for various game tasks.

Surface objects are Pygame's canvases, and can store all kinds of images. Fortunately we don't have to worry about the details of how they are stored, because when you manipulate images through a surface they all appear to be the same type.

We covered the draw module in some detail, because it is handy for visually depicting additional information in your game. For instance, you could use it to draw a little arrow over your enemy character indicating which way they are headed.

This chapter has covered *all* the ways that you can create visuals with Pygame. Armed with this information, you can create images of dungeons, alien worlds, and other game environments.

In the next chapter you will learn how to animate graphics over time.

CHAPTER 5

■■■

Making Things Move

In the real world, objects move in a variety of different ways, depending on what they are doing, and a game must approximate those motions to create a convincing virtual representation. A few games can get away with unrealistic motion—Pac-Man, for example, moves in a straight line with a constant speed and can change direction in an instant, but if you applied that kind of motion to a car in a driving game it would destroy the illusion. After all, in a driving game you would expect the car to take some time to reach full speed and it definitely shouldn't be able to turn 180 degrees in an instant!

For games with a touch of realism, the game programmer has to take into account what is making things move. Let's look at a typical driving game. Regardless of whether the vehicle is a bike, a rally car, or a semitruck, there is a force from the engine driving it forward. There are also other forces acting on it. Resistance from the wheels will vary depending on the surface you are driving on, so a vehicle will handle differently on mud than it will on tarmac. And of course there is gravity, which is constantly pulling the car toward the earth (something that the player may not notice until he tries to jump a canyon)! In actual fact there are probably hundreds of other forces that combine to create the motion of a vehicle.

Fortunately for us game programmers, we only have to simulate a few of these forces in order to create the convincing illusion of movement. And once our simulation code is written, we can apply it to many objects in the game. Gravity, for example, will affect everything (unless the game is set in space), so we can apply the gravity-related code to any object, whether it is a tossed hand grenade, a tank falling from a cliff, or an axe flying through the air.

This chapter describes how to move objects about the screen in a predictable fashion, and how to make that movement consistent on other people's computers.

Understanding Frame Rate

The first thing we need to know about movement in a computer game is that nothing really moves—at least not in any physical sense. A computer screen or television set presents us with a sequence of images, and when the time between the images is short enough, our brain blends the images together to create the illusion of fluid motion. The number of images, or *frames*, required to produce smooth motion can vary from person to person. Movies use 24 frames per second, but computer games tend to require a faster frame rate. Thirty frames per second is a good rate to aim for, but generally speaking the higher the frame rate, the smoother the motion will look—although after about 70 frames per second, few people can detect any improvement, even if they claim they can!

The frame rate for a game is also limited by the number of times per second that the display device (such as your monitor) can refresh. For instance, my LCD monitor has a refresh rate of 60 hertz, which means it refreshes the display 60 times every second. Generating frames faster than the refresh rate can lead to what is known as "tearing," where part of the next frame is combined with a previous frame.

Obtaining a good frame rate generally means compromising on visual effects, because the more work your computer is doing, the slower the frame rate will be. The good news is that the computer on your desktop is probably more than fast enough to generate the visuals you want.

Moving in a Straight Line

Let's start out by examining simple straight-line movement. If we move an image by a fixed amount each frame, then it will appear to move. To move it horizontally, we would add to the x coordinate, and to move it vertically we would add to the y coordinate. Listing 5-1 demonstrates how to move an image horizontally. It draws an image at a specified x coordinate and then adds the value of 10.0 to each frame, so that on the next frame it will have shifted a little to the right. When the x coordinate passes over the right edge of the screen, it is set back to 0 so that it doesn't disappear completely. Moving 2D images are often referred to as *sprites*.

Listing 5-1. *Simple Straight-Line Movement (simplemove.py)*

```
background_image_filename = 'sushiplate.jpg'
sprite_image_filename = 'fugu.png'

import pygame
from pygame.locals import *
from sys import exit

pygame.init()

screen = pygame.display.set_mode((640, 480), 0, 32)

background = pygame.image.load(background_image_filename).convert()
sprite = pygame.image.load(sprite_image_filename)

# The x coordinate of our sprite
x = 0.

while True:

    for event in pygame.event.get():
        if event.type == QUIT:
            exit()
```

```
screen.blit(background, (0,0))
screen.blit(sprite, (x, 100))
x+= 10.

# If the image goes off the end of the screen, move it back
if x > 640.:
    x -= 640.

pygame.display.update()
```

If you run Listing 5-1, you will see the fugu image sliding from left to right. This is exactly the effect we were looking for, but there is a flaw in the design for Listing 5-1. The problem is that we can't know exactly how long it will take to draw the image to the screen. It looks reasonably smooth because we are creating an extremely simple frame, but in a game the time to draw a frame will vary depending on how much activity there is on screen. And we don't want a game that slows down just as it is getting interesting. Another problem is that the sprite in Listing 5-1 will move more slowly on less powerful computers and more quickly on more capable machines.

It's About Time

The trick to solving this problem is to make the motion *time-based*. We need to know how much time has passed since the previous frame so we can position everything on the screen accordingly. The pygame.time module contains a Clock object that we can use to keep track of time. To create a clock object, call its constructor pygame.time.Clock:

```
clock = pygame.time.Clock()
```

Once you have a clock object, you should call its member function tick once per frame, which returns the time passed since the previous call in milliseconds (there are 1,000 milliseconds in a second):

```
time_passed = clock.tick()
```

The tick function also takes an optional parameter for the maximum frame rate. You may want to set this parameter if the game is running on the desktop so that it doesn't use all the computer's processing power:

```
# Game will run at a maximum 30 frames per second
time_passed = clock.tick(30)
```

Milliseconds are often used to time events in games because it can be easier to deal with integer values rather than fractional times, and 1,000 clock ticks per second is generally accurate enough for most game tasks. That said, I often prefer to work in seconds when dealing with things such as speeds, because 250 pixels per second makes more sense to me than .25 pixels per millisecond. Converting from milliseconds to seconds is as simple as dividing by 1,000:

```
time_passed_seconds = time_passed / 1000.0
```

■**Caution** Be sure to divide by a floating-point value of 1000.0. If you don't include the floating point, the result will be rounded down to the nearest integer!

So how do we use `time_passed_seconds` to move a sprite? The first thing we need to do is choose a speed for the sprite. Let's say that our sprite moves at 250 pixels per second. At that speed, the sprite will cover the width of a 640-pixel screen in 2.56 seconds (640 divided by 250). Next we need to work out how far the sprite has moved in the short amount of time since the last frame, and add that value to the x coordinate. The math for this is quite simple: just multiply the speed of the sprite by `time_passed_seconds`. Listing 5-2 builds on Listing 5-1 by adding time-based movement, and will move the sprite at the same speed regardless of the speed of the computer you run it on.

Listing 5-2. *Time-Based Movement (timebasedmovement.py)*

```python
background_image_filename = 'sushiplate.jpg'
sprite_image_filename = 'fugu.png'

import pygame
from pygame.locals import *
from sys import exit

pygame.init()

screen = pygame.display.set_mode((640, 480), 0, 32)

background = pygame.image.load(background_image_filename).convert()
sprite = pygame.image.load(sprite_image_filename)

# Our clock object
clock = pygame.time.Clock()

# X coordinate of our sprite
x = 0.
# Speed in pixels per second
speed = 250.

while True:

    for event in pygame.event.get():
        if event.type == QUIT:
            exit()
```

```
        screen.blit(background, (0,0))
        screen.blit(sprite, (x, 100))

        time_passed = clock.tick()
        time_passed_seconds = time_passed / 1000.0

        distance_moved = time_passed_seconds * speed
        x += distance_moved

        if x > 640.:
            x -= 640.


        pygame.display.update()
```

It is important to understand the difference between the frame rate and the speed of a sprite in the game. If you were to run Listing 5-2 side by side on a slow computer and a fast computer, then the fugu would be in about the same position on each screen, but the movement on the slow computer would be jerky compared to the fast computer. Rather than run the script on two different machines, let's write a script to simulate the difference (Listing 5-3).

Listing 5-3. *Frame Rate and Speed Comparison (frameratecompare.py)*

```
background_image_filename = 'sushiplate.jpg'
sprite_image_filename = 'fugu.png'

import pygame
from pygame.locals import *
from sys import exit

pygame.init()

screen = pygame.display.set_mode((640, 480), 0, 32)

background = pygame.image.load(background_image_filename).convert()
sprite = pygame.image.load(sprite_image_filename)

# Our clock object
clock = pygame.time.Clock()

x1 = 0.
x2 = 0.
# Speed in pixels per second
speed = 250.

frame_no = 0
```

```
while True:

    for event in pygame.event.get():
        if event.type == QUIT:
            exit()

    screen.blit(background, (0,0))
    screen.blit(sprite, (x1, 50))
    screen.blit(sprite, (x2, 250))

    time_passed = clock.tick(30)
    time_passed_seconds = time_passed / 1000.0

    distance_moved = time_passed_seconds * speed
    x1 += distance_moved

    if (frame_no % 5) == 0:
        distance_moved = time_passed_seconds * speed
        x2 += distance_moved * 5.

    # If the image goes off the end of the screen, move it back
    if x1 > 640.:
        x1 -= 640.
    if x2 > 640.:
        x2 -= 640.

    pygame.display.update()
    frame_no += 1
```

If you run Listing 5-3, you will see two sprites moving on the screen. The top one moves at 30 frames per second or as smoothly as your computer will allow; the other simulates a slow computer by updating only every five frames. You should see that although the movement is very jerky for the second sprite, it does actually move at the same average speed. So for games that use time-based motion, a slow frame rate will result in a less pleasant viewing experience but won't actually slow down the action.

■**Note** Although well-written games should still be playable at slow frame rates, people will be put off play-ing it if the motion is too jerky. Personally I wouldn't want to play a game that ran much under 15 frames per second.

Diagonal Movement

Straight-line motion is useful, but a game would likely get pretty dull if everything moved horizontally or vertically. We need to be able to move a sprite in any direction we choose, which we can do by adjusting both the x *and* the y coordinate for each frame. Listing 5-4 sets a sprite moving in diagonal direction by adding time-based movement to both coordinates. This listing also adds some trivial "collision detection." Rather than push the sprite back to an initial position when it goes over the edge, the sprite bounces in the opposite direction.

Listing 5-4. *Simple Diagonal Movement (diagonalmovement.py)*

```
background_image_filename = 'sushiplate.jpg'
sprite_image_filename = 'fugu.png'

import pygame
from pygame.locals import *
from sys import exit

pygame.init()

screen = pygame.display.set_mode((640, 480), 0, 32)

background = pygame.image.load(background_image_filename).convert()
sprite = pygame.image.load(sprite_image_filename).convert_alpha()

clock = pygame.time.Clock()

x, y = 100., 100.
speed_x, speed_y = 133., 170.

while True:

    for event in pygame.event.get():
        if event.type == QUIT:
            exit()

    screen.blit(background, (0,0))
    screen.blit(sprite, (x, y))

    time_passed = clock.tick(30)
    time_passed_seconds = time_passed / 1000.0

    x += speed_x * time_passed_seconds
    y += speed_y * time_passed_seconds
```

```
# If the sprite goes off the edge of the screen,
# make it move in the opposite direction
if x > 640 - sprite.get_width():
    speed_x = -speed_x
    x = 640 - sprite.get_width()
elif x < 0:
    speed_x = -speed_x
    x = 0.

if y > 480 - sprite.get_height():
    speed_y = -speed_y
    y = 480 - sprite.get_height()
elif y < 0:
    speed_y = -speed_y
    y = 0


pygame.display.update()
```

To accomplish this bounce, we first have to detect that we have hit an edge. This is done with some simple math on the coordinates. If the x coordinate is less than 0, we know we have gone over the left side of the screen because the coordinate of the left edge is 0. If x *plus the width* of the sprite is greater than the width of the screen, we know that the *right edge* of the sprite has hit the right edge of the screen. The code for the y coordinate is similar, but we use the height of the sprite rather than the width:

```
if x > 640 - sprite.get_width():
    speed_x = -speed_x
    x = 640 - sprite.get_width()
elif x < 0:
    speed_x = -speed_x
    x = 0.
```

We have seen that adding a time-based value to the x and y coordinates of a sprite creates a diagonal movement. In Listing 5-4 I picked values for speed_x and speed_y at random, because for this demonstration I didn't really care where the sprite would end up. In a real game, though, we would want to select a final destination for the sprite and calculate speed_x and speed_y accordingly. The best way to do this is with *vectors*.

Exploring Vectors

We used two values to generate diagonal movement: a speed for the x component of the position and another for the y component. These two values combined form what is known as a *vector*. A vector is something that game developers borrowed from mathematics and they are used in many areas, in both 2D and 3D games.

Vectors are similar to points in that they both have a value for x and y (in 2D), but they are used for different purposes. A point at coordinate (10, 20) will always be the same point on the screen, but a vector of (10, 20) means *add 10 to the x coordinate and 20 to the y coordinate from the current position.* So you could think of a point as being a vector from the origin (0, 0).

Creating Vectors

You can calculate a vector from any two points by subtracting the values in the first point from the second. Let's demonstrate with an example from a fictional game. The player character—a cybernetically enhanced soldier from the future named Alpha—has to destroy a Beta class sentry droid with a sniper rifle. Alpha is hiding behind a bush at coordinate A (10, 20) and aiming at Beta at coordinate B (30, 35). To calculate a vector AB to the target, Alpha has to subtract the components of B from A. So vector AB is (30, 35) – (10, 20), which is (20, 15). This tells us that to get from A to B we would have to go 20 units in the x direction and 15 units in the y direction (see Figure 5-1). The game would need this information in order to animate a projectile weapon or draw a laser beam between the two points.

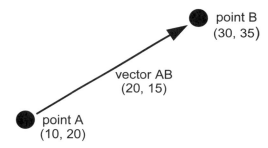

Figure 5-1. *Creating a vector*

Storing Vectors

There is no built-in vector type in Python, but you can store a vector in a tuple or list of two values, or you can define a vector class. Defining a class is probably the best option because you can refer to the components by name (x or y) rather than as an index ([0] or [1]). Listing 5-5 demonstrates how we might begin defining a vector class. I called it Vector2 because vectors are also used in 3D games and we may want to have a 3D version of the vector class called Vector3. In addition to the constructor there is a __str__ method, which turns a Vector2 object into a string when it is printed; without it, we would have to print each component individually.

Listing 5-5. *Simple Vector Definition*

```python
class Vector2(object):

    def __init__(self, x=0.0, y=0.0):
        self.x = x
        self.y = y

    def __str__(self):
        return "(%s, %s)"%(self.x, self.y)
```

To define a vector, we can now use Vector2 objects. For instance, a call to my_vector = Vector2(10, 20) produces a Vector2 object called my_vector. We can refer to the components of the vector individually as my_vector.x and my_vector.y.

The first thing we should add to our Vector2 class is a method to create a vector from two points, because this is the most common way to create a vector (see Listing 5-6).

Listing 5-6. *Vector from Points*

```
class Vector2(object):

    def __init__(self, x=0.0, y=0.0):
        self.x = x
        self.y = y

    def __str__(self):
        return "(%s, %s)"%(self.x, self.y)

    @classmethod
    def from_points(cls, P1, P2):
        return cls( P2[0] - P1[0], P2[1] - P1[1] )
```

The function from_points looks like a normal function, but the line where it is defined is preceded by @classmethod, making it a *class method*. These class methods are called from the class and not an instance of the class, such as Vector2.from_points(P1, P2). I made from_points a class method because it creates a new Vector2 object rather than modifying an existing one. Listing 5-7 shows how we would use it to create a vector between two points.

Listing 5-7. *Testing the* from_points *Method*

```
A = (10.0, 20.0)
B = (30.0, 35.0)
AB = Vector2.from_points(A, B)
print AB
```

Executing this example produces the following output:

```
(20.0, 15.0)
```

Vector Magnitude

The magnitude of a vector from A to B is the distance between those two points. Continuing with the cyber-soldier theme, Alpha has a limited amount of fuel and needs to calculate the distance from A to B to know if he can make it to B. We have already calculated vector AB as (20, 15). The magnitude will give us the distance he needs to travel.

To calculate the magnitude of a vector, square the components, add them together, and then take the square root of the result. So the magnitude of a vector (20, 15) is the square root of 20 ×20 + 15 ×15, which is 25 (see Figure 5-2). Let's add a method to our Vector2 to calculate the magnitude (Listing 5-8).

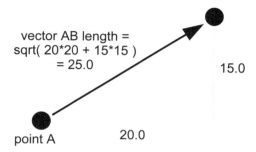

Figure 5-2. *Creating a vector*

Listing 5-8. *Vector Magnitude Function*

```
import math

class Vector2(object):

    def __init__(self, x=0.0, y=0.0):
        self.x = x
        self.y = y

    def __str__(self):
        return "(%s, %s)"%(self.x, self.y)

    @classmethod
    def from_points(cls, P1, P2):
        return Vector2(cls, P2[0] - P1[0], P2[1] - P1[1])

    def get_magnitude(self):
        return math.sqrt( self.x**2 + self.y**2 )

A = (10.0, 20.0)
B = (30.0, 35.0)
AB = Vector2.from_points(A, B)
print AB
print AB.get_magnitude()
```

```
(20.0, 15.0)
25.0
```

The line `math.sqrt(self.x**2 + self.y**2)` does the magnitude calculation. The ** operator in Python raises a value to a power, so we could just as easily have written the calculation as `math.sqrt(self.x*self.x + self.y*self.y)`.

The last few lines create a test vector, and then call the `get_magnitude` we just added. If you have some graph paper handy, you may want to plot the points A and B and verify that the distance between the two is 25.0.

Unit Vectors

Vectors actually describe two things: magnitude *and* direction. For instance, soldier Alpha can use the vector AB to figure out how far he has to travel (magnitude), but the vector also tells him in which direction to face (direction). Normally these two pieces of information are tied up together in a vector, but occasionally you only require one or the other. We have already seen how to calculate the magnitude, but we can also remove the magnitude information from the vector by dividing the components by the magnitude. This is called *normalizing* the vector, and produces a special kind of vector called a *unit vector*. Unit vectors always have a length of 1, and are often used to represent a heading. When we move into the third dimension, you will find them essential for everything from collision detection to lighting. Let's add a method to Vector2 that normalizes the vector and turns it into a unit vector (Listing 5-9).

Listing 5-9. *Testing the Unit Vector Method*

```
import math

class Vector2(object):

    def __init__(self, x=0.0, y=0.0):
        self.x = x
        self.y = y

    def __str__(self):
        return "(%s, %s)"%(self.x, self.y)

    @classmethod
    def from_points(cls, P1, P2):
        return cls( P2[0] - P1[0], P2[1] - P1[1] )

    def get_magnitude(self):
        return math.sqrt( self.x**2 + self.y**2 )

    def normalize(self):
        magnitude = self.get_magnitude()
        self.x /= magnitude
        self.y /= magnitude
```

```
A = (10.0, 20.0)
B = (30.0, 35.0)
AB = Vector2.from_points(A, B)
print "Vector AB is", AB
print "Magnitude of Vector AB is", AB.get_magnitude()
AB.normalize()
print "Vector AB normalized is", AB
```

Executing this script produces the following output:

```
Vector AB is (20.0, 15.0)
Magnitude of Vector AB is 25.0
Vector AB normalized is (0.8, 0.6)
```

Vector Addition

Vector addition combines two vectors to produce a single vector that has the combined effect of both. Let's say soldier Alpha has to rendezvous with a drop ship at point C (15, 45) after picking up whatever the droid at point B was guarding. The vector from B to C is (–15, 10), which means he has to go back 15 units in the x direction and continue on 5 units in the y direction. If we add the components of the BC vector to the AB vector, we get a vector that would take us from A to C (see Figure 5-3).

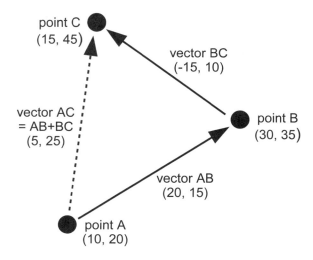

Figure 5-3. *Vector addition*

To add vector addition to our vector library, we *could* create a method called add, then call AB.add(BC) to return the result of adding AB and BC together, but it would be more natural if we could simply call AB+BC. Python provides a way for us to do this. By defining a special method called __add__, we can let Python know how to add two instances of Vector2 together.

When Python sees AB+BC, it will attempt to call AB.__add__(BC), so we should define __add__ to return a new object containing the result of the calculation. This is known as *operator overloading*. There are similar special methods for all the basic operators, such as __sub__ for subtract (–) and __mul__ for multiply (*). Listing 5-10 extends the vector class with an __add__ method.

■Caution If you use lists or tuples to store your vectors, don't try to add them together with the + operator. In Python (1, 2)+(3, 4) is *not* (4, 6); it's actually (1, 2, 3, 4)—which is not a valid 2D vector.

Listing 5-10. *Adding the* __add__ *Method to Our* Vector2 *Class*

```python
import math

class Vector2(object):

    def __init__(self, x=0.0, y=0.0):
        self.x = x
        self.y = y

    def __str__(self):
        return "(%s, %s)"%(self.x, self.y)

    @staticmethod
    def from_points(P1, P2):
        return Vector2( P2[0] - P1[0], P2[1] - P1[1] )

    def get_magnitude(self):
        return math.sqrt( self.x**2 + self.y**2 )

    def normalize(self):
        magnitude = self.get_magnitude()
        self.x /= magnitude
        self.y /= magnitude

    # rhs stands for Right Hand Side
    def __add__(self, rhs):
        return Vector2(self.x + rhs.x, self.y + rhs.y)

A = (10.0, 20.0)
B = (30.0, 35.0)
C = (15.0, 45.0)
```

```
AB = Vector2.from_points(A, B)
BC = Vector2.from_points(B, C)

AC = Vector2.from_points(A, C)
print "Vector AC is", AC

AC = AB + BC
print "AB + BC is", AC
```

Executing this script produces the following output:

```
Vector AC is (5.0, 25.0)
AB + BC is (5.0, 25.0)
```

Vector Subtraction

Subtracting a vector means going in the *opposite* direction the vector is pointing. If soldier Alpha was forced to retreat from a well-armed droid, he might calculate a vector to his adversary and then subtract it from his current position to find a point directly behind him. The math for vector subtraction is very similar to addition, but we subtract from the components rather than add. Listing 5-11 shows a method to subtract a vector from another vector, which you can add to the Vector2 class.

Listing 5-11. *Vector Subtraction Method*

```
def __sub__(self, rhs):
    return Vector2(self.x - rhs.x, self.y - rhs.y)
```

Vector Negation

Let's suppose soldier Alpha arrived at point B, only to find he had forgotten his spare batteries; how could he calculate a vector back to A (i.e., Vector BA)? He *could* do the math given the points again, but an alternative is to *negate* vector AB, which has already been calculated. Negating a vector creates a vector of the same length that points in the opposite direction. So –AB is the same as BA. To negate a vector, simply negate the components. Listing 5-12 is a member function that does negation, which you can add to the Vector2 class.

Listing 5-12. *Vector Negation*

```
def __neg__(self):
    return Vector2(-self.x, -self.y)
```

Vector Multiplication and Division

It is also possible to multiply (or divide) a vector by a *scalar* (a number), which has the effect of changing the length of the vector. Simply multiply or divide each component by the scalar value. Listing 5-13 adds two methods to our `Vector2` class to implement multiply and divide capabilities.

Listing 5-13. *Vector Multiplication and Division*

```
def __mul__(self, scalar):
    return Vector2(self.x * scalar, self.y * scalar)

def __div__(self, scalar):
    return Vector2(self.x / scalar, self.y / scalar)
```

If you multiply any vector by 2.0, it will double in size; if you divide a vector by 2.0 (or multiply by 0.5), it will halve the size. Multiplying a vector by a number greater than 0 will result in a vector that points in the same direction, but if you were to multiply by a number less than 0, the resulting vector would be "flipped" and point in the opposite direction (see Figure 5-4).

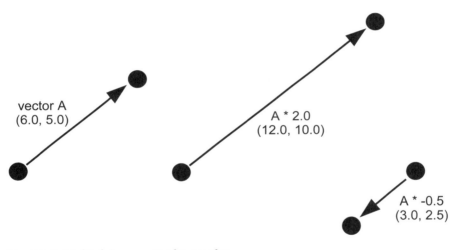

Figure 5-4. *Multiplying a vector by a scalar*

■**Note** Multiplying a vector by another vector is also possible, but it isn't used very often in games and you will probably never need it.

So how might soldier Alpha use vector multiplication—or more accurately, how would the game programmer use it? Vector multiplication is useful to break up a vector into smaller steps based on time. If we know Alpha can cover the distance from A to B in 10 seconds, we can calculate the coordinates where Alpha will be after every second by using a little vector code. Listing 5-14 shows how you might do this using the Vector2 class.

Listing 5-14. *Calculating Positions*

```
A = (10.0, 20.0)
B = (30.0, 35.0)
AB = Vector2.from_points(A, B)
step = AB * .1
position = Vector2(A.x, A.y)
for n in range(10):
    position += step
    print position
```

This produces the following output:

```
(12.0, 21.5)
(14.0, 23.0)
(16.0, 24.5)
(18.0, 26.0)
(20.0, 27.5)
(22.0, 29.0)
(24.0, 30.5)
(26.0, 32.0)
(28.0, 33.5)
(30.0, 35.0)
```

After calculating a vector between points A and B, Listing 5-14 creates a vector step that is one-tenth of the AB vector. The code inside the loop adds this value to position, which is another vector we will use to store Alpha's current location. We do this ten times, once for each second of Alpha's journey, printing out the current position vector as we go. Eventually after ten iterations we reach point B, safe and sound! If you were to take the output and plot the points, you would see that they form a perfect straight line from A to B.

Calculating intermediate positions like this is essential when moving between two points. You can also use vectors to calculate movement under gravity, external forces, and friction to create various kinds of realistic motion.

Game Objects Vector Class

The Vector2 class that we built earlier is good enough for basic vector maths, and you could use it as a starting point for your own vector class (just about every game developer has written a vector class at some point!). However, to get up and running quickly, you can use a Vector2 class I wrote as part of *Game Objects*, a framework to simplify writing games. You can download Game Objects from www.willmcgugan.com/game-objects/.

The Vector2 class is part of a larger collection of classes in the gameobjects namespace. Listing 5-15 shows a few things you can do with it.

Listing 5-15. *Using the Vector2 Class*

```
from gameobjects.vector2 import *
A = (10.0, 20.0)
B = (30.0, 35.0)
AB = Vector2.from_points(A, B)
print "Vector AB is", AB
print "AB * 2 is", AB * 2
print "AB / 2 is", AB / 2
print "AB + (-10, 5) is", AB + (-10, 5)
print "Magnitude of AB is", AB.get_magnitude()
print "AB normalized is", AB.get_normalized()
```

When you run this code it will produce the following output:

```
Vector AB is ( 20, 15 )
AB * 2 is ( 40, 30 )
AB / 2 is ( 10, 7.5 )
AB + (-10, 5) is ( 10, 20 )
Magnitude of AB is 25.0
AB normalized is ( 0.8, 0.6 )
```

Using Vectors to Create Movement

Now that we have covered vectors, we can use them to move game characters in a variety of ways, and implement simple, force-based physics that make a game more convincing.

Diagonal Movement

Let's use vectors to create more accurate diagonal movement. How would we move a sprite from one position on the screen to another, at a constant speed? The first step is to create a vector from the current position to the destination (using Vector2.from_points or something similar). We only need the direction information in this vector, but not the magnitude, so we normalize it to give us the sprite's *heading*. Inside the game loop we calculate how far the sprite has moved with speed * time_passed_seconds, then multiply it by the heading vector. The resulting vector gives us the change in x and y since the previous frame, so we add it to sprite position.

Listing 5-16 implements time-based movement using vectors. When you run it, you will see a sprite sitting motionless on the screen, but once you click the screen, the code will calculate a vector to the new position and set the sprite moving at 250 pixels per second. If you click again, a new vector will be calculated and the sprite will change its heading toward the mouse.

Listing 5-16. *Using Vectors for Time-Based Movement (vectormovement.py)*

```python
background_image_filename = 'sushiplate.jpg'
sprite_image_filename = 'fugu.png'

import pygame
from pygame.locals import *
from sys import exit
from gameobjects.vector2 import Vector2

pygame.init()

screen = pygame.display.set_mode((640, 480), 0, 32)

background = pygame.image.load(background_image_filename).convert()
sprite = pygame.image.load(sprite_image_filename).convert_alpha()

clock = pygame.time.Clock()

position = Vector2(100.0, 100.0)
speed = 250.
heading = Vector2()

while True:

    for event in pygame.event.get():
        if event.type == QUIT:
            exit()
        if event.type == MOUSEBUTTONDOWN:
            destination = Vector2(*event.pos) - Vector2(*sprite.get_size())/2.
            heading = Vector2.from_points(position, destination)
            heading.normalize()

    screen.blit(background, (0,0))
    screen.blit(sprite, position)

    time_passed = clock.tick()
    time_passed_seconds = time_passed / 1000.0

    distance_moved = time_passed_seconds * speed
    position += heading * distance_moved
    pygame.display.update()
```

The destination calculation may require a little explanation. It uses the Vector2 class to find a point that would put our sprite directly over the mouse coordinate. The * symbol, when used in front of a parameter to a function call, expands a tuple or list. So Vector2(*event.pos) is equivalent to Vector2(event.pos[0], event.pos[1]), and will create a vector with the position of the mouse. Similar code is used to create a vector containing half the dimensions of the sprite graphic. Using vectors like this could be considered an abuse of the mathematical concept, but if it saves us a little time it will be worth it. Listing 5-17 shows how we might rewrite the calculation without vector abuse.

Listing 5-17. *Calculating the Destination Coordinate the Long Way*

```
destination_x = event.pos[0] - sprite.get_width()/2.0
destination_y = event.pos[1] - sprite.get_height()/2.0
destination = (destination_x, destination_y)
```

Summary

Moving a sprite, or anything else on screen, requires that you add small values to the coordinates on each frame, but if you want the movement to be smooth and consistent it needs to be based on the current time—or more specifically, the time since the last frame. Using time-based movement is also important for running the game on as wide a range of computers as possible—computers can vary a great deal in the number of frames per second they can generate.

We've covered vectors, which are an essential part of any game developer's toolbox. Vectors simplify a great deal of the math you will do in writing your game, and you will find them remarkably versatile. If you want to take the time to build the Vector2 class we explored in this chapter, it is well worth doing, but you can use the Vector2 class in the Game Objects library to save time. This is also what we will be using in the forthcoming chapters.

The techniques for moving in two dimensions extend easily to three dimensions. You will find that the Vector3 class contains many of the methods used in the Vector2 class but with an additional component (z).

Now would be a good time to start experimenting with moving things on screen and mixing various kinds of movement. A lot of fun can be had by creating graphics of your friends and family on screen and having them slide and bounce along!

In the next chapter, you'll learn how you can connect input devices, such as the keyboard and joystick, to sprites, so that the player can interact with the game world.

■ ■ ■

## CHAPTER 6

Accepting User Input

There are a variety of ways that the player can interact with a game, and this chapter covers the various input devices in detail. In addition to retrieving information from the devices, we will also explore how to translate what the player does into meaningful events in the game. This is extremely important for any game—regardless of how good a game looks and sounds, it must also be easy to interact with.

Controlling the Game

On a typical home computer we can pretty much rely on there being a keyboard and mouse. This venerable setup is preferred by first-person shooter fans who like to control head movement (i.e., looking about) with the mouse and keep one hand on the keyboard for directional controls and firing. The keyboard is most often used as a trigger for actions such as firing, because a key operates like a switch and can only be in one of two states: pressed or not. Keyboards can also be used for motion by assigning a key for the four basic directions: up, down, left, and right. A further four directions can be indicated by pressing these keys in combination (up + right, down + right, down + left, up + left). But having eight directions is still very limiting for most games, so they aren't ideally suited for games that need a little finesse to play.

Most players will prefer an *analog* device such as the mouse. A standard mouse is ideal for a directional control since it can accurately detect anything from tiny adjustments to quick sweeps in any direction. If you have ever played a first-person shooter with just keyboard control, you will appreciate the difference. Pressing the "rotate left" key causes the player to rotate like a robot with a constant speed, which is not nearly as useful as being able to quickly turn around to shoot a monster approaching from the side.

The keyboard and mouse works well for games, which is perhaps a little ironic since neither device was designed with games in mind. Joysticks and joypads, however, were designed purely for games and have evolved alongside the games they are used to play. The first joysticks were modeled after controls used in aircraft and had simple directional sticks with a single button. They were popular with the game consoles of the day, but players found it uncomfortable to have to grip the joystick base with one hand while moving the stick with the other. This led to the development of joypads, which could be held in both hands yet still gave the player easy access to the controls with fingers and thumbs. The first joypads had a directional control on one side and trigger buttons on the other. Nowadays joypads have numerous buttons located everywhere there is a spare finger to press them, along with several sticks. The classic directional pads are still found on joypads, but most also have *analog* sticks that can detect fine adjustments. Many also have *force feedback* features, which can add an extra dimension to games by making the joypad shake or rumble in response to events on the screen. No doubt there will be other features added to joypads in the future that will further enhance the gaming experience.

There are other devices that can be used for games, but most of them mimic the standard input devices. Trackballs and touchpads, for example, are two devices that operate just like a standard mouse. So if your game can be played with the mouse, it will also be playable with these mouse-like devices. Game input devices are constantly being improved, particularly in the console market. They will make it back to home computers eventually and will likely be supported by Pygame. I am looking forward to being able to integrate the motion-sensitive Nintendo Wii controller into a Pygame project!

Understanding Keyboard Control

Most keyboards in use today are *qwerty* keyboards, so called because the initial six letters on the first letter row spell out QWERTY. There are variations between brands; keys can be slightly different shapes and sizes, but they tend to be in approximately the same position on the keyboard. This is a good thing, since computer users don't want to have to relearn how to type every time they buy a new keyboard! All keyboards I have used have had five rows for standard typing keys: one row for function keys F1–F12 and four *cursor* keys for moving a caret around the screen. They also tend to have a "numpad," which is a block of keys for entering numbers and doing sums, and a few other miscellaneous keys. The numpad is often omitted on laptop keyboards to save space, since the number keys are duplicated on the main part of the keyboard. We can detect all of these keys with the `pygame.key` module.

■**Note** Although it is the most common, *qwerty* isn't the only keyboard layout; there are other keyboards such as AZERTY and Dvorak. The same keyboard constants may be used, but the keys may be at a different location on the keyboard. If you give the player the option of selecting their own keys for use in the game, they can select the controls that are most appropriate for their keyboard.

Detecting Key Presses

There are two ways to detect a key press in Pygame. One way is to handle `KEYDOWN` events, which are issued when a key is pressed, and `KEYUP` events, which are issued when the key is released. This is great for typing text because we will always get keyboard events even if a key has been pressed *and* released in the time since the last frame. Events will also capture very quick taps of the key for fire buttons. But when we use keyboard input for movement, we simply need to know if the key is pressed or not before we draw the next frame. In this case, we can use the `pygame.key` module more directly.

Every key on the keyboard has a *key constant* associated with it, which is a value we can use to identify the key in code. Each constant begins with `K_`. There are letters (`K_a` to `K_z`), numbers (`K_0` to `K_9`), and many other constants such as `K_f1`, `K_LEFT`, and `K_RETURN`. See the Pygame documentation for a complete list (`www.pygame.org/docs/ref/key.html`). Since there are constants for K_a to K_z, you may expect there to be equivalent uppercase versions—but there aren't any. The reason for this is that capital letters are the result of combining keys together (Shift + key). If you need to detect capital letters, or other Shifted keys, use the unicode parameter in key events that contain the result of such key combinations.

We can use the pygame.key.get_pressed function to detect whether a key is pressed. It returns a list of booleans (True or False values), one for each of the key constants. To look up a particular key, use its constant as an index into the pressed list. For example, if we were using the spacebar as a fire button, we might write the trigger code like this:

```
pressed_keys = pygame.key.get_pressed()
if pressed_keys[K_SPACE]:
    # Space key has been pressed
    fire()
```

Let's write a script to experiment with the keyboard. Listing 6-1 uses the get_pressed function to detect any pressed keys and displays a list of them on the screen.

■Caution Due to limitations of the hardware, some combinations of keys cannot be detected. See www.sjbaker.org/steve/omniv/keyboards_are_evil.html, which explains why this is the case.

Listing 6-1. *Testing Pressed Keys (keydemo.py)*

```
import pygame
from pygame.locals import *
from sys import exit

pygame.init()
screen = pygame.display.set_mode((640, 480), 0, 32)

font = pygame.font.SysFont("arial", 32);
font_height = font.get_linesize()

while True:

    for event in pygame.event.get():
        if event.type == QUIT:
            exit()

    screen.fill((255, 255, 255))

    pressed_key_text = []
    pressed_keys = pygame.key.get_pressed()
    y = font_height
```

```
for key_constant, pressed in enumerate(pressed_keys):
    if pressed:
        key_name = pygame.key.name(key_constant)
        text_surface = font.render(key_name+" pressed", True, (0,0,0))
        screen.blit(text_surface, (8, y))
        y+= font_height

pygame.display.update()
```

After Listing 6-1 gets the pressed keys as a list of booleans, it enters a for loop that iterates through each value. You'll notice that the loop iterates over the pressed keys indirectly by calling enumerate, which is a built-in function that returns a tuple of the index (the first value is 0, second is 1, and so on) and the value from the iterated list. If the iterated value (pressed) is True, then that key has been pressed, and we enter a small code block to display it on screen. This code block uses another function in the keyboard module, pygame.key.name, which takes a key constant and returns a string with a description of the key (i.e., it turns K_SPACE into "space").

When I first ran Listing 6-1, it displayed numlock pressed even though I wasn't touching it at the time. This is because numlock is a special key that switches a state in the keyboard. When it's on, the numpad can be used to enter numbers. But when it is off, the numpad is used for other keys that do scrolling and navigating text. Another key that works like this is the Caps Lock key. If you tap Caps Lock, Listing 6-1 will display caps lock pressed even when it has been released. Tap it again to disable the Caps Lock state. Another key that does this is Scroll Lock (on a PC keyboard), which doesn't get used much these days. These three keys shouldn't be used as triggers because Pygame can't change this behavior.

Let's go over the pygame.key module in more detail:

- key.get_focused—A Pygame window only receives key events when the window is focused, usually by clicking on the window title bar. This is true of all top-level windows. The get_focused function returns True if the window has focus and can receive key events; otherwise, it returns False. When Pygame is running in full-screen mode, it will always have focus since it doesn't have to share the screen with other applications.

- key.get_pressed—Returns a list of boolean values for each key. If any of the values are set to True, the key for that index is pressed.

- key.get_mods—Returns a single value that indicates which of the modifier keys are pressed. Modifier keys are keys such as Shift, Alt, and Ctrl that are used in combination with other keys. To check if a modifier key is pressed, use the bitwise AND operator (&) with one of the KMOD_ constants. For example, to check if the left Shift key is pressed, you would use pygame.key.get_mods() & KMOD_LSHIFT.

- pygame.key.set_mods—You can also set one of the modifier keys to mimic the effect of a key being pressed. To set one or more modifier keys, combine the KMOD_ constants with the bitwise OR operator (|). For example, to set the Shift and Alt keys you could use pygame.key.set_mods(KMOD_SHIFT | KMOD_ALT).

- pygame.key.set_repeat—If you open your favorite text editor and hold down a letter key, you will see that after a short delay the key starts repeating, which is useful if you want to enter a character several times without pressing and releasing many times. You can ask Pygame to send you repeated KEY_DOWN events with the set_repeat function, which takes a value for the initial delay before a key repeats and a value for the delay between repeated keys. Both values are in milliseconds (1,000 milliseconds in a second). You can disable key repeat by calling set_repeat with no parameters.

- pygame.key.name—This function takes a KEY_ constant and returns a descriptive string for that value. It is useful for debugging because when the code is running we can only see the value for a key constant and not its name. For instance, if I get a KEY_DOWN event for a key with a value of 103, I can use key.name to print out the name of the key (which in this case is "g").

Directional Movement with Keys

You can move a sprite on the screen with the keyboard by assigning a key for up, down, left, and right. Any keys may be used for directional movement, but the most obvious keys to use are the *cursor* keys, since they are designed for directional movement and are positioned in just the right place to operate with one hand. First-person shooter fans will also be accustomed to using the W, A, S, and D keys to move about.

So how do we turn key presses into directional movement? As with most types of movement, we need to create a heading vector that points in the direction we want to go. If only one of the four direction keys is pressed, the heading vector is quite simple. Table 6-1 lists the four basic direction vectors.

Table 6-1. *Simple Direction Vectors*

Direction	Vector
Left	(-1.0, 0.0)
Right	(1.0, 0.0)
Up	(0.0, -1.0)
Down	(0.0, 1.0)

In addition to horizontal and vertical movement, we want the user to be able to move diagonally by pressing two keys at the same time. For example, if the Up and Right keys are pressed, the sprite should move diagonally toward the top right of the screen. We can create this diagonal vector by adding two of the simple vectors. If we add Up (0.0, -1.0) and Right (1.0, 0,0), we get (1.0, -1.0), which points up *and* right, but we can't use this as a heading vector since it is no longer a unit vector (length 1). If we were to use it as a heading vector, we would find that our sprite moves faster diagonally than it does either vertically or horizontally, which is not that useful.

Before we use our calculated heading, we should turn it back into a unit vector by normalizing it, which gives us a heading of approximately (0.707, -0.707). See Figure 6-1 for a visual depiction of the diagonal vectors that are calculated from simple vectors.

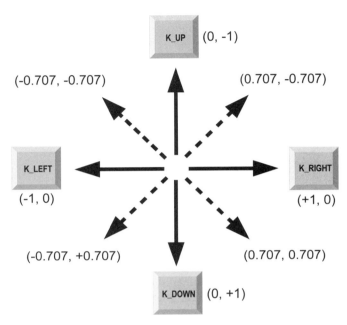

Figure 6-1. *Diagonal vectors by combining simple vectors*

Listing 6-2 implements this directional movement. When you run it, you will see a sprite that can be moved horizontally or vertically by pressing any of the cursor keys, or moved diagonally by pressing two cursor keys in combination.

Listing 6-2. *Simple Directional Movement (keymovement.py)*

```
background_image_filename = 'sushiplate.jpg'
sprite_image_filename = 'fugu.png'

import pygame
from pygame.locals import *
from sys import exit
from gameobjects.vector2 import Vector2

pygame.init()

screen = pygame.display.set_mode((640, 480), 0, 32)
```

```
background = pygame.image.load(background_image_filename).convert()
sprite = pygame.image.load(sprite_image_filename).convert_alpha()

clock = pygame.time.Clock()

sprite_pos = Vector2(200, 150)
sprite_speed = 300.

while True:

    for event in pygame.event.get():
        if event.type == QUIT:
            exit()

    pressed_keys = pygame.key.get_pressed()

    key_direction = Vector2(0, 0)
    if pressed_keys[K_LEFT]:
        key_direction.x = -1
    elif pressed_keys[K_RIGHT]:
        key_direction.x = +1
    if pressed_keys[K_UP]:
        key_direction.y = -1
    elif pressed_keys[K_DOWN]:
        key_direction.y = +1

    key_direction.normalize()

    screen.blit(background, (0,0))
    screen.blit(sprite, sprite_pos)

    time_passed = clock.tick(30)
    time_passed_seconds = time_passed / 1000.0

    sprite_pos += key_direction * sprite_speed * time_passed_seconds

    pygame.display.update()
```

Listing 6-2 cheats a little in calculating the direction vector. It sets the x component to –1 or +1 if K_LEFT or K_RIGHT is pressed and the y component to –1 or +1 if K_UP or K_DOWN is pressed. This gives us the same result as adding two of the simple horizontal and vertical heading vectors together. If you ever see a mathematical shortcut that lets you do something with less code, feel free to try it out—game developers find that they accumulate many such time-saving gems!

You may have noticed that there are only eight vectors used for this vector movement. If we were to precalculate these vectors and insert them into the code directly, we could reduce the amount of work done when running the script. It's worth doing as an exercise if you like a challenge, but since calculating the heading vector is only ever done once per frame, speeding it up will make no noticeable difference to the frame rate. Keep your eye out for situations like this; reducing the amount of work the game must do to creating a frame is called *optimizing* and gets more important when there is a lot of action on the screen.

Rotational Movement with Keys

Moving in eight directions is a little artificial in that you don't see many things moving like this in real life. Most mobile things can rotate freely, but move in the direction they are pointing, or perhaps backward—but definitely in more than eight compass directions. We can still use the same Up, Down, Left, and Right keys to simulate this, but we have to change what the keys control. What we want to do is have keys for left and right that control rotation and keys for forward and back movement, which would give our sprite the ability to move in any direction. Listing 6-3 uses exactly the same set of keys but uses this free rotation control to move the sprite around the screen.

Listing 6-3. *Free Rotation Control (keyrotatemovement.py)*

```
background_image_filename = 'sushiplate.jpg'
sprite_image_filename = 'fugu.png'

import pygame
from pygame.locals import *
from sys import exit
from gameobjects.vector2 import Vector2
from math import *

pygame.init()

screen = pygame.display.set_mode((640, 480), 0, 32)

background = pygame.image.load(background_image_filename).convert()
sprite = pygame.image.load(sprite_image_filename).convert_alpha()

clock = pygame.time.Clock()

sprite_pos = Vector2(200, 150)
sprite_speed = 300.
sprite_rotation = 0.
sprite_rotation_speed = 360. # Degrees per second

while True:

    for event in pygame.event.get():
        if event.type == QUIT:
            exit()
```

```
pressed_keys = pygame.key.get_pressed()

rotation_direction = 0.
movement_direction = 0.

if pressed_keys[K_LEFT]:
    rotation_direction = +1.0
if pressed_keys[K_RIGHT]:
    rotation_direction = -1.0
if pressed_keys[K_UP]:
    movement_direction = +1.0
if pressed_keys[K_DOWN]:
    movement_direction = -1.0

screen.blit(background, (0,0))

rotated_sprite = pygame.transform.rotate(sprite, sprite_rotation)
w, h = rotated_sprite.get_size()
sprite_draw_pos = Vector2(sprite_pos.x-w/2, sprite_pos.y-h/2)
screen.blit(rotated_sprite, sprite_draw_pos)

time_passed = clock.tick()
time_passed_seconds = time_passed / 1000.0

sprite_rotation += rotation_direction * sprite_rotation_speed *➥
time_passed_seconds

heading_x = sin(sprite_rotation*pi/180.0)
heading_y = cos(sprite_rotation*pi/180.0)
heading = Vector2(heading_x, heading_y)
heading *= movement_direction

sprite_pos+= heading * sprite_speed * time_passed_seconds

pygame.display.update()
```

Listing 6-3 works in a similar way to the previous example, but it calculates the heading differently. Rather than create a heading vector from whatever keys are pressed, we create the heading from the rotation of the sprite (stored in the variable sprite_rotation). It is this value that we modify when the appropriate key is pressed. When the Right key is pressed, we add to the sprite rotation, turning it one way. And when the Left key is pressed, we subtract from the rotation to turn it in the opposite direction.

To calculate the heading vector from the rotation, we must calculate the *sine* and *cosine* of the angle, which we can do with the sin and cos functions found in the math module. The sin function calculates the x component, and cos calculates the y component. Both functions take an angle in *radians* (there are 2 * pi radians in a circle), but since Listing 6-3 uses degrees it has to convert the rotation to radians by multiplying by pi and dividing by 180. After we assemble the heading vector from the two components, it can be used as before to give us time-based movement.

Before Listing 6-3 displays the sprite, the sprite is rotated visually so we can see which way it is facing. This is done with a function from the transform module called rotate, which takes a surface plus an angle and returns a new surface containing the rotated sprite. A problem with this function is that the returned sprite may not have the same dimensions as the original (see Figure 6-2), so we can't blit it to the same coordinate as the unrotated sprite or it will be drawn in the wrong position on screen. A way to work around this is to draw the sprite in a position that puts the center of the sprite image underneath the sprite's position on screen. That way, the sprite will be in the same position on the screen regardless of the size of the rotated surface.

Figure 6-2. *Rotating a surface changes its size.*

Implementing Mouse Control

The mouse has been around for almost as long as the keyboard. Mouse design didn't change much for many years—the devices became a little more ergonomic (hand-shaped) but the design remained the same. Classic mice have a rubber-coated ball underneath that rolls over the desk or mousepad. The movement of the ball is picked up by two rollers inside the mouse that are in contact with the ball.

In recent years, though, mice design has undergone a revival. More buttons have been added to the original design. Nowadays most mice have at least three buttons, and some have buttons on the side that can be programmed to mimic keys. Another recent addition is the mouse wheel, which is a roller in the center of the mouse that can be used to scroll a page up and down. Many have done away with the typical mouse ball and roller method of picking up movement and replaced it with a high-tech laser that detects movement from tiny imperfections on the desk (or pad).

Games often make use of these mice innovations. Extra buttons always come in handy for quick access to game controls, and the mouse wheel could have been made for switching weapons in a first-person shooter! And of course the extra accuracy of laser mice always comes in handy when picking off enemies with a sniper rifle.

Rotational Movement with the Mouse

You have seen that drawing a mouse cursor on the screen is quite straightforward: you simply need to get the coordinates of the mouse from a MOUSEMOTION event or directly from the pygame.mouse.get_pos function. Either method is fine if you just want to display a mouse cursor, but mouse movement can also be used to control something other than an absolute position, such as rotating or looking up and down in a 3D game. In this case, we can't use the mouse position directly because the coordinates would be restricted to the edges of the screen, and we don't want the player to be restricted in how many times he turns left or right! In these situations, we want to get the relative movement of the mouse, often called the mouse *mickeys*, which just means how far the mouse has moved since the previous frame. Listing 6-4 adds mouse rotation movement to the sprite demo. In addition to the cursor keys, the sprite will rotate when the mouse is moved left or right.

Listing 6-4. *Rotational Mouse Movement (mouserotatemovement.py)*

```
background_image_filename = 'sushiplate.jpg'
sprite_image_filename = 'fugu.png'

import pygame
from pygame.locals import *
from sys import exit
from gameobjects.vector2 import Vector2
from math import *

pygame.init()
screen = pygame.display.set_mode((640, 480), 0, 32)

background = pygame.image.load(background_image_filename).convert()
sprite = pygame.image.load(sprite_image_filename).convert_alpha()

clock = pygame.time.Clock()

pygame.mouse.set_visible(False)
pygame.event.set_grab(True)

sprite_pos = Vector2(200, 150)
sprite_speed = 300.
sprite_rotation = 0.
sprite_rotation_speed = 360. # Degrees per second

while True:

    for event in pygame.event.get():
        if event.type == QUIT:
            exit()
        if event.type == KEYDOWN:
            if event.key == K_ESCAPE:
                exit()
```

```
    pressed_keys = pygame.key.get_pressed()
    pressed_mouse = pygame.mouse.get_pressed()

    rotation_direction = 0.
    movement_direction = 0.

    rotation_direction = pygame.mouse.get_rel()[0] / 3.

    if pressed_keys[K_LEFT]:
        rotation_direction = +1.
    if pressed_keys[K_RIGHT]:
        rotation_direction = -1.
    if pressed_keys[K_UP] or pressed_mouse[0]:
        movement_direction = +1.
    if pressed_keys[K_DOWN] or pressed_mouse[2]:
        movement_direction = -1.

    screen.blit(background, (0,0))

    rotated_sprite = pygame.transform.rotate(sprite, sprite_rotation)
    w, h = rotated_sprite.get_size()
    sprite_draw_pos = Vector2(sprite_pos.x-w/2, sprite_pos.y-h/2)
    screen.blit(rotated_sprite, sprite_draw_pos)

    time_passed = clock.tick()
    time_passed_seconds = time_passed / 1000.0

    sprite_rotation += rotation_direction * sprite_rotation_speed ➥
* time_passed_seconds

    heading_x = sin(sprite_rotation*pi/180.)
    heading_y = cos(sprite_rotation*pi/180.)
    heading = Vector2(heading_x, heading_y)
    heading *= movement_direction

    sprite_pos+= heading * sprite_speed * time_passed_seconds

    pygame.display.update()
```

To use the mouse to control sprite rotation, Listing 6-4 has to enable *virtual infinite area* for the mouse, which prevents Pygame from restricting the mouse to the physical screen area. This is done with the following two lines:

```
pygame.mouse.set_visible(False)
pygame.event.set_grab(True)
```

The call to `set_visible(False)` switches off the mouse cursor and the call to `set_grab(True)` *grabs* the mouse so that Pygame has complete control over it. A side effect of this is that you cannot use the mouse to close the window, so you must provide an alternative way of closing the script (Listing 6-4 exits if the Esc key is pressed). Using the mouse in this way also makes it difficult to use other applications, which is why it is usually best used in full-screen mode.

The following line in Listing 6-4 gets the mouse mickeys for the x axis (at index [0]). It divides them by 5, because I found that using the value directly rotated the sprite too quickly. You can adjust this value to change the mouse sensitivity (the greater the number, the less sensitive the mouse control will be). Games often let the player adjust the mouse sensitivity in a preferences menu.

```
rotation_direction = pygame.mouse.get_rel()[0] / 5.
```

In addition to rotating with the mouse, the buttons are used to move the sprite forward (left mouse button) and backward (right mouse button). Detecting pressed mouse buttons is similar to keys. The function `pygame.mouse.get_pressed()` returns a tuple of three booleans for the left mouse button, the middle mouse button, and the right mouse button. If any are `True`, then the corresponding mouse button was held down at the time of the call. An alternative way to use this function is the following, which unpacks the tuple into three values:

```
lmb, mmb, rmb = pygame_mouse.get_pressed()
```

Let's look at `pygame.mouse` in more detail. It is another simple module, and has only eight functions:

- `pygame.mouse.get_pressed`—Returns the mouse buttons pressed as a tuple of three booleans, one for the left, middle, and right mouse buttons.

- `pygame.mouse.get_rel`—Returns the relative mouse movement (or mickeys) as a tuple with the x and y relative movement.

- `pygame.mouse.get_pos`—Returns the mouse coordinates as a tuple of the x and y values.

- `pygame.mouse.set_pos`—Sets the mouse position. Takes the coordinate as a tuple or list for x and y.

- `pygame.mouse.set_visible`—Changes the visibility of the standard mouse cursor. If `False`, the cursor will be invisible

- `pygame.mouse.get_focused`—Returns `True` if the Pygame window is receiving mouse input. When Pygame runs in a window, it will only receive mouse input when the window is selected and at the front of the display.

- `pygame.mouse.set_cursor`—Sets the standard cursor image. This is rarely needed since better results can be achieved by blitting an image to the mouse coordinate.

- `pyGame.mouse.get_cursor`—Gets the standard cursor image. See the previous item.

Mouse Gameplay

The humble mouse can allow you to be quite creative in a game. Even a simple cursor can be a great gameplay tool for puzzle and strategy games, where the mouse is often used to pick and drop game elements in the game arena. These elements could be anything from laser-reflecting mirrors to bloodthirsty ogres, depending on the game. The actual mouse pointer doesn't need to be an arrow. For a god game, it would probably be the omnipotent hand of a deity or perhaps a mysterious alien probe. The classic *point 'n' click* adventure games also made excellent use of the mouse. In these games, the game character would walk over to whatever the player clicked on and have a look at it. If it was a useful object, it could be stored away for use later in the game.

For games with more direct control of the player character, the mouse is used for rotation or movement. A flight sim may use the x and y axes of the mouse to adjust the pitch and yaw of the aircraft so that the player can make fine adjustments to the trajectory. A simple way to do this in Pygame would be to add the mouse onto the angle of the aircraft. I also like to use the mouse for first-person shooters and use the x axis for rotating left and right, and the y axis for looking up and down. This feels quite natural because heads tend to move in that way; I can rotate my head to either side as well as look up and down. I can also tilt my head to either side, but I don't do it very often!

You can also combine mouse and keyboard controls. I especially like games that use the keyboard for movement and the mouse for aiming. A tank, for example, might be moved about with the cursor keys, but use the mouse to rotate the turret so that you can fire on an enemy without facing in the same direction.

Of course, you are not limited to using the mouse in the same way as other games. Be as creative as you wish—just be sure to test it on a few of your friends first!

Implementing Joystick Control

Joysticks have not been limited by the need to use them in nongames computing and have been completely free to innovate, so modern joysticks have a smooth molded design and make use of every spare digit players have at their disposal. Although the word *joystick* is often used to mean a game controller of any kind, it more technically describes a flight stick as used in flight simulations. Nowadays the joypad is most popular with game players and often comes with new computers. They fit comfortably in two hands and have many buttons, in addition to a directional pad and two thumb-operated analog sticks.

Pygame's joystick module supports all kinds of controllers with the same interface and doesn't distinguish between the various devices available. This is a good thing because we don't want to have to write code for every game controller out there!

Joystick Basics

Let's start by looking at the pygame.joystick module, which contains just five simple functions:

- pygame.joystick.init—Initializes the joystick module. This is called automatically by pygame.init, so you rarely need to call it yourself.

- pygame.joystick.quit—Uninitializes the joystick module. Like init, this function is called automatically and so is not often needed.

- pygame.joystick.get_init—Returns True if the joystick module has been initialized. If it returns False, the following joystick functions won't work.

- pygame.joystick.get_count—Returns the number of joysticks currently plugged into the computer.

- pygame.joystick.Joystick—Creates a new joystick object that is used to access all information for that stick. The constructor takes the ID of the joystick—the first joystick is ID 0, then ID 1, and so on, up to the number of joysticks available on the system.

The first three functions in the joystick module are used in the initialization process and aren't often called manually. The other two functions are more important because we will need them to find out how many joysticks are plugged into the computer and to create joystick objects for any of the sticks we want to use. These joystick objects can be used to query information about the joystick as well as get the state of any buttons and the position of any analog sticks. Here's how we might get the first joystick plugged into the computer:

```
joystick = None
if pygame.joystick.get_count() > 0:
    joystick = pygame.joystick.Joystick(0)
```

This code uses a variable called joystick that will reference the first joystick. It is set to None initially because it is possible that there are no joysticks plugged into the computer. If there is at least one plugged in (pygame.joystick.get_count() > 0), a joystick object is created for the first joystick ID, which is always 0. We have to be careful when working this way because if we try to use joystick when it is None, Python will throw an exception. So you should first test whether there is a joystick by using if joystick is not None before you attempt to use it.

Joystick Buttons

Joysticks have so many buttons that few games can use them all. For a typical joypad there are four buttons on the right side that are most often used as fire buttons, or for performing the most basic of actions in the game, and one or two buttons in the middle that are used for things like select, start, or pause. There are also generally two or four *shoulder* buttons, which are elongated buttons on the edge of the joypad underneath where the index and forefinger would naturally be placed. I find these buttons are good for actions that require the button to be held down. A racing game, for example, would probably use the shoulder buttons for accelerate and break. Shoulder buttons can also be good in a first-person shooter to *strafe* (sidestep) left and right. Some pads also have an extra two buttons hidden away on the underside of the pad, which can be a little difficult to access and so are probably best for infrequently need actions. Finally, there are usually two buttons that are located underneath the analog sticks so that you have to press the stick down to activate them. These are probably best used to activate something that is being moved with the stick, because it will spring back to the center if the player was to press another button. Not many games make use of these stick buttons, because few games players are even aware of them!

As with the other input devices, you have two options when accessing the joypad: either through events or by querying the state of the pad directly. When a button is pressed on the pad, Pygame issues a JOYBUTTONDOWN event that contains the joystick ID and the index of the button (buttons are numbered from 0 on). You can get the number of buttons on the joystick from the get_numbuttons member function of joystick objects. When a button is released, Pygame issues a corresponding JOYBUTTONDOWN event with the same information.

Let's adapt the events script (Listing 3-2) from Chapter 3 to see the joystick events as they are generated. Listing 6-5 is similar to the original code but initializes all joysticks currently plugged in and filters out any non-joystick-related events.

Listing 6-5. *Displaying the Joystick Events (events.py)*

```
import pygame
from pygame.locals import *
from sys import exit

pygame.init()

SCREEN_SIZE = (640, 480)
screen = pygame.display.set_mode( SCREEN_SIZE, 0, 32)

font = pygame.font.SysFont("arial", 16);
font_height = font.get_linesize()
event_text = []

joysticks = []
for joystick_no in xrange(pygame.joystick.get_count()):
    stick = pygame.joystick.Joystick(joystick_no)
    stick.init()
    joysticks.append(stick)
```

```
while True:

    event = pygame.event.wait()
    if event.type in (JOYAXISMOTION,
                        JOYBALLMOTION,
                        JOYHATMOTION,
                        JOYBUTTONUP,
                        JOYBUTTONDOWN):
        event_text.append(str(event))

    event_text = event_text[-SCREEN_SIZE[1]/font_height:]

    if event.type == QUIT:
        exit()

    screen.fill((255, 255, 255))

    y = SCREEN_SIZE[1]-font_height
    for text in reversed(event_text):
        screen.blit( font.render(text, True, (0, 0, 0)), (0, y) )
        y-=font_height

    pygame.display.update()
```

When you run Listing 6-5 and press some of the buttons on your joystick, you should see
the JOYBUTTONDOWN and corresponding JOYBUTTONUP for each button press (see Figure 6-3). If you
wiggle the analog sticks and press the directional pad, you will also see a variety of other events,
which we will cover in the next section.

Detecting the state of joypad buttons differs slightly from keys and mouse buttons. Rather
than return a list of boolean values, you use the get_button member function in joystick
objects that takes the index of the button and returns its state. Even though you can find the
state of a joystick button at any time, it is often a good idea to get a snapshot of the state of
the buttons at the start of each frame. That way, you can be sure that the state won't change as
you are drawing the screen. Here's how we might get a list of booleans for the button states:

```
joystick_buttons = []
for button_no in range(joystick.get_numbuttons()):
    joystick_buttons.append( joystick.get_button(button_no) )
```

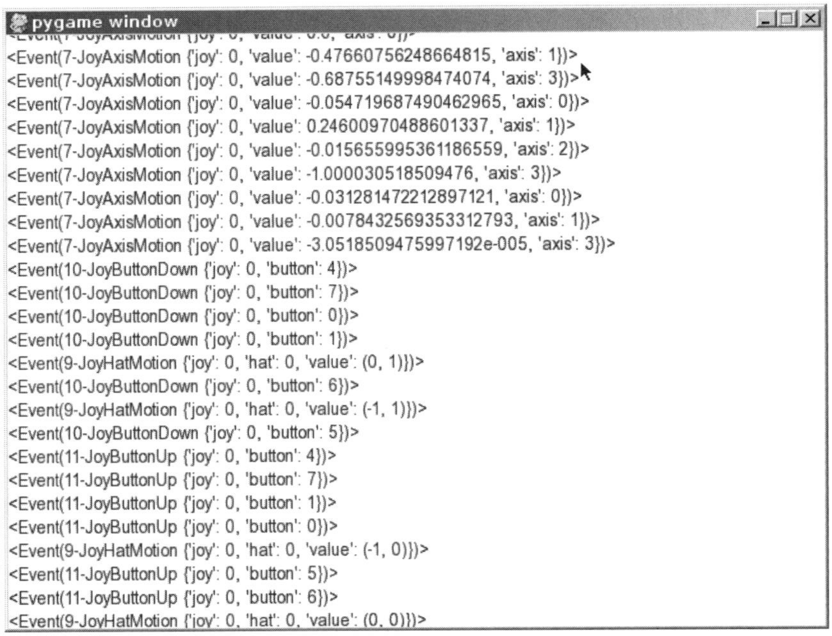

Figure 6-3. *Displaying the joystick events*

Joystick Direction Controls

Whereas buttons on a joystick are most often used for activating actions, we still need some way of moving about or aiming in a game. This is where the directional controls come in. There are typically two forms of direction control on a joystick: the directional pad (d-pad) and the analog stick. Which one you use is heavily dependent on the type of game. Often one is obviously better, but they can also be used in combination for some games. This section covers both, and explains how to convert input from the directional controls into in-game motion.

D-pads

The d-pad, a small circular or cross-shaped button on the joypad, is used to indicate a direction by pressing an edge, usually with the thumb. If you were to look underneath the d-pad, you would see that there are four switches arranged in a cross. When you press the pad in any direction, you also push down one or two of these switches, which are interpreted like cursor keys to give eight directions. D-pads may be old technology, but they are often the best choice for certain game actions. I like using d-pads for selecting menus, panning maps, and jumping around in platform games.

Pygame refers to d-pads as "hats" because classic joysticks had a d-pad-like control directly on top of the stick. For our purposes, though, the *hat* and *d-pad* are the same thing.

When you press the d-pad, Pygame sends you a JOYHATMOTION event. This event contains three values: joy, hat, and value. The first, joy, is the index of the joystick the event came from;

hat is the index of the hat that was pressed; and value indicates which way it was pressed. The hat value is actually a tuple of the changes in the x and y axes—negative number for an axis indicates left or down, and a positive number indicates right or up.

■**Note** There aren't any up and down events for the d-pad because when it is released, it springs back to the middle and another JOYHATMOTION event is sent.

We can also bypass the events for the d-pad and ask Pygame for the current state of the d-pad. The first step is to find out how many d-pads a joystick has (there could be none), which we can do with the get_numhats member function of joystick objects. Then we can get the state of each d-pad with a call to get_hat, which takes the hat index and returns the axis tuple.

This tuple is very similar to the key_direction vector we went to the trouble of creating in Listing 6-2, and we can very conveniently create a heading vector out of it simply by making a Vector2 object from its values and normalizing the result! Listing 6-6 uses this method to scroll an image around the screen.

Listing 6-6. *Using the D-pad to Scroll (hatscroll.py)*

```
picture_file = 'cat.jpg'

import pygame
from pygame.locals import *
from sys import exit
from gameobjects.vector2 import Vector2

pygame.init()
screen = pygame.display.set_mode((640, 480), 0, 32)

picture = pygame.image.load(picture_file).convert()
picture_pos = Vector2(0, 0)
scroll_speed = 1000.

clock = pygame.time.Clock()

joystick = None
if pygame.joystick.get_count() > 0:
    joystick = pygame.joystick.Joystick(0)
    joystick.init()

if joystick is None:
    print "Sorry, you need a joystick for this!"
    exit()
```

```
while True:

    for event in pygame.event.get():
        if event.type == QUIT:
            exit()

    scroll_direction = Vector2(*joystick.get_hat(0))
    scroll_direction.normalize()

    screen.fill((255, 255, 255))
    screen.blit(picture, (-picture_pos.x, picture_pos.y))

    time_passed = clock.tick()
    time_passed_seconds = time_passed / 1000.0

    picture_pos += scroll_direction * scroll_speed * time_passed_seconds

    pygame.display.update()
```

You will need an image file for Listing 6-6. I used a picture of my sister's cat, but you can use any image by editing the value of picture_file at the top of the script. I recommend using a large image so that you can pan around it, *Blade Runner* style.

Analog Sticks

All modern joypads will have at least one analog stick, which are like spring-mounted buttons that can be moved around with the thumbs. Gamers have tended to favor these over the d-pad because they offer finer control and feel more natural for games with a higher level of realism.

Pygame treats analog sticks as two individual axes: one for x (left and right) and one for y (up and down). The reason for treating them separately is that the same functions are used for other devices that may have just a single axis, although analog sticks are by far the most common.

The event for analog stick movement is JOYAXISMOVEMENT, which supplies three pieces of information: joy, axis, and value. The first of these, joy, is the ID of the joystick object; axis is an index for the axis; and value indicates the current position of the axis, which varies between –1 (left or down) and +1 (right or up).

■**Note** The y axis always follows the x axis, so the first stick will use axis index 0 and 1. If there is a second analog stick available, it will use slot 2 and 3.

In addition to the JOYAXISMOVEMENT event, you can get the state of any axis from the joystick object. Use get_numaxis to query the number of axes on the joystick and get_axis to retrieve its current value. Let's expand on Listing 6-6 by adding the ability to scroll with an analog stick (which will make it easier to accurately pan the image).

Listing 6-7 calculates an additional vector, analog_scroll, from the x and y axes. This vector isn't normalized because we will be using it to indicate *how fast* we want to move, in addition to the *direction* we want to move in. We still need to multiply by a value for speed, because the axes range from –1 to +1, which would result in very slow movement.

Listing 6-7. *Scrolling with the Analog Stick (analoghatscroll.py)*

```
picture_file = 'cat.jpg'

import pygame
from pygame.locals import *
from sys import exit
from gameobjects.vector2 import Vector2

pygame.init()
screen = pygame.display.set_mode((640, 480), 0, 32)

picture = pygame.image.load(picture_file).convert()
picture_pos = Vector2(0, 0)
scroll_speed = 1000.

clock = pygame.time.Clock()

joystick = None
if pygame.joystick.get_count() > 0:
    joystick = pygame.joystick.Joystick(0)
    joystick.init()

if joystick is None:
    print "Sorry, you need a joystick for this!"
    exit()

while True:

    for event in pygame.event.get():
        if event.type == QUIT:
            exit()
```

```
    scroll_direction = Vector2(0, 0)
    if joystick.get_numhats() > 0:
        scroll_direction = Vector2(*joystick.get_hat(0))
        scroll_direction.normalize()

    analog_scroll = Vector2(0, 0)
    if joystick.get_numaxes() >= 2:
        axis_x = joystick.get_axis(0)
        axis_y = joystick.get_axis(1)
        analog_scroll = Vector2(axis_x, -axis_y)

    screen.fill((255, 255, 255))
    screen.blit(picture, (-picture_pos.x, picture_pos.y))

    time_passed = clock.tick()
    time_passed_seconds = time_passed / 1000.0

    picture_pos += scroll_direction * scroll_speed * time_passed_seconds
    picture_pos += analog_scroll * scroll_speed * time_passed_seconds

    pygame.display.update()
```

Although Listing 6-7 simply pans an image around the screen, it could be the basis for a scrolling map in a strategy or god game.

Dealing with Joystick Dead Zones

Because analog sticks and other axis devices are mechanical things, they tend to suffer from wear and tear, and even brand-new controllers can have imperfections. This can result in the stick wobbling a tiny amount when it is not being manipulated. If you see a constant stream of JOYAXISMOTION events without touching anything, then your controller suffers from this. Don't throw it away just yet, though—this problem is easily handled in code. If the values for the axis are very close to zero, then set them to zero. This creates what is called a *dead zone* in the center of the stick, where no movement will be detected. It should be small enough that the player won't notice it but still mask any noise from worn-out sticks.

Add the following snippet to the previous listing (just after axis_x and axis_y are assigned) to create a dead zone:

```
if abs(axis_x) < 0.1:
    axis_x = 0.
if abs(axis_y) < 0.1:
    axis_y = 0.
```

Joystick Objects

Joystick objects hold all the information that you need from a joystick. There can be one for each joystick or game controller you have plugged in. Let's take a look at joystick objects in more detail. They contain the following methods:

- `joystick.init`—Initializes the joystick. Must be called prior to other functions in the joystick object.

- `joystick.quit`—Uninitializes the joystick. After a call to this, Pygame won't send any more joystick-related events from the device.

- `joystick.get_id`—Retrieves the ID of the joystick (the same ID that was given to the Joystick constructor).

- `joystick.get_name`—Retrieves the name of the joystick (usually a string supplied by the manufacturer). This string will be unique for all the joysticks.

- `joystick.get_numaxes`—Retrieves the number of axes on the joystick.

- `joystick.get_axis`—Retrieves a value between –1 and +1 for an axis. This function takes the index of the axis you are interested in.

- `joystick.get_numballs`—Retrieves the number of trackballs on the joystick. A trackball is similar to a mouse but only gives relative motion.

- `joystick.get_ball`—Retrieves a tuple containing the relative motion in the x and y axes of a ball since the previous call to get_ball. Takes the index of the ball you are interested in.

- `joystick.get_button`—Retrieves the state of a button, which will either be True (for pressed) or False (for not pressed). This function takes the index of the button you are interested in.

- `joystick.get_numhats`—Retrieves the number of d-pads on a joystick.

- `joystick.get_hat`—Retrieves the state of hat as a tuple of two values for the x and y axes. This function takes an index of the hat you are interested in.

Seeing Joysticks in Action

Let's write a script to help you play with the `pygame.joystick` module. Listing 6-8 draws a crude representation of the current state of your joystick, including the axes, the d-pads, and all the buttons. You can switch between joysticks you have plugged in by pressing the number keys (0 is the first joystick, 1 is the second, and so on).

If you ever have trouble getting a joystick to work in a game, test it with Listing 6-8 (see Figure 6-4). You will easily be able to tell if a button or control isn't working properly.

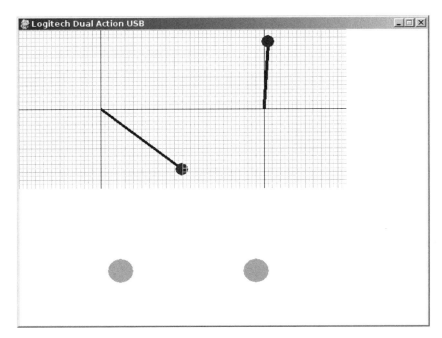

Figure 6-4. *The joystick demo script in action*

Listing 6-8. *Joystick Demo (joystickdemo.py)*

```
import pygame
from pygame.locals import *
from sys import exit

pygame.init()
screen = pygame.display.set_mode((640, 480), 0, 32)

# Get a list of joystick objects
joysticks = []
for joystick_no in xrange(pygame.joystick.get_count()):
    stick = pygame.joystick.Joystick(joystick_no)
    stick.init()
    joysticks.append(stick)

if not joysticks:
    print "Sorry! No joystick(s) to test."
    exit()

active_joystick = 0
```

```
pygame.display.set_caption(joysticks[0].get_name())

def draw_axis(surface, x, y, axis_x, axis_y, size):

    line_col = (128, 128, 128)
    num_lines = 40
    step = size / float(num_lines)
    for n in xrange(num_lines):
        line_col = [(192, 192, 192), (220, 220, 220)][n&1]
        pygame.draw.line(surface, line_col, (x+n*step, y), (x+n*step, y+size))
        pygame.draw.line(surface, line_col, (x, y+n*step), (x+size, y+n*step))

    pygame.draw.line(surface, (0, 0, 0), (x, y+size/2), (x+size, y+size/2))
    pygame.draw.line(surface, (0, 0, 0), (x+size/2, y), (x+size/2, y+size))

    draw_x = int(x + (axis_x * size + size) / 2.)
    draw_y = int(y + (axis_y * size + size) / 2.)
    draw_pos = (draw_x, draw_y)
    center_pos = (x+size/2, y+size/2)
    pygame.draw.line(surface, (0, 0, 0), center_pos, draw_pos, 5)
    pygame.draw.circle(surface, (0, 0, 255), draw_pos, 10)


def draw_dpad(surface, x, y, axis_x, axis_y):

    col = (255, 0, 0)
    if axis_x == -1:
        pygame.draw.circle(surface, col, (x-20, y), 10)
    elif axis_x == +1:
        pygame.draw.circle(surface, col, (x+20, y), 10)

    if axis_y == -1:
        pygame.draw.circle(surface, col, (x, y+20), 10)
    elif axis_y == +1:
        pygame.draw.circle(surface, col, (x, y-20), 10)


while True:

    joystick = joysticks[active_joystick]

    for event in pygame.event.get():
        if event.type == QUIT:
            exit()
        if event.type == KEYDOWN:
            if event.key >= K_0 and event.key <= K_1:
```

```
                        num = event.key - K_0
                        if num < len(joysticks):
                            active_joystick = num
                            name = joysticks[active_joystick].get_name()
                            pygame.display.set_caption(name)

    # Get a list of all the axis
    axes = []
    for axis_no in xrange(joystick.get_numaxes()):
        axes.append( joystick.get_axis(axis_no) )

    axis_size = min(256, 640 / (joystick.get_numaxes()/2))

    pygame.draw.rect(screen, (255, 255,255), (0, 0, 640, 480))

    # Draw all the axes (analog sticks)
    x = 0
    for axis_no in xrange(0, len(axes), 2):
        axis_x = axes[axis_no]
        if axis_no+1 < len(axes):
            axis_y = axes[axis_no+1]
        else:
            axis_y = 0.
        draw_axis(screen, x, 0, axis_x, axis_y, axis_size)
        x += axis_size


    # Draw all the hats (d-pads)
    x, y = 50, 300
    for hat_no in xrange(joystick.get_numhats()):
        axis_x, axis_y = joystick.get_hat(hat_no)
        draw_dpad(screen, x, y, axis_x, axis_y)
        x+= 100


    #Draw all the buttons
    x, y = 0.0, 390.0
    button_width = 640 / joystick.get_numbuttons()
    for button_no in xrange(joystick.get_numbuttons()):
        if joystick.get_button(button_no):
            pygame.draw.circle(screen, (0, 255, 0), (int(x), int(y)), 20)
        x += button_width

    pygame.display.update()
```

Summary

There are three modules for controls in Pygame: `pygame.keyboard`, `pygame.mouse`, and `pygame.joystick`. Between them, you will be able to support just about any device the player wants to use in a game. You don't have to support all three, and you can always give the player a choice if there is no clear winner for a control method.

Sometimes the controls influence the player character instantly, so that it will obey exactly what the player tells it to do. Classic *shoot-'em-ups* were like this; you pressed left, the ship instantly went left, and vice versa. For a little more realism, though, the controls should affect the player character indirectly by applying forces like thrust and break. Now that you know how to read information from game controllers, the following chapters will teach you how to use this information to manipulate objects in more realistic gaming worlds.

The controls for a game are how the player *interfaces* with the gaming universe. Since we can't jack into the game, *Matrix* style, the controls should feel as natural as possible. When considering control methods for a game, it is a good idea to take a look at how similar games are played. Controls don't vary a great deal for games of a similar genre. This is not because game designers lack imagination; it's just that game players have come to expect games to work in similar ways. If you do use more creative control methods, be ready to justify it to the players or offer them a more standard alternative!

In the next chapter we will explore the topic of artificial intelligence and you will learn how to add nonplayer characters to a game.

■ ■ ■

## CHAPTER 7

Take Me to Your Leader

Placing a player character in a convincing world is only part of creating a game. To make a game fun, you need to present the player with a number of challenges. These may come in the form of traps and obstacles, but to really entertain your players you need to have them interact with nonplayer characters (NPCs)—characters that appear to act with a degree of intelligence or awareness in the game. The process of creating these NPCs is called artificial intelligence (AI). In this chapter, we will explore some simple techniques that you can use to give your game characters a life of their own.

Creating Artificial Intelligence for Games

You may have looked in the Pygame documentation for a `pygame.ai` module. There isn't one, because each game can have vastly different requirements when it comes to creating NPCs. The code for an ape that throws barrels at plumbers wouldn't require much work—all the ape needs to determine is whether it should throw the barrel to the left or right, something you could probably simulate in a single line of Python code! Creating a convincing enemy combatant in a futuristic first-person shooter may take a little more effort. The AI player would have to plan routes from one part of the map to another, and at the same time aim weapons and dodge enemy fire. It may also have to make decisions based on the ammo supply and armor inventory. The better it does all of this, the better AI player it will be and the greater the challenge for the player.

Although most AI in games is used to create convincing opponents to play against, it is becoming increasingly popular to use AI techniques for altogether more peaceful purposes. NPCs need not always be enemies that must be dispatched on sight; they may also be characters placed in the game world to add depth to the gameplay. Some NPCs may even be friends of the player that should be protected from harm because they actively assist in the quest. Other games, such as the phenomenally successful The Sims, don't require a player character at all, and are entirely populated with NPCs.

AI is also useful for making the game world more convincing by adding background characters that aren't directly involved in the gameplay (the game equivalent of movie extras). We can apply a few AI techniques to make birds flock together, or crowds of people flee from an out-of-control car in a racing game. It's this kind of attention to detail that truly connects a player to the game world. The trick is to convince the player that the game world would exist even if they weren't currently playing.

AI has a reputation for being difficult, which it doesn't really deserve. Much of the code you create for AI can be reused in various combinations to create a large variety of different types of NPCs. In fact, most games will use the same code for every character in a game and you have to tweak just a few values to modify behavior.

This chapter won't cover a great deal of the theory of artificial intelligence (which could easily consume an entire book). Rather, it will give you a number of techniques that you can apply to many situations in games.

What Is Intelligence?

Intelligence is a difficult thing to define, even for AI programmers. I'm confident that I am intelligent and self-aware, but I can only assume that others are intelligent because they are like me in many ways. Other people talk, move, check their e-mail, and take out their trash like I do—so I *assume* they are intelligent. Similarly, in a game if a character behaves in a way that an intelligent thing would, then the player will assume it is intelligent. The programmer may know that the actions of a character are simply a result of a few pages of computer code, but the player will be oblivious to that fact. As far as the player is concerned, if it walks like a zombie, moans like a zombie, and eats people like a zombie, then it's a zombie!

So intelligence in a game is an illusion (it may be in real life as well). The code to create this illusion doesn't differ a great deal from the code in the previous chapters. You will use the same basic tools of Python strings, lists, dictionaries, and so forth to build classes that are effectively the *brains* of your NPCs. In fact, Python is probably one of the best languages for writing AI because of its large range of built-in objects.

Exploring AI

Artificial intelligence isn't essential to creating an entertaining game. I used to love to play classic platform games where the hero has to leap from platform to platform and brazenly jump on the heads of monsters.

Although the monsters in these games are NPCs, their actions are a little rudimentary to be considered AI. Let's look inside the head of a typical platform game monster (Listing 7-1). This listing is *pseudocode*, which is code that's used to demonstrate a technique but that doesn't actually run.

Listing 7-1. *Pseudocode for a platform monster*

```
self.move_forward()
if self.hit_wall():
    self.change_direction()
```

The particular monster in Listing 7-1 doesn't have any awareness of its surroundings other than being able to detect if it has hit a wall, and it certainly won't react in any way to the player character that is about to land on its head. Generally speaking, a requirement for AI is that the NPC must have awareness of other entities in the games, especially the player character. Let's consider another type of game monster: a fireball-throwing imp from the underworld. The imp has a simple mission in life: to find the player and hurl a fireball in his direction. Listing 7-2 is the pseudocode for the imp's brain.

Listing 7-2. *Pseudocode for Imp AI*

```
if self.state == "exploring":
    self.random_heading()
    if self.can_see(player):
        self.state = "seeking"

elif self.state == "seeking":
    self.head_towards("player")
    if self.in_range_of(player):
        self.fire_at(player)
    if not self.can_see(player):
        self.state = "exploring"
```

The imp can be in one of two states: *exploring* or *seeking*. The current state of the imp is stored in the value of self.state, and indicates which block of code currently controls the imp's actions. When the imp is exploring (i.e., self.state == "exploring"), it will walk aimlessly around the map by picking a random heading. But if it sees the player, it will switch to the second state of "seeking". An imp that is in seeking mode will head toward the player and fire as soon as it is in range. It will keep doing this as long as the player can be seen, but if the cowardly player retreats, the imp will switch back to the exploring state.

Our imp is certainly no deep thinker, but it does have an awareness of its surroundings (i.e., where the player is) and takes actions accordingly. Even with two states, the imp will be intelligent enough to be a stock enemy in a first-person shooter. If we were to add a few more states and define the conditions to switch between them, we could create a more formidable enemy. This is a common technique in game AI and is known as a *state machine*.

■**Note** This imp is not the smartest of underworld denizens. If the player can no longer be seen, the imp will stop seeking, even if the player has just hidden behind a tree! Fortunately we can build on the state machine to create a smarter class of imp.

Implementing State Machines

The two states for the imp's brain form a very simple state machine. A state generally defines two things:

- What the NPC is doing at that moment

- At what point it should switch to another state

The condition to get from the *exploring* state to the *seeking* state is self.can_see(player)—in other words, "Can I (the imp) see the player?" The opposite condition (not self.can_see(player)) is used to get back from *seeking* to *exploring*. Figure 7-1 is a diagram of the imp's state machine, which is effectively its brain. The arrows define the links between the states and the conditions that must be satisfied to switch states. Links in a state machine are always one-way, but there may be another link that returns to the original state. There may also be several intermediate states before returning to the original state, depending on the complexity of the NPC's behavior.

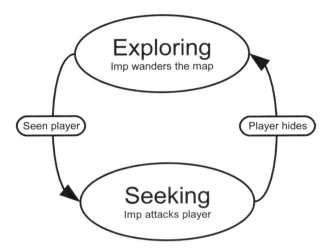

Figure 7-1. *Imp state machine*

In addition to the current behavior and conditions, states may also contain *entry actions* and *exit actions*. An entry action is something that is done prior to entering a new state, and is typically used to perform one-time actions needed by the state to run. For the seeking state in the imp's state machine, an entry action might calculate a heading toward the player and play a noise to indicate that it has seen the player—or anything else required to ready the imp for battle. Exit actions, the opposite of entry actions, are performed when leaving a state.

Let's create a slightly more interesting state machine so we can put this into practice. We are going to create a simulation of an ant's nest. Insects are often used when experimenting with AI because they have quite simple behaviors that are easy to model. In our simulation universe, we are going to have three *entities*: leaves, spiders, and the ants themselves. The leaves will grow in random spots on the screen and will be harvested by the ants and returned to the nest. Spiders wander over the screen, and are tolerated by the ants as long as they don't come near the nest. If a spider enters the nest, it will be chased and bitten until it either dies or manages to get far enough away.

■**Note** Even though we are using an insect theme for this simulation, the AI code we will be writing is applicable to many scenarios. If we were to replace the ants, spiders, and leaves with giant "mech" robots, tanks, and fuel drops, then the simulation would still make sense.

Game Entities

Although we have three different types of entities, it is a good idea to come up with a *base* class for a game entity that contains common properties and actions. That way, we won't need to duplicate code for each of the entities, and we can easily add other entities without much extra work.

An entity will need to store its name ("ant", "leaf", or "spider"), as well as its current location, destination, speed, and the image used to represent it on screen. You may find it odd that the "leaf" entity will have a destination and speed. We aren't going to have magic walking leaves; we will simply set their speed to zero so that they don't move. That way, we can still treat leaves in the same way as the other entities. In addition to this information, we need to define a few common functions for game entities. We will need a function to render entities to the screen and another to process the entity (i.e., update its position on screen). Listing 7-3 shows the code to create a GameEntity class, which will be used as the base for each of the entities.

Listing 7-3. *The Base Class for a Game Entity*

```
class GameEntity(object):

    def __init__(self, world, name, image):

        self.world = world
        self.name = name
        self.image = image
        self.location = Vector2(0, 0)
        self.destination = Vector2(0, 0)
        self.speed = 0.

        self.brain = StateMachine()

        self.id = 0

    def render(self, surface):

        x, y = self.location
        w, h = self.image.get_size()
        surface.blit(self.image, (x-w/2, y-h/2))

    def process(self, time_passed):

        self.brain.think()

        if self.speed > 0 and self.location != self.destination:
```

```
        vec_to_destination = self.destination - self.location
        distance_to_destination = vec_to_destination.get_length()
        heading = vec_to_destination.get_normalized()
        travel_distance = min(distance_to_destination, time_passed * self.speed)
        self.location += travel_distance * heading
```

The GameEntity class also keeps a reference to a world, which is an object we will use to store the positions of all the entities. This World object is important because it is how the entity knows about other entities in the simulation. Entities also require an ID to identify it in the world and a StateMachine object for its brain (which we will define later).

The render function for GameEntity simply blits the entities' image to the screen, but first adjusts the coordinates so that the current location is under the center of the image rather than the top left. We do this because the entities will be treated as circles with a point and a radius, which will simplify the math when we need to detect interactions with other entities.

The process function of GameEntity objects first calls self.brain.think, which will run the state machine to control the entity (typically by changing its destination). Only the ant will use a state machine in this simulation, but we *could* add AI to any entity. If we haven't built a state machine for the entity, this call will simply return without doing anything. The rest of the process function moves the entity toward its destination, if it is not there already.

Building Worlds

Now that we have created a GameEntity class, we need to create a *world* for the entities to live in. There is not much to the world for this simulation—just a nest, represented by a circle in the center of the screen, and a number of game entities of varying types. The World class (Listing 7-4) draws the nest and manages its entities.

Listing 7-4. *World Class*

```
class World(object):

    def __init__(self):

        self.entities = {} # Store all the entities
        self.entity_id = 0 # Last entity id assigned
        # Draw the nest (a circle) on the background
        self.background = pygame.surface.Surface(SCREEN_SIZE).convert()
        self.background.fill((255, 255, 255))
        pygame.draw.circle(self.background, (200, 255, 200), NEST_POSITION, ➡
int(NEST_SIZE))

    def add_entity(self, entity):

        # Stores the entity then advances the current id
        self.entities[self.entity_id] = entity
        entity.id = self.entity_id
        self.entity_id += 1
```

```
def remove_entity(self, entity):

    del self.entities[entity.id]

def get(self, entity_id):

    # Find the entity, given its id (or None if it is not found)
    if entity_id in self.entities:
        return self.entities[entity_id]
    else:
        return None

def process(self, time_passed):

    # Process every entity in the world
    time_passed_seconds = time_passed / 1000.0
    for entity in self.entities.itervalues():
        entity.process(time_passed_seconds)

def render(self, surface):

    # Draw the background and all the entities
    surface.blit(self.background, (0, 0))
    for entity in self.entities.values():
        entity.render(surface)

def get_close_entity(self, name, location, range=100.):

    # Find an entity within range of a location
    location = Vector2(*location)

    for entity in self.entities.values():
        if entity.name == name:
            distance = location.get_distance_to(entity.location)
            if distance < range:
                return entity
    return None
```

Since we have a number of GameEntity objects, it would be perfectly natural to use a Python list object to store them. Although this could work, we would run into problems; when an entity needs to be removed from the world (i.e., it died), we would have to search through the list to find its index, and then call del to delete it. Searching through lists can be slow, and would only get slower as the list grows. A better way to store entities is with a Python dictionary, which can efficiently find an entity even if there are many of them.

To store entities in a dictionary, we need a value to use as a key, which could be a string, a number, or another value. Thinking of a name for each ant would be difficult, so we will simply number the ants sequentially: the first ant is #0, the second is #1, and so on. This number is the entity's id, and is stored in every GameEntity object so that we can always locate the object in the dictionary (see Figure 7-2).

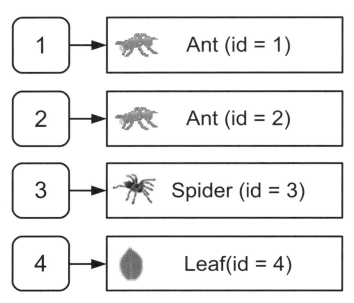

Figure 7-2. *The entities dictionary*

Most of the functions in the World class are responsible for managing the entities in some way. There is an add_entity function to add an entity to the world, a remove_entity function to remove it from the world, and a get function that looks up the entity given its id. If get can't find the id in the entities dictionary, it will return None. This is useful because it will tell us that an entity has been removed (id values are never reused). Consider the situation where a group of ants are in hot pursuit of a spider that has invaded the nest. Each ant object stores the id of the spider it is chasing and will look it up (with get) to retrieve the spider's location. At some point, though, the unfortunate spider will be dispatched and removed from the world. When this happens, any call to the get function with the spider's id will return None, so the ants will know they can stop chasing and return to other duties.

Also in the World class we have a process and a render function. The process function of the World object calls the process function of each entity to give it a chance to update its position. The render function is similar; in addition to drawing the background, it calls the corresponding render function of each entity to draw the appropriate graphic at its location.

Finally in the World class there is a function called get_close_entity, which finds an entity that is within a certain distance of a location in the world. This will be used in several places in the simulation.

■**Note** When implementing an NPC, you should generally limit the information available to it, because like real people NPCs may not necessarily be aware of everything that is going on in the world. We simulate this with the ants, by only letting them *see* objects within a limited distance.

Ant Entity Class

Before we model the brain for the ants, let's look at the Ant class (Listing 7-5). It derives from GameEntity, so that it will have all the capabilities of a GameEntity, together with any additional functions we add to it.

Listing 7-5. *The Ant Entity Class*

```
class Ant(GameEntity):

    def __init__(self, world, image):

        # Call the base class constructor
        GameEntity.__init__(self, world, "ant", image)

        # Create instances of each of the states
        exploring_state = AntStateExploring(self)
        seeking_state = AntStateSeeking(self)
        delivering_state = AntStateDelivering(self)
        hunting_state = AntStateHunting(self)

        # Add the states to the state machine (self.brain)
        self.brain.add_state(exploring_state)
        self.brain.add_state(seeking_state)
        self.brain.add_state(delivering_state)
        self.brain.add_state(hunting_state)

        self.carry_image = None

    def carry(self, image):

        self.carry_image = image

    def drop(self, surface):
```

```
        # Blit the 'carry' image to the background and reset it
        if self.carry_image:
            x, y = self.location
            w, h = self.carry_image.get_size()
            surface.blit(self.carry_image, (x-w, y-h/2))
            self.carry_image = None

    def render(self, surface):

        # Call the render function of the base class
        GameEntity.render(self, surface)

        # Extra code to render the 'carry' image
        if self.carry_image:
            x, y = self.location
            w, h = self.carry_image.get_size()
            surface.blit(self.carry_image, (x-w, y-h/2))
```

The constructor for our Ant class (__init__) first calls the constructor for the base class with the line GameEntity.__init__(self, world, "ant", image). We have to call it this way because if we were to call self.__init__ Python would call the constructor in Ant—and end up in an infinite loop! The remaining code in the ant's constructor creates the state machine (covered in the next section) and also sets a member variable called carry_image to None. This variable is set by the carry function and is used to store the image of an object that the ant is carrying; it could be a leaf or a dead spider. If the drop function is called, it will set carry_image back to None, and it will no longer be drawn.

Because of the ability to *carry* other images, ants have an extra requirement when it comes to rendering the sprite. We want to draw the image the ant is carrying in addition to its own image, so ants have a *specialized* version of render, which calls the render function in the base class and then renders carry_image, if it is not set to None.

Building the Brains

Each ant is going to have four states in its state machine, which should be enough to simulate ant-like behavior. The first step in defining the state machine is to work out what each state should do, which are the *actions* for the state (see Table 7-1).

Table 7-1. *Actions for the Ant States*

State	Actions
Exploring	Walk toward a random point in the world.
Seeking	Head toward a leaf.
Delivering	Deliver something to the nest.
Hunting	Chase a spider.

We also need to define the links that connect states together. These take the form of a condition and the name of the state to switch to if the condition is met. The exploring state, for example, has two such links (see Table 7-2).

Table 7-2. *Links from Exploring State*

Condition	Destination State
Seen a leaf?	Seeking
Spider attacking base?	Hunting

Once we have defined the links between the states, we have a state machine that can be used as the brain for an entity. Figure 7-3 shows the complete state machine that we will be building for the ant. Drawing a state machine out on paper like this is a great way of visualizing how it all fits together, and will help you when you need to turn it into code.

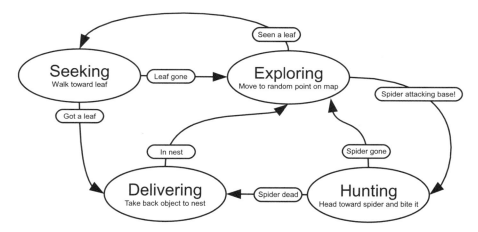

Figure 7-3. *Ant state machine*

Let's put this into practice and create the code for the state machine. We will begin by defining a base class for an individual state (Listing 7-6). Later we will create another class for the state machine as a whole that will manage the states it contains.

The base State class doesn't actually do anything other than store the name of the state in the constructor. The remaining functions in State do nothing—the pass keyword simply tells Python that you intentionally left the function blank. We need these empty functions because not all of the states we will be building will implement all of the functions in the base class. The exploring state, for example, has no exit actions. When we come to implement the AntStateExploring class, we can omit the exit_actions function because it will safely fall back to the do-nothing version of the function in the base class (State).

Listing 7-6. *Base Class for a State*

```
class State(object):

    def __init__(self, name):
        self.name = name

    def do_actions(self):
        pass

    def check_conditions(self):
        pass

    def entry_actions(self):
        pass

    def exit_actions(self):
        pass
```

Before we build the states, we need to build a class that will manage them. The StateMachine class (Listing 7-7) stores an instance of each of the states in a dictionary and manages the currently active state. The think function runs once per frame, and calls the do_actions on the active state—to do whatever the state was designed to do; the exploring state will select random places to walk to, the *seeking* state will move toward the leaf, and so forth. The think function also calls the state's check_conditions function to check all of the link conditions. If check_conditions returns a string, a new active state will be selected and any exit and entry actions will run.

Listing 7-7. *The State Machine Class*

```
class StateMachine(object):

    def __init__(self):

        self.states = {}      # Stores the states
        self.active_state = None     # The currently active state

    def add_state(self, state):

        # Add a state to the internal dictionary
        self.states[state.name] = state

    def think(self):
```

```
    # Only continue if there is an active state
        if self.active_state is None:
            return

        # Perform the actions of the active state, and check conditions
        self.active_state.do_actions()

        new_state_name = self.active_state.check_conditions()
        if new_state_name is not None:
            self.set_state(new_state_name)

    def set_state(self, new_state_name):

        # Change states and perform any exit / entry actions
        if self.active_state is not None:
            self.active_state.exit_actions()

        self.active_state = self.states[new_state_name]
        self.active_state.entry_actions()
```

Now that we have a functioning state machine class, we can start implementing each of the individual states by deriving from the State class and implementing some of its functions. The first state we will implement is the exploring state, which we will call AntStateExploring (see Listing 7-8). The entry actions for this state give the ant a random speed and set its destination to a random point on the screen. The main actions, in the do_actions function, select another random destination if the expression randint(1, 20) == 1 is true, which will happen in about 1 in every 20 calls, since randint (in the random module) selects a random number that is greater than or equal to the first parameter, and less than or equal to the second. This gives us the antlike random searching behavior we are looking for.

The two outgoing links for the exploring state are implemented in the check_conditions function. The first condition looks for a leaf entity that is within 100 pixels from an ant's location (because that's how far our ants can see). If there is a nearby leaf, then check_conditions records its id and returns the string seeking, which will instruct the state machine to switch to the seeking state. The remaining condition will switch to hunting if there are any spiders inside the nest *and* within 100 pixels of the ant's location.

■**Caution** Random numbers are a good way to make your game more fun, because predictable games can get dull after a while. But be careful with random numbers—if something goes wrong, it may be difficult to reproduce the problem!

Listing 7-8. *The Exploring State for Ants (AntStateExploring)*

```
class AntStateExploring(State):

    def __init__(self, ant):

        # Call the base class constructor to initialize the State
        State.__init__(self, "exploring")
        # Set the ant that this State will manipulate
        self.ant = ant

    def random_destination(self):

        # Select a point in the screen
        w, h = SCREEN_SIZE
        self.ant.destination = Vector2(randint(0, w), randint(0, h))

    def do_actions(self):

        # Change direction, 1 in 20 calls
        if randint(1, 20) == 1:
            self.random_destination()

    def check_conditions(self):

        # If there is a nearby leaf, switch to seeking state
        leaf = self.ant.world.get_close_entity("leaf", self.ant.location)
        if leaf is not None:
            self.ant.leaf_id = leaf.id
            return "seeking"
        # If there is a nearby spider, switch to hunting state
        spider = self.ant.world.get_close_entity("spider", NEST_POSITION, NEST_SIZE)
        if spider is not None:
            if self.ant.location.get_distance_to(spider.location) < 100.:
                self.ant.spider_id = spider.id
                return "hunting"

        return None

    def entry_actions(self):

        # Start with random speed and heading
        self.ant.speed = 120. + randint(-30, 30)
        self.random_destination()
```

As you can see from Listing 7-8, the code for an individual state need not be very complex because the states work together to produce something that is more than the sum of its parts. The other states are similar to AntStateExploring in that they pick a destination based on the goal of that state and switch to another state if they have accomplished that goal, or it no longer becomes relevant.

There is not a great deal left to do in the main loop of the game. Once the World object has been created, we simply call process and render once per frame to update and draw everything in the simulation. Also in the main loop are a few lines of code to create leaf entities at random positions in the world and occasionally create spider entities that wander in from the left side of the screen.

Listing 7-9 shows the entire simulation. When you run it, you will see something like Figure 7-4; the ants roam around the screen collecting leaves and killing spiders, which they will pile up in the nest. You can see that the ants satisfy the criteria of being AIs because they are aware of their environment—in a limited sense—and take actions accordingly.

Although there is no *player* character in this simulation, this is the closest we have come to a true game. We have a world, an entity framework, and artificial intelligence. It could be turned into a game with the addition of a player character. You could define a completely new entity for the player, perhaps a praying mantis that has to eat the ants, or add keyboard control to the spider entity and have it collect eggs from the nest. Alternatively, the simulation is a great starting point for a strategy game where groups of ants can be sent to collect leaves or raid neighboring nests. Game developers should be as imaginative as possible!

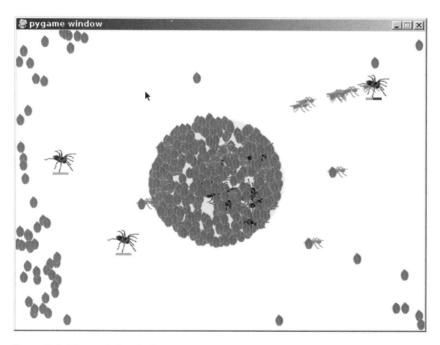

Figure 7-4. *The ant simulation*

Listing 7-9. *The Complete AI Simulation (antstatemachine.py)*

```
# Some constants you can modify
SCREEN_SIZE = (640, 480)
NEST_POSITION = (320, 240)
ANT_COUNT = 20
NEST_SIZE = 100.

import pygame
from pygame.locals import *

from random import randint, choice
from gameobjects.vector2 import Vector2

class State(object):

    def __init__(self, name):
        self.name = name

    def do_actions(self):
        pass

    def check_conditions(self):
        pass

    def entry_actions(self):
        pass

    def exit_actions(self):
        pass


class StateMachine(object):

    def __init__(self):

        self.states = {}
        self.active_state = None

    def add_state(self, state):

        self.states[state.name] = state

    def think(self):

        if self.active_state is None:
            return
```

```
            self.active_state.do_actions()

            new_state_name = self.active_state.check_conditions()
            if new_state_name is not None:
                self.set_state(new_state_name)

    def set_state(self, new_state_name):

        if self.active_state is not None:
            self.active_state.exit_actions()

        self.active_state = self.states[new_state_name]
        self.active_state.entry_actions()


class World(object):

    def __init__(self):

        self.entities = {}
        self.entity_id = 0
        self.background = pygame.surface.Surface(SCREEN_SIZE).convert()
        self.background.fill((255, 255, 255))
        pygame.draw.circle(self.background, (200, 255, 200), NEST_POSITION,➥
int(NEST_SIZE))

    def add_entity(self, entity):

        self.entities[self.entity_id] = entity
        entity.id = self.entity_id
        self.entity_id += 1

    def remove_entity(self, entity):

        del self.entities[entity.id]

    def get(self, entity_id):

        if entity_id in self.entities:
            return self.entities[entity_id]
        else:
            return None

    def process(self, time_passed):
```

```python
        time_passed_seconds = time_passed / 1000.0
        for entity in self.entities.values():
            entity.process(time_passed_seconds)

    def render(self, surface):

        surface.blit(self.background, (0, 0))
        for entity in self.entities.itervalues():
            entity.render(surface)

    def get_close_entity(self, name, location, range=100.):

        location = Vector2(*location)

        for entity in self.entities.itervalues():
            if entity.name == name:
                distance = location.get_distance_to(entity.location)
                if distance < range:
                    return entity
        return None


class GameEntity(object):

    def __init__(self, world, name, image):

        self.world = world
        self.name = name
        self.image = image
        self.location = Vector2(0, 0)
        self.destination = Vector2(0, 0)
        self.speed = 0.

        self.brain = StateMachine()

        self.id = 0

    def render(self, surface):

        x, y = self.location
        w, h = self.image.get_size()
        surface.blit(self.image, (x-w/2, y-h/2))

    def process(self, time_passed):

        self.brain.think()
```

```
        if self.speed > 0. and self.location != self.destination:

            vec_to_destination = self.destination - self.location
            distance_to_destination = vec_to_destination.get_length()
            heading = vec_to_destination.get_normalized()
            travel_distance = min(distance_to_destination, time_passed * self.speed)
            self.location += travel_distance * heading


class Leaf(GameEntity):

    def __init__(self, world, image):
        GameEntity.__init__(self, world, "leaf", image)


class Spider(GameEntity):

    def __init__(self, world, image):
        GameEntity.__init__(self, world, "spider", image)

        # Make a 'dead' spider image by turning it upside down
        self.dead_image = pygame.transform.flip(image, 0, 1)

        self.health = 25
        self.speed = 50. + randint(-20, 20)

    def bitten(self):

        # Spider as been bitten
        self.health -= 1
        if self.health <= 0:
            self.speed = 0.
            self.image = self.dead_image
        self.speed = 140.

    def render(self, surface):

        GameEntity.render(self, surface)

        # Draw a health bar
        x, y = self.location
        w, h = self.image.get_size()
        bar_x = x - 12
        bar_y = y + h/2
        surface.fill( (255, 0, 0), (bar_x, bar_y, 25, 4))
        surface.fill( (0, 255, 0), (bar_x, bar_y, self.health, 4))
```

```python
    def process(self, time_passed):

        x, y = self.location
        if x > SCREEN_SIZE[0] + 2:
            self.world.remove_entity(self)
            return

        GameEntity.process(self, time_passed)


class Ant(GameEntity):

    def __init__(self, world, image):

        GameEntity.__init__(self, world, "ant", image)

        # State classes are defined below
        exploring_state = AntStateExploring(self)
        seeking_state = AntStateSeeking(self)
        delivering_state = AntStateDelivering(self)
        hunting_state = AntStateHunting(self)

        self.brain.add_state(exploring_state)
        self.brain.add_state(seeking_state)
        self.brain.add_state(delivering_state)
        self.brain.add_state(hunting_state)

        self.carry_image = None

    def carry(self, image):

        self.carry_image = image

    def drop(self, surface):

        if self.carry_image:
            x, y = self.location
            w, h = self.carry_image.get_size()
            surface.blit(self.carry_image, (x-w, y-h/2))
            self.carry_image = None

    def render(self, surface):

        GameEntity.render(self, surface)
```

```
        if self.carry_image:
            x, y = self.location
            w, h = self.carry_image.get_size()
            surface.blit(self.carry_image, (x-w, y-h/2))


class AntStateExploring(State):

    def __init__(self, ant):

        State.__init__(self, "exploring")
        self.ant = ant

    def random_destination(self):

        w, h = SCREEN_SIZE
        self.ant.destination = Vector2(randint(0, w), randint(0, h))

    def do_actions(self):

        if randint(1, 20) == 1:
            self.random_destination()

    def check_conditions(self):

        # If ant sees a leaf, go to the seeking state
        leaf = self.ant.world.get_close_entity("leaf", self.ant.location)
        if leaf is not None:
            self.ant.leaf_id = leaf.id
            return "seeking"

        # If the ant sees a spider attacking the base, go to hunting state
        spider = self.ant.world.get_close_entity("spider", NEST_POSITION, NEST_SIZE)
        if spider is not None:
            if self.ant.location.get_distance_to(spider.location) < 100.:
                self.ant.spider_id = spider.id
                return "hunting"

        return None

    def entry_actions(self):

        self.ant.speed = 120. + randint(-30, 30)
        self.random_destination()
```

```python
class AntStateSeeking(State):

    def __init__(self, ant):

        State.__init__(self, "seeking")
        self.ant = ant
        self.leaf_id = None

    def check_conditions(self):

        # If the leaf is gone, then go back to exploring
        leaf = self.ant.world.get(self.ant.leaf_id)
        if leaf is None:
            return "exploring"

        # If we are next to the leaf, pick it up and deliver it
        if self.ant.location.get_distance_to(leaf.location) < 5.0:

            self.ant.carry(leaf.image)
            self.ant.world.remove_entity(leaf)
            return "delivering"

        return None

    def entry_actions(self):

        # Set the destination to the location of the leaf
        leaf = self.ant.world.get(self.ant.leaf_id)
        if leaf is not None:
            self.ant.destination = leaf.location
            self.ant.speed = 160. + randint(-20, 20)


class AntStateDelivering(State):

    def __init__(self, ant):

        State.__init__(self, "delivering")
        self.ant = ant


    def check_conditions(self):
```

```
        # If inside the nest, randomly drop the object
        if Vector2(*NEST_POSITION).get_distance_to(self.ant.location) < NEST_SIZE:
            if (randint(1, 10) == 1):
                self.ant.drop(self.ant.world.background)
                return "exploring"

        return None


    def entry_actions(self):

        # Move to a random point in the nest
        self.ant.speed = 60.
        random_offset = Vector2(randint(-20, 20), randint(-20, 20))
        self.ant.destination = Vector2(*NEST_POSITION) + random_offset


class AntStateHunting(State):

    def __init__(self, ant):

        State.__init__(self, "hunting")
        self.ant = ant
        self.got_kill = False

    def do_actions(self):

        spider = self.ant.world.get(self.ant.spider_id)

        if spider is None:
            return

        self.ant.destination = spider.location

        if self.ant.location.get_distance_to(spider.location) < 15.:

            # Give the spider a fighting chance to avoid being killed!
            if randint(1, 5) == 1:
                spider.bitten()

                # If the spider is dead, move it back to the nest
                if spider.health <= 0:
                    self.ant.carry(spider.image)
                    self.ant.world.remove_entity(spider)
                    self.got_kill = True
```

```python
    def check_conditions(self):

        if self.got_kill:
            return "delivering"

        spider = self.ant.world.get(self.ant.spider_id)

        # If the spider has been killed then return to exploring state
        if spider is None:
            return "exploring"

        # If the spider gets far enough away, return to exploring state
        if spider.location.get_distance_to(NEST_POSITION) > NEST_SIZE * 3:
            return "exploring"

        return None

    def entry_actions(self):

        self.speed = 160. + randint(0, 50)

    def exit_actions(self):

        self.got_kill = False


def run():

    pygame.init()
    screen = pygame.display.set_mode(SCREEN_SIZE, 0, 32)

    world = World()

    w, h = SCREEN_SIZE

    clock = pygame.time.Clock()

    ant_image = pygame.image.load("ant.png").convert_alpha()
    leaf_image = pygame.image.load("leaf.png").convert_alpha()
    spider_image = pygame.image.load("spider.png").convert_alpha()

    # Add all our ant entities
    for ant_no in xrange(ANT_COUNT):
```

```
        ant = Ant(world, ant_image)
        ant.location = Vector2(randint(0, w), randint(0, h))
        ant.brain.set_state("exploring")
        world.add_entity(ant)


    while True:

        for event in pygame.event.get():
            if event.type == QUIT:
                return

        time_passed = clock.tick(30)

        # Add a leaf entity 1 in 20 frames
        if randint(1, 10) == 1:
            leaf = Leaf(world, leaf_image)
            leaf.location = Vector2(randint(0, w), randint(0, h))
            world.add_entity(leaf)

        # Add a spider entity 1 in 100 frames
        if randint(1, 100) == 1:
            spider = Spider(world, spider_image)
            spider.location = Vector2(-50, randint(0, h))
            spider.destination = Vector2(w+50, randint(0, h))
            world.add_entity(spider)

        world.process(time_passed)
        world.render(screen)

        pygame.display.update()

if __name__ == "__main__":
    run()
```

Summary

Making a nonplayer character behave in a realistic fashion is the goal of artificial intelligence in games. Good AI adds an extra dimension to the game because players will feel that they are in a real world rather than a computer program. Poor AI can destroy the illusion of realism as easily as glitches in the graphics or unrealistic sounds—possibly even more so. A player might be able to believe that a crudely drawn stick figure is a real person, but only as long as it doesn't bump into walls!

The apparent intelligence of an NPC is not always related to the amount of code used to simulate it. Players will tend to attribute intelligence to NPCs that is not really there. In the ant simulation that we created for this chapter, the ants will form an orderly queue when chasing the spider. A friend of mine saw this and remarked that they were cooperating in the hunt—but of course the ants were acting completely independently. Sometimes it can take surprisingly little work to convince the player that something is smart.

State machines are a practical and easy way of implementing game AI because they break down a complex system (i.e., a brain) into smaller chunks that are easy to implement. They aren't difficult to design because we are accustomed to imagining what other people or animals are thinking when they do things. It may not be practical to turn every thought into computer code, but you only need to approximate behavior to simulate it in a game.

The simple state machine framework we created in this chapter can be used in your own games to build convincing AI. As with the ant simulation, start out by defining what the actions for your NPC are and then figure out what would make it switch between these actions. Once you have this laid out on paper (as in Figure 7-3), you can start building the individual states in code.

The next chapter is a gentle introduction to rendering three-dimensional graphics with Pygame.

■ ■ ■

## CHAPTER 8

Moving into the
Third Dimension

Games generally try to mimic the real world, or create a world that is not so far from reality that the player will still in some way be able to identify with it. In the past this required a real leap of faith on behalf of the player because technology wasn't yet capable of creating visuals that looked much like reality. But as the technology advanced, game designers began to push the hardware to create more convincing graphics.

Initially everything was in two dimensions because drawing a 2D sprite is a fairly simple operation that consoles and computers can do rather well. Even with only 2D capabilities, game designers attempted to create a three-dimensional look with shading and movement. Eventually gaming hardware became capable of creating more convincing 3D graphics, and developers were free to experiment with an extra dimension. Early 3D games had crude graphics, generated with lines and flat, unshaded triangles, but soon these graphics evolved into rich scenes with thousands of multilayered polygons and realistic lighting.

Nowadays the majority of games are in 3D, and home computers have graphics cards with hardware dedicated to creating 3D visuals. The computer on your desktop can generate 3D images in a fraction of a second—something that would have taken hours a few decades ago—and you can access these capabilities in your Pygame application. This chapter covers the basics of storing 3D information and creating an image out of it.

Creating the Illusion of Depth

Like just about everything else in a computer game, 3D is an illusion. Televisions and monitors are still only capable of displaying a two-dimensional image. If you move your head from side to side when playing a game, you won't see any more of the scene, because it is essentially flat and has no real depth. The illusion can be quite a convincing one because our brains are highly tuned to recognize characteristics of a three-dimensional world. The main way that our brains judge the depth of what we are viewing is by combining the two images from each eye. But even if you close one eye, you will find that you are able to judge distances and get around without bumping into things (even if it is a little harder than before). This is because visual clues such as perspective and shading are also used to make sense of the image from each eye, and our brains subconsciously use this information to help us understand depth. So even if the image on screen is flat, it still appears to have depth if it contains perspective and shading.

Games with 3D graphics must have objects that move in the way you would expect them to in the real world. Sometimes it is enough that objects move in a plausible way to create the illusion of depth. Listing 8-1 is an example of how movement alone can create visuals with an apparent third dimension.

Listing 8-1. *Illusion of Depth (parallaxstars.py)*

```
import pygame
from pygame.locals import *
from random import randint

class Star(object):

    def __init__(self, x, y, speed):

        self.x = x
        self.y = y
        self.speed = speed


def run():

    pygame.init()
    screen = pygame.display.set_mode((640, 480), FULLSCREEN)

    stars = []

    # Add a few stars for the first frame
    for n in xrange(200):

        x = float(randint(0, 639))
        y = float(randint(0, 479))
        speed = float(randint(10, 300))
        stars.append( Star(x, y, speed) )

    clock = pygame.time.Clock()

    white = (255, 255, 255)

    while True:

        for event in pygame.event.get():
            if event.type == QUIT:
                return
            if event.type == KEYDOWN:
                return
```

```
    # Add a new star
    y = float(randint(0, 479))
    speed = float(randint(10, 300))
    star = Star(640., y, speed)
    stars.append(star)

    time_passed = clock.tick()
    time_passed_seconds = time_passed / 1000.

    screen.fill((0, 0, 0))

    # Draw the stars
    for star in stars:

        new_x = star.x - time_passed_seconds * star.speed
        pygame.draw.aaline(screen, white, (new_x, star.y), (star.x+1., star.y))
        star.x = new_x

    def on_screen(star):
        return star.x > 0

    # Remove stars that are no longer visible
    stars = filter(on_screen, stars)

    pygame.display.update()


if __name__ == "__main__":
    run()
```

When you run Listing 8-1, you will see a fairly convincing star field with stars at various distances moving past the screen. Although the star field looks 3D, you won't find anything particularly unfamiliar in the code; all it does is move a number of points across the screen at varying speeds. The impression of depth is a result of your brain assuming that quick objects are close to you and slower objects are farther away.

Understanding 3D Space

To store the position of an entity in a 2D game, you use a *coordinate system* with two components, x and y, that correspond to the physical pixels on the screen. For a 3D game you need to use a coordinate system with an additional component called z (see Figure 8-1). This extra component is used to measure the distance *into*, or *out from*, the screen. Of course, Pygame can't actually draw anything using 3D coordinates because the screen is flat. So 3D coordinates will eventually have to be converted to 2D before they are used to render anything to the screen. We will cover how to do this later in the chapter, but first we need to know how to store a 3D coordinate with Python.

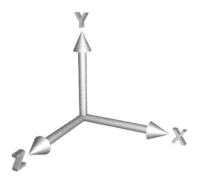

Figure 8-1. *A three-dimensional coordinate system*

In a 3D coordinate system, x points right and y points up. This is different from the coordinate system we have been using to create 2D graphics, where y points *down* the screen. In 3D, if you increase the y component, the coordinate will move *up* the screen and not down.

The z axis in a 3D coordinate system can point in one of two ways depending on the graphics technology used; either it points *into* the screen (away from the viewer), or it points *out of* the screen (toward the viewer). In this book, we will be using a coordinate system with a positive z that points out of the screen. Figure 8-2 shows a 3D coordinate system with a spy droid—represented by a circle—at coordinate (7, 5, 10). Since this isn't a pop-up book, the extra axis is represented as a diagonal line.

The units for a 3D coordinate could represent anything depending on the scale of the game. If you are writing a first-person shooter, the units may be meters or even centimeters, but for a space game the units may represent a much larger scale (maybe light-years)! Assuming that the droid's coordinates are in meters and soldier alpha (the player character) is standing at coordinate (0, 0, 0) facing along the negative z axis, the droid would be hovering 10 meters in the air, behind and to the right of the player.

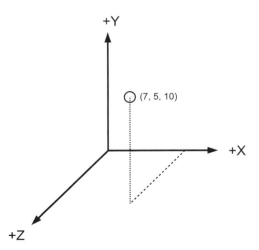

Figure 8-2. *A droid in a 3D coordinate system*

Using 3D Vectors

By now you will be comfortable with the two-dimensional vectors we have been using to represent positions and headings in the 2D samples. Vectors in 3D are similar to their 2D counterparts but with three components rather than two. These 3D vectors have many of the same capabilities as 2D; they can be added, subtracted, scaled, and so forth. Three-dimensional vectors can be stored in a tuple or list, but using a dedicated class will make calculations easier. Listing 8-2 shows how we might begin to define a 3D Vector class.

Listing 8-2. *Beginning a 3D Vector Class*

```
from math import sqrt

class Vector3(object):

    def __init__(self, x, y, z):

        self.x = x
        self.y = y
        self.z = z

    def __add__(self, x, y, z):

        return Vector3(self.x + x, self.y + y, self.z + z)

    def get_magnitude(self):

        return sqrt(self.x ** 2 + self.y ** 2 + self.z ** 2)
```

Most operations that can be done in 3D can be extended to take into account the z component. The __add__ function, for example, is very similar to the 2D version, but it also adds the z component of the two vectors.

We will be using the Vector3 class defined in the Game Objects library for the 3D code. Listing 8-3 shows how we would import and use this class.

Listing 8-3. *Using the Game Objects Vector3 Class*

```
from gameobjects.vector3 import *

A = Vector3(6, 8, 12)
B = Vector3(10, 16, 12)

print "A is", A
print "B is", B
print "Magnitude of A is", A.get_magnitude()
print "A+B is", A+B
print "A-B is", A-B
```

```
print "A normalized is", A.get_normalized()
print "A*2 is", A * 2
```

Running this code generates the following output:

```
A is (6, 8, 12)
B is (10, 16, 12)
Magnitude of A is 15.6204993518
A+B is (16, 24, 24)
A-B is (-4, -8, 0)
A normalized is (0.384111, 0.512148, 0.768221)
A*2 is (12, 16, 24)
```

Time-Based Movement in 3D

We can use the Vector3 class to do time-based movement in 3D in much the same way as we do in two dimensions. As an example, let's use a little 3D vector math to calculate a target vector and work out the intermediate coordinates for a projectile weapon (see Figure 8-3).

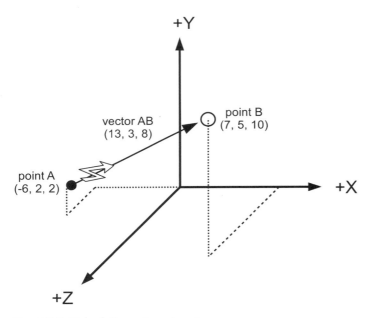

Figure 8-3. *Calculating a target vector*

Soldier Alpha has walked a few meters away from his original position in Figure 8-2, and is now standing at point (–6, 2, 0). The spy droid is still hovering at (7, 5, 10), monitoring Alpha's actions. Fortunately Alpha's acute hearing (or the player's speakers) pick up the faint whirring noise of its antigravity engine and he decides to take out the droid. To fire at the droid, Alpha needs to calculate a vector from his shoulder-mounted plasma rifle to the droid's location.

Alpha may be standing over point (–6, 2, 0), but his shoulder is 2 meters above the ground at point (–6, 2, 2), so this is the starting point for the vector calculation. The vector to his target is produced by subtracting the droid's position—point B at (7, 5, 10)—from the starting point A at (–6, 2, 2), giving us a target vector of (13, 3, 8). Normalizing this vector produces a heading vector that can be used in time-based movement. Listing 8-4 shows how to do these calculations in code.

Listing 8-4. *Creating a Target Vector*

```
from gameobjects.vector3 import *

A = (-6, 2, 2)
B = (7, 5, 10)
plasma_speed = 100. # meters per second

AB = Vector3.from_points(A, B)
print "Vector to droid is", AB

distance_to_target = AB.get_magnitude()
print "Distance to droid is", distance_to_target, "meters"

plasma_heading = AB.get_normalized()
print "Heading is", plasma_heading
```

Running Listing 8-4 produces this output:

```
Vector to droid is (13, 3, 8)
Distance to droid is 15.5563491861 meters
Heading is (0.835672, 0.192847, 0.514259)
```

If we use these values to render a plasma bolt in a game, we can calculate how far the plasma bolt has moved since the previous frame by multiplying the heading vector by the time passed since the previous frame and the speed of the plasma bolt. Adding the result to the bolt's current location gives us its new location. The code would look something like this:

```
bolt_location += plasma_heading * time_passed_seconds * plasma_speed
```

Before you can create 3D projectiles in a Pygame application, you first have to learn how to turn a 3D coordinate into a 2D coordinate in order to render it to the screen—which is the topic of the next section.

Projecting 3D Points

Storing points in 3D space is as simple as creating a tuple of three values, or a Vector3 object, but we can't use either in Pygame's drawing functions because they all take coordinates as 2D points. In order to draw anything at a 3D coordinate, we first have to *project* it onto a 2D screen.

Parallel Projections

One way to convert a 3D coordinate into a 2D coordinate is to simply discard the z component, which is known a *parallel projection*. Listing 8-5 shows a very simple function that we can use to convert a 3D coordinate into 2D with a parallel projection.

Listing 8-5. *Function That Performs a Parallel Projection*

```
def parallel_project(vector3):

    return (vector3.x, vector3.y)
```

Although parallel projections are quick and easy to do, they are not often used in games because by ignoring the z component there is no impression of depth. A 3D scene rendered with a parallel projection is kind of like looking through a zoom lens with a high level of magnification; the world appears flat, and objects at varying distances seem as though they are next to each other. Figure 8-4 shows a cube rendered with a parallel projection.

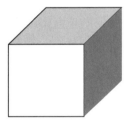

Figure 8-4. *A cube rendered with a parallel projection*

Perspective Projections

A far more common projection in games and 3D computer graphics in general is the *perspective projection*, because it takes into account the distance of an object from the viewer. A perspective projection replicates the way that objects farther from the viewer appear smaller than objects close up. Objects rendered with a perspective projection will also appear to narrow toward the horizon, an effect known as *foreshortening* (see Figure 8-5). Listing 8-6 is a function that projects a 3D coordinate with a perspective projection and returns the result.

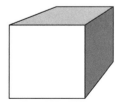

Figure 8-5. *A cube rendered with a perspective projection*

Listing 8-6. *Function That Performs a Perspective Projection*

```
def perspective_project(vector3, d):

    x, y, z = vector3
    return (x * d/z, -y * d/z)
```

There's a little more math involved in perspective projection than there is for a simple parallel projection. The `perspective_project` function multiplies the x and y coordinates by the d value (which we will discuss later), and divides by the z component. It also negates the y component (–y) since the y axis is in the opposite direction in 2D.

The d value in `perspective_project` is the *viewing distance*, which is the distance from the camera to where units in the 3D world units correspond directly to the pixels on the screen. For instance, if we have an object at coordinate (10, 5, 100), projected with a viewing distance of 100, and we move it one unit to the right at (11, 5, 100), then it will appear to have moved exactly one pixel on screen. If its z value is anything but 100, it will move a different distance relative to the screen.

Figure 8-6 shows how the viewing distance relates to the width and height of the screen. Assuming the player (indicated by the smiley face) is sitting directly in front of the screen, then the viewing distance would be approximately the distance, in pixel units, from the screen to the player's head.

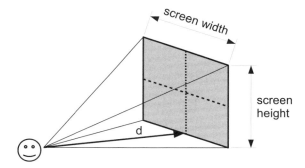

Figure 8-6. *The viewing distance in a perspective projection*

Field of View

So how do we select a good value for the viewing distance (d)? We could just experiment to find a value that makes the 3D scene look convincing, but we can take the guesswork out of it by calculating d from the *field of view (fov)*, which is the angular range of the scene that is visible at one moment. For human beings, the fov is the range from the left eye to the right eye, which is about 180 degrees. Figure 8-7 shows the relationship between fov and viewing distance. When the fov angle increases (grows wider), the viewing distance *decreases* as more of the scene becomes visible. The opposite happens when the fov decreases (becomes narrower); viewing distance increases and less of the scene is visible.

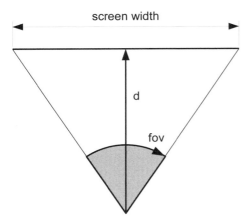

Figure 8-7. *Field of view*

Field of view is a better way to define how much perspective there will be in your 3D scene, but we still need a value for d in the perspective projection. To calculate d from the fov, we need to use a little trigonometry. Listing 8-7 is a function that takes the fov plus the screen width, and uses the tan function in the math module to calculate the viewing distance.

■**Tip** You can accomplish a lot in 3D graphics by looking up formulas on the Internet, but occasionally you may need to work out a little math yourself. Don't let that scare you if math is not your strong point—you only need the basics, particularly in trigonometry.

Listing 8-7. *Calculating the Viewing Distance*

```
from math import tan

def calculate_viewing_distance(fov, screen_width):

    d = (screen_width/2.0) / tan(fov/2.0)
    return d
```

I usually use a value between 45 and 60 degrees for my fov, which gives a natural-looking perspective. Higher values may be good for racing games, because the increased perspective tends to exaggerate the effect of speed. Lower values may be better for strategy games because they show more of the scene.

You may also want to adjust the fov depending on what is happening in the game. A great sniper rifle effect can be achieved by quickly narrowing the fov so that the camera zooms in, then moving it back when the player fires.

A 3D World

Let's write an application to test the concepts we have covered so far. Because we haven't yet explored how to draw 3D objects, we will build a scene by drawing an image at 3D points projected on the 2D screen. This will create a recognizable 3D scene, even though the images don't change size as they approach the camera (see Figure 8-8).

If you run Listing 8-8, you will see a cube formed from a number of sphere images along its edges. By pressing the cursor keys you can pan the "camera" horizontally and vertically; pressing Q and A will move forward and back in the scene. The W and S keys adjust the viewing distance of the perspective projection. You can see the effect this has from how the cube looks and by viewing the diagram (in green). Experiment with the viewing distance and fov—notice that a wide fov makes the cube appear elongated, and a narrow fov makes the cube appear flatter.

■**Note** A *camera* in a 3D scene is just the current viewpoint; it may be the view from the player character's eyes, or any other view in the game.

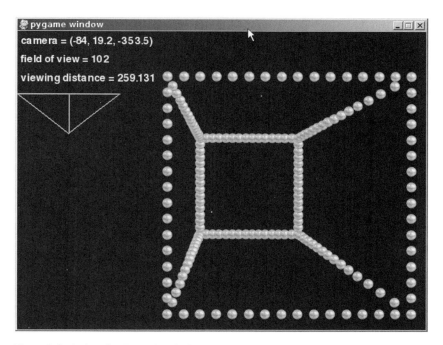

Figure 8-8. *A simple 3D engine in Pygame*

Listing 8-8. *Simple 3D Engine (simple3d.py)*

```
SCREEN_SIZE =  (640, 480)
POINT_COUNT = 300
CUBE_SIZE = 300

import pygame
from pygame.locals import *
from gameobjects.vector3 import Vector3

from math import *
from random import randint

def calculate_viewing_distance(fov, screen_width):

    d = (screen_width/2.0) / tan(fov/2.0)
    return d


def run():

    pygame.init()
    screen = pygame.display.set_mode(SCREEN_SIZE, 0)

    default_font = pygame.font.get_default_font()
    font = pygame.font.SysFont(default_font, 24)

    ball = pygame.image.load("ball.png").convert_alpha()

    # The 3D points
    points = []

    fov = 90. # Field of view
    viewing_distance = calculate_viewing_distance(radians(fov), SCREEN_SIZE[0])

    # Create a list of points along the edge of a cube
    for x in xrange(0, CUBE_SIZE+1, 20):
        edge_x = x == 0 or x == CUBE_SIZE

        for y in xrange(0, CUBE_SIZE+1, 20):
            edge_y = y == 0 or y == CUBE_SIZE

            for z in xrange(0, CUBE_SIZE+1, 20):
                edge_z = z == 0 or z == CUBE_SIZE
```

```
            if sum((edge_x, edge_y, edge_z)) >= 2:

                point_x = float(x) - CUBE_SIZE/2
                point_y = float(y) - CUBE_SIZE/2
                point_z = float(z) - CUBE_SIZE/2

                points.append(Vector3(point_x, point_y, point_z))

# Sort points in z order
def point_z(point):
    return point.z
points.sort(key=point_z, reverse=True)

center_x, center_y = SCREEN_SIZE
center_x /= 2
center_y /= 2

ball_w, ball_h = ball.get_size()
ball_center_x = ball_w / 2
ball_center_y = ball_h / 2

camera_position = Vector3(0.0, 0.0, -700.)
camera_speed = Vector3(300.0, 300.0, 300.0)

clock = pygame.time.Clock()

while True:

    for event in pygame.event.get():
        if event.type == QUIT:
            return

    screen.fill((0, 0, 0))

    pressed_keys = pygame.key.get_pressed()

    time_passed = clock.tick()
    time_passed_seconds = time_passed / 1000.

    direction = Vector3()
    if pressed_keys[K_LEFT]:
        direction.x = -1.0
    elif pressed_keys[K_RIGHT]:
        direction.x = +1.0
```

```python
        if pressed_keys[K_UP]:
            direction.y = +1.0
        elif pressed_keys[K_DOWN]:
            direction.y = -1.0

        if pressed_keys[K_q]:
            direction.z = +1.0
        elif pressed_keys[K_a]:
            direction.z = -1.0

        if pressed_keys[K_w]:
            fov = min(179., fov+1.)
            w = SCREEN_SIZE[0]
            viewing_distance = calculate_viewing_distance(radians(fov), w)
        elif pressed_keys[K_s]:
            fov = max(1., fov-1.)
            w = SCREEN_SIZE[0]
            viewing_distance = calculate_viewing_distance(radians(fov), w)

        camera_position += direction * camera_speed * time_passed_seconds

        # Draw the 3D points
        for point in points:

            x, y, z = point - camera_position

            if z > 20.:
                x =  x * viewing_distance / z
                y = -y * viewing_distance / z
                x += center_x
                y += center_y
                screen.blit(ball, (x-ball_center_x, y-ball_center_y))

        # Draw the field of view diagram
        diagram_width = SCREEN_SIZE[0] / 4
        col = (50, 255, 50)
        diagram_points = []
        diagram_points.append( (diagram_width/2, 100+viewing_distance/4) )
        diagram_points.append( (0, 100) )
        diagram_points.append( (diagram_width, 100) )
        diagram_points.append( (diagram_width/2, 100+viewing_distance/4) )
        diagram_points.append( (diagram_width/2, 100) )
        pygame.draw.lines(screen, col, False, diagram_points, 2)
```

```
    # Draw the text
    white = (255, 255, 255)
    cam_text = font.render("camera = " + str(camera_position), True, white)
    screen.blit(cam_text, (5, 5))
    fov_text = font.render("field of view = %i" % int(fov), True, white)
    screen.blit(fov_text, (5, 35))
    txt = "viewing distance = %.3f" % viewing_distance
    d_text = font.render(txt, True, white)
    screen.blit(d_text, (5, 65))

    pygame.display.update()


if __name__ == "__main__":
    run()
```

Listing 8-8 starts out by creating a list of Vector3 objects with coordinates along the edges of a cube. The points are then sorted by their z components, so that when they are rendered, the points nearer the viewer are drawn first. Otherwise, distance points may overlap those that are close to the viewer and it will break the illusion of 3D.

Inside the main loop, the camera position is changed depending on which keys are currently pressed. You can see that the code to move a 3D point is very similar to moving a 2D sprite, with only an additional z component that moves forward and back in the 3D scene. The code to update the position with time-based movement is actually identical to the 2D calculation; it just used Vector3 objects rather than Vector2 objects.

Next in the code is a loop that draws all the points in the scene. First, the point is adjusted so that it is relative to the camera by subtracting the camera_position variable. If the resulting z component is greater than 0, it means that the point is in front of the camera and may be visible—otherwise, there is no point in drawing it. When the point is in front of the camera, it is projected by multiplying the x and y components by the viewing distance and dividing by the z component. The y axis is also flipped to point in the right direction for the 2D drawing functions. Finally the 2D coordinate is adjusted to place the "world" in the center of the screen by adding half the width (center_x) to the x component and half the height (center_y) to the y component.

The remaining code draws a small diagram that shows how the viewing distance relates to the width of the screen and the fov. It also displays a few pieces of information on screen so that you can see what effect the key presses have.

If you want to experiment with this demonstration, try adding other lists of points that create other objects, such as pyramids and spheres. You might also want to make these "objects" move in 3D in the same way as we have done with 2D sprites in the preceding chapters.

Summary

Games with 3D visuals have the most potential to draw players in and keep them entertained. This is true not because the graphics are more realistic—early 3D games actually looked crude in comparison to their 2D counterparts—but because they feel more *natural*. Objects in a 3D game can rotate and be viewed at different angles, just like in the real world.

Storing information about 3D points and directions is a simple extension to 2D; we just need an extra component for the extra dimension. If you use the Vector3 class from the Game Objects library, you will find that much of the math is virtually identical to 2D because the vector class handles the extra component. All that we have done differently so far in the move to 3D is to *project* the points onto the screen in order to use Pygame's drawing capabilities. There are actually many types of projection, but perspective projection is by far the most common because it creates natural-looking scenes.

In the next chapter we will explore how to create rich 3D scenes with OpenGL, the technology behind many commercial games, including the Quake series. You will discover that some of what we have covered in this chapter is actually done automatically by OpenGL, but I haven't wasted your time—understanding projection and field of view will help you when you're creating OpenGL-powered visuals.

CHAPTER 9

∎∎∎

Exploring the Third Dimension

You've seen how to take a point in three-dimensional space and *project* it onto the screen so that it can be rendered. Projection is only part of the process of rendering a 3D scene; you also need to manipulate the points in the game to update the scene from frame to frame. This chapter introduces the *matrix*, which is a kind of mathematical shortcut used to manipulate the position and orientation of objects in a game.

You will also learn how to use Pygame with OpenGL to access the 3D graphics capabilities of your graphics card to create impressive visuals, on par with commercial games.

What Is a Matrix?

Long before *that movie*, mathematicians and game programmers were using matrices. A matrix is a grid of numbers that can be any size, but in 3D graphics the most useful matrix is the 4 ×4 matrix. This section covers how to use matrices to position objects in a 3D world.

It takes a few different pieces of information to describe how a 3D object will look in a game, but its basic shape is defined by a collection of points. In the previous chapter we created a *model* of cube by building a list of points along its edges. More typically the list of points for a game model is read from a file created with specialized software. However the model is created, it has to be placed at a location in the game world, pointing in an appropriate direction and possibly scaled to a new size. These *transformations* of the points in a 3D model are done with matrices.

Understanding how matrices work would require a lot of math that is beyond the scope of this book. Fortunately you don't need to know how they work to be able to use them. It is more important to understand what matrices do, and how they relate to the 3D graphics on screen. This is something that is generally not covered well in textbooks, and is probably why matrices have a reputation for being a little mysterious. Let's take a look at a matrix and try to make sense of it. The following is one of the simplest types of matrix:

```
[ 1 0 0 0 ]
[ 0 1 0 0 ]
[ 0 0 1 0 ]
[ 0 0 0 1 ]
```

This matrix consists of 16 numbers arranged into four rows and four columns. For most matrices used in 3D graphics, only the first three columns will differ; the fourth column will consist of three zeros followed by a 1.

■**Note** Matrices can contain any number of rows and columns, but when I use the word *matrix* in this book I am referring to the 4 ×4 matrix, commonly used in 3D graphics.

The first three rows represent an axis in 3D space, which is simply three vectors that point in the x, y, and z directions of the transformation. It helps to think of these three vectors as *right*, *up*, and *forward* to avoid confusion with the x, y, and z axes of the world. These vectors are always relative to the object being transformed. For example, if the game character was a humanoid male, then the matrix may be in the center of his chest somewhere. The right vector would point out from his right arm, the up vector would point out of the top of his head, and the forward vector would point forward through his chest.

The fourth row is the matrix *translation*, which is where the coordinate (0, 0, 0) would end up if it were transformed with this matrix. Since most 3D objects are modeled around the origin, you can think of the translation as the position of the object, once it has been transformed.

If we transformed a tank with this matrix, where would it end up? Well, the translation is (0, 0, 0) so it would be in the center of the screen. The *right* vector is (1, 0, 0), which would mean that the right side of the tank was facing in the direction of the x axis. The *up* vector is (0, 1, 0), which faces the top of the screen in the positive y direction. Finally, the *forward* vector is (0, 0, 1), which would place the turret of the tank pointing directly out of the screen. See Figure 9-1 for a breakdown of the parts of a matrix.

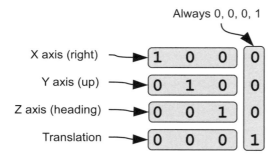

Figure 9-1. *Components of a matrix*

■**Note** Some books display matrices with the rows and columns flipped, so that the translation part is in the right column rather than the bottom row. Game programmers typically use the same convention as this book because it can be more efficient to store matrices in memory this way.

Using the Matrix Class

The Game Objects library contains a class named Matrix44 that we can use with Pygame. Let's experiment with it in the interactive interpreter. The following code shows how you would import Matrix44 and start using it:

```
>>> from gameobjects.matrix44 import *
>>> identity = Matrix44()
>>> print identity
```

The first line imports the Matrix44 class from the gameobjects.matrix44 module. The second line creates a Matrix44 object, which defaults to the identity matrix, and names it identity. The third line prints the value of identity to the console, which results in the following output:

```
[ 1 0 0 0 ]
[ 0 1 0 0 ]
[ 0 0 1 0 ]
[ 0 0 0 1 ]
```

Let's see what happens if we use the identity matrix to transform a point. The following code creates a tuple (1.0, 2.0, 3.0) that we will use to represent a point (a Vector3 object would also work here). It then uses the transform function of the matrix object to transform the point and return the result as another tuple:

```
>>> p1 = (1.0, 2.0, 3.0)
>>> identity.transform(p1)
```

This produces the following output:

```
(1.0, 2.0, 3.0)
```

The point that was returned is the same as p1, which is what we would expect from the identity matrix. Other matrices have more interesting (and useful) effects, which we will cover in this chapter.

Matrix Components

It is possible to access the components of a matrix individually (see Figure 9-2). You can access individual values using the index operator ([ ]), which takes the row and column of the value in the matrix you are interested in. For example, matrix[3, 1] returns the value at row 3, column 1 and matrix[3, 1] = 2.0 would set that same value to 2.0. This value is actually the y component of the translation part of the matrix, so changing it would alter the height of an object over the ground.

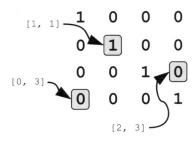

Figure 9-2. *Matrix components*

Individual rows of the matrix can be extracted by calling the get_row method, which returns the row as a tuple of four values. For example, matrix.get_row(0) returns row zero (top row, x axis), and matrix.get_row(3) returns the last row. There is also an equivalent set_row method, which takes the index of the row you want to set, and a sequence of up to four values to copy into the row. As with most methods of the Matrix44 class, get_row and set_row work with Vector3 objects as well as the built-in types.

The Matrix44 class also contains a number of attributes you can use to retrieve rows, which can be more intuitive than using the row index. For instance, rather than doing m.get_row(3) to retrieve the translation part of a matrix, you can use the attribute m.translate, which has the same effect. You can also replace m.set_row(3, (1, 2, 3)) with m.translate = (1, 2, 3)— both will set the first three values of row 3 to (1, 2, 3). Table 9-1 lists the attributes you can use to access rows in a matrix.

Table 9-1. *Row Attributes for Matrix44 Objects*

Matrix Attribute	Alias
x_axis	Row 0
y_axis	Row 1
z_axis	Row 2
right	Row 0
up	Row 1
forward	Row 2
translate	Row 3

You can also get and set the columns of a matrix with get_column and set_column, which work in the same way as the row methods. They are perhaps less useful, because columns don't give you as much relevant information as the rows do. One use for get_column is to check that the right column is (0, 0, 0, 1), because anything else may indicate an error in your code. Listing 9-1 is an example of how to check a matrix for validity. It uses Python's assert keyword to check column 3 of the matrix. If the third column is (0, 0, 0, 1), then nothing happens; otherwise, Python will throw an AssertionError. You should never catch these types of exceptions; they are Python's way of telling you that something is wrong with your code and that you should investigate the problem.

■**Tip** Try to get into the habit of writing assert conditions. They are a good way of catching problems in your code early on. If you want Python to ignore assert statements in the code, invoke the script with python -O.

Listing 9-1. *Checking That a Matrix Is Valid*

```
assert matrix.get_column(3) == (0, 0, 0, 1), "Something is wrong with this matrix!"
```

Translation Matrix

A *translation matrix* is a matrix that adds a vector to the point being transformed. If we transform the points of a 3D model by a translation matrix, it will move the model so that its center is at a new coordinate in the world. You can create a translation matrix by calling Matrix44.translation, which takes the translation vector as three values. The following code creates and displays a translation matrix:

```
>>> p1 = (1.0, 2.0, 3.0)
>>> translation = Matrix44.translation(10, 5, 2)
>>> print translation
>>> translation.transform(p1)
```

This produces the following output:

```
[ 1  0  0  0 ]
[ 0  1  0  0 ]
[ 0  0  1  0 ]
[ 10 5  2  1 ]
(11.0, 7.0, 5.0)
```

The first three rows of a translation matrix are the same as the identity matrix; the translation vector is stored in the last row. When p1 is transformed, its components are added to the translation—in the same way as vector addition. Every object in a 3D game must be translated; otherwise, everything would be located in the center of the screen!

Manipulating the matrix translation is the primary way of moving a 3D object. You can treat the translation row of a matrix as the object's coordinate and update it with time-based movement. Listing 9-2 is an example of how you might move a 3D model (in this case, a tank) forward, based on its current speed.

Listing 9-2. *Example of Moving a 3D Object*

```
tank_heading = Vector3(tank_matrix.forward)
tank_matrix.translation += tank_heading * tank_speed * time_passed
```

The first line in Listing 9-2 retrieves the tank's heading. Assuming that the tank is moving in the same direction as it is pointing, its heading is the same as its forward vector (z axis). The second line calculates the distance the tank has moved since the previous frame by multiplying its heading by the tank's speed and the time passed. The resulting vector is then added to the matrix translation. If this were done in every frame, the tank would move smoothly in the direction it is pointing.

■**Caution**   You can only treat the forward vector as a heading if the matrix has not been scaled (see the next section). If it has, then you must normalize the forward vector so that it has a length of one. If the tank in Listing 9-2 was scaled, you could calculate a forward heading with Vector3(tank_matrix.forward).get_normalized().

Scale Matrix

A scale matrix is used to change the size of a 3D object, which can create useful effects in a game. For example, if you have a survival horror game with many zombies wandering about a desolate city, it might look a little odd if they were all exactly the same size. A little variation in height would make the hoards of undead look more convincing. Scale can also be varied over time to produce other visual effects; a crowd-pleasing fireball effect can be created by rapidly scaling a red sphere so that it engulfs an enemy and then slowly fades away.

The following code creates a scale matrix that would double the dimensions of an object. When we use it to transform p1, we get a point with components that are twice the original:

```
>>> scale = Matrix44.scale(2.0)
>>> print scale
>>> scale.transform(p1)
```

This produces the following output:

```
[ 2 0 0 0 ]
[ 0 2 0 0 ]
[ 0 0 2 0 ]
[ 0 0 0 1 ]
(2.0, 4.0, 6.0)
```

The scale value can also be less than one, which would make the model smaller. For example, `Matrix44.scale(0.5)` will create a matrix that makes a 3D object half the size.

■**Note** If you create a scale matrix with a negative scale value, it will have the effect of flipping everything so that left becomes right, top becomes bottom, and front becomes back!

You can also create a scale matrix with three different values for each axis, which scales the object differently in each direction. For example, `Matrix44.scale(2.0, 0.5, 3.0)` will create a matrix that makes an object twice as wide, half as tall, and three times as deep! You are unlikely to need this very often, but it can be useful. For example, to simulate a plume of dust from a car tire, you could scale a model of a cloud of dust unevenly so that it looks like the tires are kicking it up.

To deduce the scale of a matrix, look at the axis vectors in the top left 3 ×3 values. In an unscaled matrix, each vector of the axis has a length of one. For a scale matrix, the length (i.e., magnitude) of each vector is the scale for the corresponding axis. For example, the first axis vector in the `scale` matrix is (2, 0, 0), which has a length of two. The length may not be as obvious as this in all matrices, so this code demonstrates how to go about finding the scale of the x axis:

```
>>> x_axis_vector = Vector3(scale.x_axis)
>>> print x_axis_vector.get_magnitude()
```

This produces the following result:

```
2.0
```

Rotation Matrix

Every object in a 3D game will have to be rotated at some point so that it faces in an appropriate direction. Most things face in the direction they are moving, but you can orient a 3D object in any direction you wish. Rotation is also a good way to draw attention to an object. For example, *power-ups* (ammo, extra lives, etc.) often rotate around the y axis so they stand out from the background scenery.

The simplest type of rotation matrix is a rotation about the x, y, or z axis, which you can create with the `x_rotation`, `y_rotation`, and `z_rotation` class methods in `Matrix44` (see Figure 9-3).

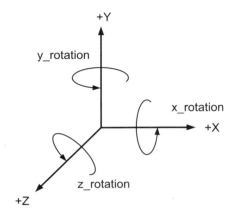

Figure 9-3. *Rotation matrices*

To predict which way a point will rotate, visualize yourself looking along the axis of rotation. Positive rotations go *counterclockwise* and negative rotations go *clockwise*. Let's experiment with this in the interactive interpreter. We are going to rotate a point at (0, 10, 0), –45 degrees around the z axis (see Figure 9-4).

```
>>> z_rotate = Matrix44.z_rotation(radians(-45))
>>> print z_rotate
>>> a = (0, 10, 0)
>>> z_rotate.transform(a)
```

This displays a z rotation matrix, and the result of using it to translate the point (0, 10, 0):

```
[ 0.707107  -0.707107 0        0 ]
[ 0.707107  0.707107  0        0 ]
[ 0         0         1        0 ]
[ 0         0         0        1 ]
(7.0710678118654746, 7.0710678118654755, 0.0)
```

If the original point were the end of a watch hand at 12 o'clock, then the transformed point would be halfway between 1 and 2.

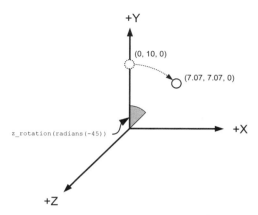

Figure 9-4. *A rotation about the z axis*

When working with 3D rotation, I find it helpful to visualize an axis for my head, where (0, 0, 0) is in my brain somewhere. The x axis points out of my right ear, the y axis points out the top of my head, and the z axis points out of my nose. If I were to rotate my head around the x axis, I would nod my head up and down. Rotating around the y axis would make me turn my head left or right. A rotation around the z axis would make me tilt my head quizzically from side to side. Alternatively, you can use your thumb and first two fingers to point along the positive direction of each axis and physically rotate your hand when you are thinking about rotations.

Matrix Multiplication

Often in a game you will need to do several transformations to a 3D object. For a tank game you would likely want to *translate* it to a position in the world and then *rotate* it to face the direction it is heading. You could transform the tank with both matrices, but it is possible to create a single matrix that has the combined effect by using *matrix multiplication*. When you multiply a matrix by another, you get a single matrix that does both transformations. Let's test that by multiplying two translation matrices together:

```
>>> translate1 = Matrix44.translation(5, 10, 2)
>>> translate2 = Matrix44.translation(-7, 2, 4)
>>> print translate1 * translate2
```

This prints the result of multiplying `translate1` with `translate2`:

```
[ 1  0  0  0 ]
[ 0  1  0  0 ]
[ 0  0  1  0 ]
[ -2 12 6  1 ]
```

The result is also a translation matrix. The last row (the translation part) in the matrix is (–2, 12, 6), which is the combined effect of translating by (5, 10, 2) and (–7, 2, 4). Matrices do not need to be of the same type to be multiplied together. Let's try multiplying a rotation matrix by a translation matrix. The following code creates two matrices, `translate` and `rotate`, and a single matrix, `translate_rotate`, that has the effect of both:

```
>>> translate = Matrix44.translation(5, 10, 0)
>>> rotate = Matrix44.y_rotation(radians(45))
>>> translate_rotate = translate * rotate
>>> print translate_rotate
```

This displays the result of multiplying the two matrices:

```
[ 0.707107  0        -0.707107 0 ]
[ 0         1        0         0 ]
[ 0.707107  0        0.707107  0 ]
[ 5         10       0         1 ]
```

If we were to transform a tank with `translate_rotate`, it would place it at the coordinate (5, 10, 0), rotated 45 degrees around the y axis.

Although matrix multiplication is similar to multiplying numbers together, there is a significant difference: the order of multiplication matters. With numbers, the result of A*B is the same as B*A, but this would not be true if A and B were matrices. The `translate_rotate` matrix we produced first translates the object to (5, 10, 0), then rotates it around its center point. If we do the multiplication in the opposite order, the resulting matrix will be different. The following code demonstrates this:

```
>>> rotate_translate = rotate * translate
>>> print rotate_translate
```

This will display the following matrix:

```
[ 0.707107  0        -0.707107 0 ]
[ 0         1        0         0 ]
[ 0.707107  0        0.707107  0 ]
[ 3.535534  10       -3.535534 1 ]
```

As you can see, this results in a different matrix. If we transformed a model with `rotate_translate`, it would first rotate it around the y axis and *then* translate it, but because translation happens relative to the rotation, the object would end up somewhere entirely different. As a rule of thumb, you should do translations first, followed by the rotation, so that you can predict where the object will end up.

Matrices in Action

Enough theory for the moment; now let's apply our knowledge of matrices and transforms to produce an interesting demonstration. When you run Listing 9-3 you will see another cube rendered with sprites along its edges. The matrix used to transform the cube is displayed in the top-left corner of the screen. Initially the transformation is the identity matrix, which places the cube directly in the middle of the screen with its z axis facing you. If instead of a cube we had a model of a tank, then it would be facing *out of* the screen, toward you.

Pressing the Q and A keys rotates the cube around the x axis; pressing W and S rotates it around the y axis; and pressing E and D rotates it around the z axis. The resulting transformation matrix is displayed as the cube rotates (see Figure 9-5). Look at the code (in bold) that creates the matrix; it first creates an x rotation and then multiplies it by a y rotation, followed by a z rotation.

■**Tip** A quicker way to create a transformation about all three axes is to use the `xyz_rotation` function, which takes three angles.

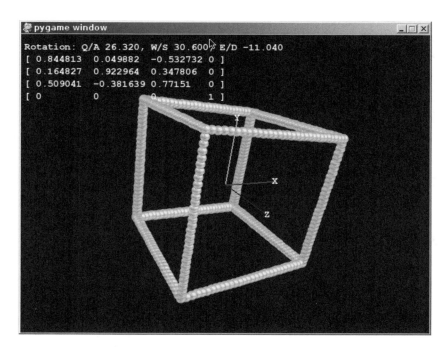

Figure 9-5. *3D transformations in action*

Listing 9-3. *Matrix transformation in action (rotation3d.py)*

```
SCREEN_SIZE =  (640, 480)
CUBE_SIZE = 300

import pygame
from pygame.locals import *
from gameobjects.vector3 import Vector3
from gameobjects.matrix44 import Matrix44 as Matrix

from math import *
from random import randint

def calculate_viewing_distance(fov, screen_width):

    d = (screen_width/2.0) / tan(fov/2.0)
    return d


def run():

    pygame.init()
    screen = pygame.display.set_mode(SCREEN_SIZE, 0)

    # 'courier new' is a fixed width font
    font = pygame.font.SysFont("courier new", 16, True)
    ball = pygame.image.load("ball.png").convert_alpha()

    points = []

    fov = 75. # Field of view
    viewing_distance = calculate_viewing_distance(radians(fov), SCREEN_SIZE[0])

    # Create a list of points along the edge of a cube
    for x in xrange(0, CUBE_SIZE+1, 10):
        edge_x = x == 0 or x == CUBE_SIZE

        for y in xrange(0, CUBE_SIZE+1, 10):
            edge_y = y == 0 or y == CUBE_SIZE

            for z in xrange(0, CUBE_SIZE+1, 10):
                edge_z = z == 0 or z == CUBE_SIZE

                if sum((edge_x, edge_y, edge_z)) >= 2:
```

```
                point_x = float(x) - CUBE_SIZE/2
                point_y = float(y) - CUBE_SIZE/2
                point_z = float(z) - CUBE_SIZE/2

                points.append(Vector3(point_x, point_y, point_z))
def point_z(point):
    return point[2]

center_x, center_y = SCREEN_SIZE
center_x /= 2
center_y /= 2

ball_w, ball_h = ball.get_size()
ball_center_x = ball_w / 2
ball_center_y = ball_h / 2

camera_position = Vector3(0.0, 0.0, 600.)

rotation = Vector3()
rotation_speed = Vector3(radians(20), radians(20), radians(20))

clock = pygame.time.Clock()

# Some colors for drawing
red = (255, 0, 0)
green = (0, 255, 0)
blue = (0, 0, 255)
white = (255, 255, 255)

# Labels for the axes
x_surface = font.render("X", True, white)
y_surface = font.render("Y", True, white)
z_surface = font.render("Z", True, white)

while True:

    for event in pygame.event.get():
        if event.type == QUIT:
            return

    screen.fill((0, 0, 0))

    time_passed = clock.tick()
    time_passed_seconds = time_passed / 1000.
```

```
rotation_direction = Vector3()

#Adjust the rotation direction depending on key presses
pressed_keys = pygame.key.get_pressed()

if pressed_keys[K_q]:
    rotation_direction.x = +1.0
elif pressed_keys[K_a]:
    rotation_direction.x = -1.0

if pressed_keys[K_w]:
    rotation_direction.y = +1.0
elif pressed_keys[K_s]:
    rotation_direction.y = -1.0

if pressed_keys[K_e]:
    rotation_direction.z = +1.0
elif pressed_keys[K_d]:
    rotation_direction.z = -1.0

# Apply time based movement to rotation
rotation += rotation_direction * rotation_speed * time_passed_seconds

# Build the rotation matrix
rotation_matrix = Matrix.x_rotation(rotation.x)
rotation_matrix *= Matrix.y_rotation(rotation.y)
rotation_matrix *= Matrix.z_rotation(rotation.z)

transformed_points = []

# Transform all the points and adjust for camera position
for point in points:

    p = rotation_matrix.transform_vec3(point) - camera_position

    transformed_points.append(p)

transformed_points.sort(key=point_z)

# Perspective project and blit all the points
for x, y, z in transformed_points:

    if z < 0:
        x = center_x + x * -viewing_distance / z
        y = center_y + -y * -viewing_distance / z
```

```
        screen.blit(ball, (x-ball_center_x, y-ball_center_y))


    # Function to draw a single axis, see below
    def draw_axis(color, axis, label):

        axis = rotation_matrix.transform_vec3(axis * 150.)
        SCREEN_SIZE =  (640, 480)
        center_x = SCREEN_SIZE[0] / 2.0
        center_y = SCREEN_SIZE[1] / 2.0
        x, y, z = axis - camera_position

        x = center_x + x * -viewing_distance / z
        y = center_y + -y * -viewing_distance / z

        pygame.draw.line(screen, color, (center_x, center_y), (x, y), 2)

        w, h = label.get_size()
        screen.blit(label, (x-w/2, y-h/2))

    # Draw the x, y and z axes
    x_axis = Vector3(1, 0, 0)
    y_axis = Vector3(0, 1, 0)
    z_axis = Vector3(0, 0, 1)

    draw_axis(red, x_axis, x_surface)
    draw_axis(green, y_axis, y_surface)
    draw_axis(blue, z_axis, z_surface)

    # Display rotation information on screen
    degrees_txt = tuple(degrees(r) for r in rotation)
    rotation_txt = "Rotation: Q/A %.3f, W/S %.3f, E/D %.3f" % degrees_txt
    txt_surface = font.render(rotation_txt, True, white)
    screen.blit(txt_surface, (5, 5))

    # Display the rotation matrix on screen
    matrix_txt = str(rotation_matrix)
    txt_y = 25
    for line in matrix_txt.split('\n'):
        txt_surface = font.render(line, True, white)
        screen.blit(txt_surface, (5, txt_y))
        txt_y += 20

    pygame.display.update()
```

```
if __name__ == "__main__":
    run()
```

The matrices in Listing 9-3 transform the points of a cube to their final positions on screen. Games will do many such transforms in the process of rendering a 3D world, and tend to have more sophisticated graphics than can be produced with 2D sprites. In the following section, you will learn how to *join up* the points in a model and use lighting to create solid-looking 3D models.

Introducing OpenGL

Today's graphics cards come with chips that are dedicated to the task of drawing 3D graphics, but that wasn't always the case; in the early days of 3D games on home computers, the programmer had to write code to draw the graphics for each game. Drawing polygons (shapes used in games) in software is time consuming, as the processor has to calculate each pixel individually. When graphics cards with 3D acceleration became popular, they freed up the processor to do work on other aspects of the game, such as artificial intelligence, resulting in better-looking games with richer gameplay.

OpenGL is an application programming interface (API) for working with the 3D capabilities of graphics cards. There are other APIs for 3D, such as Microsoft's Direct3D, but we will be using OpenGL, because it is well supported across platforms; OpenGL-powered games can be made to run on many different computers and consoles. It comes installed by default on all major platforms that Pygame runs on, usually as part of your graphics drivers.

There is a downside to using OpenGL with Pygame. With an OpenGL game, you can't blit from a surface to the screen, or draw directly to it with any of the `pygame.draw` functions. You *can* use any of the other Pygame modules that don't draw to the screen, such as `pygame.key`, `pygame.time`, and `pygame.image`. The event loop and general structure of a Pygame script doesn't change when using OpenGL, so you can still apply what you have learned in the previous chapters.

Installing PyOpenGL

Although OpenGL is probably already on your system, you will still need to install PyOpenGL, which is a module that interfaces the OpenGL drivers on your computer with the Python language. PyOpenGL is available as a Python *egg* file, which is an increasingly standard way of packaging Python modules. To use Python eggs, first download the Easy Install module from `http://peak.telecommunity.com/DevCenter/EasyInstall` (if you don't already have it). After you run the `ez_setup.py` script, you can download and install PyOpenGL from the command shell with the following line:

```
easy_install PyOpenGL
```

For more information regarding PyOpenGL, see the project's web site at `http://pyopengl.sourceforge.net/`. For the latest news on OpenGL, see `http://www.opengl.org/`.

■**Tip** Easy Install is a very useful tool, because it can find and install a huge number of Python modules automatically.

Initializing OpenGL

The PyOpenGL module consists of a number of functions, which can be imported with a single line:

```
from OpenGL.GL import *
```

This line imports the OpenGL functions, which begin with gl, for example, glVertex, which we will cover later. This is all you need to start using OpenGL, but you may also want to import the OpenGL Utility library (GLU), which contains a number of convert functions that simplify some common tasks. This line imports the GLU functions, which begin with glu:

```
from OpenGL.GLU import *
```

Before you can use any of the functions in these two modules, you must first tell Pygame to create an OpenGL display surface. Although this surface is different from a typical 2D display surface, it is created in the usual way with the pygame.display.set_mode function. The following line creates a 640 ×480 OpenGL surface called screen:

```
screen = pygame.display.set_mode((640, 480), HWSURFACE|OPENGL|DOUBLEBUF)
```

The OPENGL flag tells Pygame to create an OpenGL surface; HWSURFACE creates it in hardware, which is important for accelerated 3D; and DOUBLEBUF makes it double-buffered, which reduces flickering. You may also want to add FULLSCREEN to expand the display to fill the entire screen, but it is convenient to work in windowed mode when developing.

OpenGL Primer

OpenGL contains several matrices that are applied to the coordinates of what you draw to the screen. The two that are most commonly used are called GL_PROJECTION and GL_MODELVIEW. The projection matrix (GL_PROJECTION) takes a 3D coordinate and projects it onto 2D space so that it can be rendered to the screen. We've been doing this step manually in our experiments with 3D—it basically does the multiplication by the *view distance* and divides by the z component. The *model view* matrix is actually a combination of two matrices: the *model* matrix transforms (translates, scales, rotates, etc.) the model to its position in the world and the *view* matrix adjusts the objects to be relative to the camera (usually the player character's viewpoint).

Resizing the Display

Before we begin drawing anything to the screen, we first have to tell OpenGL about the dimensions of the display and set up the GL_PROJECTION and GL_MODELVIEW matrices (see Listing 9-4).

Listing 9-4. *Resizing the Viewport*

```
def resize(width, height):

    glViewport(0, 0, width, height)
    glMatrixMode(GL_PROJECTION)
    glLoadIdentity()
    gluPerspective(60., float(width)/height, 1., 10000.)
    glMatrixMode(GL_MODELVIEW)
    glLoadIdentity()
```

The resize function in Listing 9-4 takes the width and height of the screen, and should be called when the display is initialized or the screen dimensions change. The call to glViewport tells OpenGL that we want to use the area of the screen from coordinate (0, 0), with a size of (width, height), that is, the entire screen. The next line calls glMatrixMode(GL_PROJECTION), which tells OpenGL that all further calls that work with matrices will apply to the projection matrix. It is followed by a call to glLoadIdentity, which resets the projection matrix to identity, and a call to gluPerspective (from the GLU library), which sets a standard perspective projection matrix. This function takes four parameters: the field of view of the camera, the aspect ratio (width divided by height), followed by the near and far clipping planes. These clipping planes define the range of distances that can be "seen"; anything outside that range won't be visible to the player. The viewable area in the 3D screen is called the viewing *frustum* (see Figure 9-6), which resembles a pyramid with a portion of the top cut off.

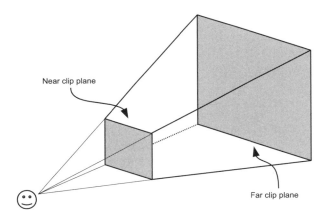

Figure 9-6. *The viewing frustum*

Initializing OpenGL Features

The resize function is enough to start using OpenGL functions to render to the screen, but there are a few other things we should set to make it more interesting (see Listing 9-5).

Listing 9-5. *Initializing OpenGL*

```
def init():

    glEnable(GL_DEPTH_TEST)
    glClearColor(1.0, 1.0, 1.0, 0.0)

    glShadeModel(GL_FLAT)
    glEnable(GL_COLOR_MATERIAL)

    glEnable(GL_LIGHTING)
    glEnable(GL_LIGHT0)
    glLight(GL_LIGHT0, GL_POSITION,  (0, 1, 1, 0))
```

The first thing that the init function does is call glEnable with GL_DEPTH_TEST, which tells OpenGL to enable the *Z buffer*. This ensures that objects that are far from the camera aren't drawn over objects that are near to the camera, regardless of the order that we draw them in code.

The glEnable function is used to enable OpenGL features, and glDisable is used to disable them. Both functions take one of a number of uppercase constants, beginning with GL_. We will cover a number of these that you can use in your games in this book, but see the OpenGL documentation for a complete list.

The second line in init sets the *clear color*, which is the color of the parts of the screen that aren't drawn to (the equivalent of automatically calling screen.fill in the 2D sample code). In OpenGL, colors are given as four values for the red, green, blue, and alpha components, but rather than a value between 0 and 255, it uses values between 0 and 1.

The remaining lines in the function initialize OpenGL's lighting capabilities, which automatically shades 3D objects depending on the position of a number of lights in the 3D world. The call to glShadeModel sets the shade model to GL_FLAT, which is used to shade faceted objects like cubes, or anything with edged surfaces. An alternative setting for the shade model is GL_SMOOTH, which is better for shading curved objects. The call to glEnable(GL_COLOR_MATERIAL) tells OpenGL that we want to enable *materials*, which are settings that define how a surface interacts with a light source. For instance, we could make a sphere appear highly polished like marble, or softer like a piece of fruit, by adjusting its material properties.

The remaining portion of Listing 9-5 enables lighting (glEnable(GL_LIGHTING)) and light zero (glEnable(GL_LIGHT0)). There are a number of different lights that you can switch on in OpenGL; they are numbered GL_LIGHT0, GL_LIGHT1, GL_LIGHT2, and so on. In a game, you would have at least one light (probably for the sun), and additional lights for other things such as headlights, lamps, or special effects. Placing a light source inside a fireball effect, for example, will ensure that it illuminates the surrounding terrain.

The last line sets the position of light zero to (0, 1, 1, 0). The first three values in this tuple are the x, y, and z coordinates of the light; the last value tells OpenGL to make it a *directional* light, which creates a light source with parallel light rays, similar to the sun. If the last value is 1, OpenGL creates a point light source, which looks like a close-up light, such as a bulb, candle, or plasma fireball. See Figure 9-7 for the differences between point and directional light sources.

Tip You can get the number of lights that your OpenGL driver supports with
glGetInteger(GL_MAX_LIGHTS). Typically you will get eight, but it can vary depending on your platform.

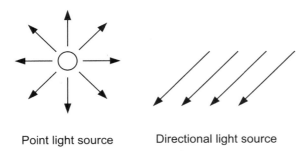

Point light source   Directional light source

Figure 9-7. *OpenGL light sources*

Drawing in Three Dimensions

Now that we have initialized OpenGL and created a light source, we can start drawing 3D shapes. OpenGL supports a number of *primitives* that you can use to build a 3D scene, such as points, lines, and triangles. Each takes a number of pieces of information, depending on the type of primitive and the OpenGL features that are enabled. Because of this, there aren't single functions for each primitive as there are in 2D Pygame. The information is given in a number of function calls, and when OpenGL has all the information it needs, it can draw the primitive.

To draw a primitive in OpenGL, first call glBegin, with one of the primitive constants (see Table 9-2). Next, send OpenGL the information it needs to draw the primitive. At a minimum it will need a number of 3D points, specified with the glVertex function (a *vertex* is a point that forms part of a shape), but you can give it other information, such as color with the glColor function. Once all the information has been given, call glEnd, which tells OpenGL that all the information has been provided and it can be used to draw the primitive.

Note The call to glVertex should always come after other information for a vertex is given.

Table 9-2. *OpenGL primitives*

Constant	Primitive
GL_POINTS	Draws dots
GL_LINES	Draws individual lines
GL_LINE_STRIP	Draws connected lines
GL_LINE_LOOP	Draws connected lines, with the last point joined to the first

Constant	Primitive
GL_TRIANGLES	Draws triangles
GL_TRIANGLE_STRIPS	Draws triangles where each additional vertex forms a new triangle with two previous vertices
GL_QUADS	Draws quads (shapes with four vertices)
GL_QUAD_STRIP	Draws quad strips where every two vertices are connected to the previous two vertices
GL_POLYGON	Draws polygons (shapes with any number of vertices)

Listing 9-6 is an example of how you might draw a red square with OpenGL. The first line tells OpenGL that you want to draw quads (shapes with four points). The next line sends the color red (1.0, 0.0, 0.0), so all vertices will be red until the next call to glColor. The four calls to glVertex send the coordinates of each of the corners of the square, and finally, the call to glEnd tells OpenGL that you have finished sending vertex information. With four vertices, OpenGL can draw a single quad, but if you were to give it more, it would draw a quad for every four vertices you send it.

Listing 9-6. *Pseudocode for Drawing a Red Square*

```
glBegin(GL_QUADS)

glColor(1.0, 0.0, 0.0) # Red

glVertex(100.0, 100.0, 0.0) # Top left
glVertex(200.0, 100.0, 0.0) # Top right
glVertex(200.0, 200.0, 0.0) # Bottom right
glVertex(100.0, 200.0, 0.0) # Bottom left

glEnd()
```

Normals

If you have OpenGL lighting enabled, you will need to send an additional piece of information for primitives called a *normal*, which is a unit vector (a vector of length 1.0) that faces outward from a 3D shape. This vector is necessary for calculating the shading from lights in the scene. For example, if you have a cube in the center of the screen aligned along the axis, the normal for the front face is (0, 0, 1) because it is facing along the positive z axis, and the normal for the right face is (1, 0, 0) because it faces along the x axis (see Figure 9-8).

To send a normal to OpenGL, use the glNormal3d function, which takes three values for the normal vector, or the glNormal3dv function, which takes a *sequence* of three values. For example, if the square in Listing 9-6 was the front face of a cube you would set the normal with glNormal3d(0, 0, 1) or glNormal3dv(front_vector). The latter is useful because it can be used with Vector3 objects. If you are using flat shading (glShadeModel(GL_FLAT)), you will need one normal per face. For smooth shading (glShadeModel(GL_SMOOTH)), you will need to supply a normal per vertex.

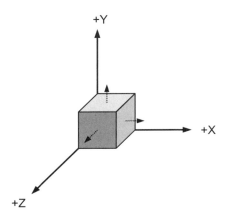

+Y

+X

+Z

Figure 9-8. *Normals of a cube*

Display Lists

If you have many primitives to draw—which is typically the case for a 3D game—then it can be slow to make all the calls necessary to draw them all. It is faster to send many primitives to OpenGL in one go, rather than one at a time. There are several ways of doing this, but one of the easiest ways is to use *display lists*.

You can think of a display list as a number of OpenGL function calls that have been recorded and can be played back at top speed. To create a display list, first call glGenLists(1), which returns an id value to identify the display list. Then call glNewList with the id and the constant GL_COMPILE, which begins *compiling* the display list. When you have finished sending primitives to OpenGL, call glEndList to end the compile process. Once you have compiled the display list, call glCallList with the id to draw the recorded primitives at maximum speed. Display lists will let you create games that run as fast as commercial products, so it is a good idea to get into the habit of using them! Listing 9-7 is an example of how you might create a display list to draw a tank model. It assumes that there is a function draw_tank, which sends the primitives to OpenGL.

Once you have created a display list, you can draw it many times in the same scene by setting a different transformation matrix before each call to glCallList(tank_display_id).

Listing 9-7. *Creating a Display List*

```
# Create a display list
tank_display_list = glGenLists(1)
glNewList(tank_display_list, GL_COMPILE)

draw_tank()

# End the display list
glEndList()
```

Storing a 3D Model

3D objects are a collection of primitives, typically either triangles or quads, that form part of a larger shape. For instance, a cube can be created with six quads, one for each side. More complex shapes, particularly organic shapes like people or bug-eyed aliens, take many more primitives to create. The most efficient way to store a model is to keep a list of vertices, and additional information about which points to use to draw the faces (primitives). For instance, a cube could be stored as six vertices (one for each corner), and the faces would be stored as four indexes into that list (see Figure 9-9).

This is typically how models are stored in files produced by 3D editing software. Although there are a variety of different formats, they will all contain a list of vertices and a list of indices that connect vertices together with primitives. We'll cover how to read these models later in this book.

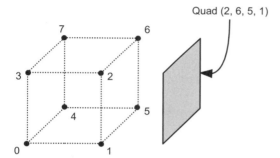

Figure 9-9. *Faces and vertices*

Seeing OpenGL in Action

We've covered enough theory for one chapter; let's put what we have learned into practice. We are going to use OpenGL to create a very simple *world* composed of cubes, and give the player the ability to fly around and explore it.

When you run Listing 9-8, you will find yourself in a colorful maze. Use the left and right cursor keys to pan around, and the Q and A keys to move forward and back. The effect is much like a first-person shooter, but if you press the up or down cursor key, you will find that you can actually fly above, or below, the 3D world (see Figure 9-10). If you press the Z or X key, you can also *roll* the camera.

So how is this world created? The Map class in Listing 9-8 reads in a small bitmap (map.png) and goes through each pixel. When it finds a nonwhite pixel, it creates a colored cube at a corresponding point in 3D. The Cube class contains a list of vertices, normals, and *normal indices* that define which vertices are used in each side of the cube, and it uses this information to draw the six sides.

The whole world is transformed with a single camera matrix (camera_matrix), which is modified as the user presses keys. This matrix is multiplied by a rotation matrix when the user rotates the camera, and the translate row is adjusted to move the camera forward and back. Both rotation and translation use the familiar time-based calculations to give a consistent speed.

Before the 3D world is rendered, we must send the camera matrix to OpenGL. The following line *uploads* the camera matrix to OpenGL:

```
glLoadMatrixd(camera_matrix.get_inverse().to_opengl())
```

The get_inverse function returns the *inverse* of the matrix, which is a matrix that does the exact opposite of the original. The reason we use the inverse, and not the original, is because we want to transform everything in the world to be relative to the camera. To explain it another way, if you are looking directly at an object and you turn your head to the right, that object is now on the *left* side of your vision. It's the same with the camera matrix; the world is transformed in the opposite way.

The to_opengl function of Matrix44 converts the matrix into a single list, which is the format that the glLostMatrixd requires to send the matrix to OpenGL. Once that matrix has been sent, everything in the 3D world will be transformed to be relative to the camera.

■**Note** It may seem a little odd, but when you move a camera about in a 3D world, you are actually transforming the world and not the camera!

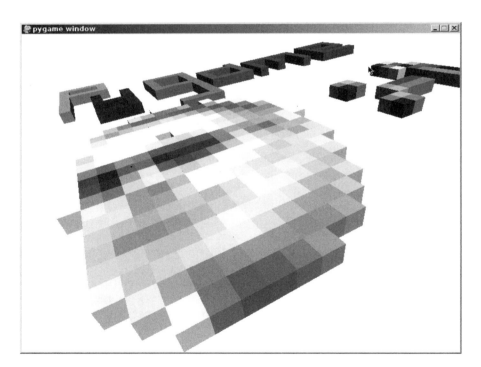

Figure 9-10. *Cube world*

Listing 9-8. *Flying Around Cube World! (firstopengl.py)*

```python
SCREEN_SIZE = (800, 600)

from math import radians

from OpenGL.GL import *
from OpenGL.GLU import *

import pygame
from pygame.locals import *

from gameobjects.matrix44 import *
from gameobjects.vector3 import *


def resize(width, height):

    glViewport(0, 0, width, height)
    glMatrixMode(GL_PROJECTION)
    glLoadIdentity()
    gluPerspective(60.0, float(width)/height, .1, 1000.)
    glMatrixMode(GL_MODELVIEW)
    glLoadIdentity()


def init():

    glEnable(GL_DEPTH_TEST)

    glShadeModel(GL_FLAT)
    glClearColor(1.0, 1.0, 1.0, 0.0)

    glEnable(GL_COLOR_MATERIAL)

    glEnable(GL_LIGHTING)
    glEnable(GL_LIGHT0)
    glLight(GL_LIGHT0, GL_POSITION,  (0, 1, 1, 0))
```

```python
class Cube(object):

    def __init__(self, position, color):

        self.position = position
        self.color = color

    # Cube information

    num_faces = 6

    vertices = [ (0.0, 0.0, 1.0),
                 (1.0, 0.0, 1.0),
                 (1.0, 1.0, 1.0),
                 (0.0, 1.0, 1.0),
                 (0.0, 0.0, 0.0),
                 (1.0, 0.0, 0.0),
                 (1.0, 1.0, 0.0),
                 (0.0, 1.0, 0.0) ]

    normals = [ (0.0, 0.0, +1.0),  # front
                (0.0, 0.0, -1.0),  # back
                (+1.0, 0.0, 0.0),  # right
                (-1.0, 0.0, 0.0),  # left
                (0.0, +1.0, 0.0),  # top
                (0.0, -1.0, 0.0) ] # bottom

    vertex_indices = [ (0, 1, 2, 3),  # front
                       (4, 5, 6, 7),  # back
                       (1, 5, 6, 2),  # right
                       (0, 4, 7, 3),  # left
                       (3, 2, 6, 7),  # top
                       (0, 1, 5, 4) ] # bottom

    def render(self):

        # Set the cube color, applies to all vertices till next call
        glColor( self.color )

        # Adjust all the vertices so that the cube is at self.position
        vertices = []
        for v in self.vertices:
            vertices.append( tuple(Vector3(v)+ self.position) )
```

```python
        # Draw all 6 faces of the cube
        glBegin(GL_QUADS)

        for face_no in xrange(self.num_faces):

            glNormal3dv( self.normals[face_no] )

            v1, v2, v3, v4 = self.vertex_indices[face_no]

            glVertex( vertices[v1] )
            glVertex( vertices[v2] )
            glVertex( vertices[v3] )
            glVertex( vertices[v4] )

        glEnd()


class Map(object):

    def __init__(self):

        map_surface = pygame.image.load("map.png")
        map_surface.lock()

        w, h = map_surface.get_size()

        self.cubes = []

        # Create a cube for every non-white pixel
        for y in range(h):
            for x in range(w):

                r, g, b, a = map_surface.get_at((x, y))

                if (r, g, b) != (255, 255, 255):

                    gl_col = (r/255.0, g/255.0, b/255.0)
                    position = (float(x), 0.0, float(y))
                    cube = Cube( position, gl_col )
                    self.cubes.append(cube)


        map_surface.unlock()

        self.display_list = None
```

```python
    def render(self):

        if self.display_list is None:

            # Create a display list
            self.display_list = glGenLists(1)
            glNewList(self.display_list, GL_COMPILE)

            # Draw the cubes
            for cube in self.cubes:
                cube.render()

            # End the display list
            glEndList()

        else:

            # Render the display list
            glCallList(self.display_list)


def run():

    pygame.init()
    screen = pygame.display.set_mode(SCREEN_SIZE, HWSURFACE|OPENGL|DOUBLEBUF)

    resize(*SCREEN_SIZE)
    init()

    clock = pygame.time.Clock()

    # This object renders the 'map'
    map = Map()

    # Camera transform matrix
    camera_matrix = Matrix44()
    camera_matrix.translate = (10.0, .6, 10.0)

    # Initialize speeds and directions
    rotation_direction = Vector3()
    rotation_speed = radians(90.0)
    movement_direction = Vector3()
    movement_speed = 5.0
```

```
while True:

    for event in pygame.event.get():
        if event.type == QUIT:
            return
        if event.type == KEYUP and event.key == K_ESCAPE:
            return

    # Clear the screen, and z-buffer
    glClear(GL_COLOR_BUFFER_BIT | GL_DEPTH_BUFFER_BIT);

    time_passed = clock.tick()
    time_passed_seconds = time_passed / 1000.

    pressed = pygame.key.get_pressed()

    # Reset rotation and movement directions
    rotation_direction.set(0.0, 0.0, 0.0)
    movement_direction.set(0.0, 0.0, 0.0)

    # Modify direction vectors for key presses
    if pressed[K_LEFT]:
        rotation_direction.y = +1.0
    elif pressed[K_RIGHT]:
        rotation_direction.y = -1.0
    if pressed[K_UP]:
        rotation_direction.x = -1.0
    elif pressed[K_DOWN]:
        rotation_direction.x = +1.0
    if pressed[K_z]:
        rotation_direction.z = -1.0
    elif pressed[K_x]:
        rotation_direction.z = +1.0
    if pressed[K_q]:
        movement_direction.z = -1.0
    elif pressed[K_a]:
        movement_direction.z = +1.0

    # Calculate rotation matrix and multiply by camera matrix
    rotation = rotation_direction * rotation_speed * time_passed_seconds
    rotation_matrix = Matrix44.xyz_rotation(*rotation)
    camera_matrix *= rotation_matrix
```

```
        # Calculate movement and add it to camera matrix translate
        heading = Vector3(camera_matrix.forward)
        movement = heading * movement_direction.z * movement_speed
        camera_matrix.translate += movement * time_passed_seconds

        # Upload the inverse camera matrix to OpenGL
        glLoadMatrixd(camera_matrix.get_inverse().to_opengl())

        # Light must be transformed as well
        glLight(GL_LIGHT0, GL_POSITION,  (0, 1.5, 1, 0))

        # Render the map
        map.render()

        # Show the screen
        pygame.display.flip()

if __name__ == "__main__":
    run()
```

Summary

We've covered a lot of ground with this chapter. We started out with matrices, which are an important topic because they are used everywhere in 3D games, including handhelds and consoles. The math for working with matrices can intimidating, but if you use a prebuilt matrix class, such as gameobjects.Matrix44, you won't need to know the details of how they work (most game programmers aren't mathematicians)! It's more important that you know how to combine translation, rotation, and scaling to manipulate objects in a game. Visualizing a matrix from its grid of numbers is also a useful skill to have, and will help you fix bugs if anything goes wrong with your games.

You also learned how to work with OpenGL to create 3D visuals. OpenGL is a large, powerful API, and we have only touched on a portion of it. We covered the basics of how to store a 3D model and send it to OpenGL for rendering, which we can make use of even when more OpenGL features are enabled. Later chapters will describe how to add textures and transparency to create visuals that will really impress!

Listing 9-8 is a good starting point for any experiments with OpenGL. Try tweaking some of the values to produce different effects, or add more interesting shapes to the *cube world*. You could even turn it into a game by adding a few enemies (see Chapter 7).

In the next chapter we will take a break from 3D to explore how you can use sound with Pygame.

CHAPTER 10

■■■

Making Things Go Boom

Sound is an essential component of any game as it gives instant *feedback* from the virtual world. If you were to play a game with the audio turned down, you would likely find it a very passive experience because we expect events to be accompanied by sound.

Like other aspects of creating a game, good sound effects require a lot of creativity. Selecting an appropriate set of sound effects for in-game action can make the difference between the visuals working or completely failing to impress.

This chapter explores the Pygame modules you can use to add sound effects and music to your game. We will also cover how to use free software to create and edit your sounds.

What Is Sound?

Sound is essentially vibrations, typically traveling through the air but potentially through water or other substances. Just about everything can vibrate and pass vibrations to the air in the form of sound. For instance, as I type I can hear a "clack-clack" noise caused by the plastic keys colliding with the surface underneath. The plastic vibrates very quickly and pushes the surrounding air molecules, which in turn push other molecules, and send out a chain reaction that eventually reaches my ears, to be interpreted as sound.

The more energy in a vibration, the louder the sound will be. A key press is relatively quiet because not much force is required to push a key down, but if I were to strike the keyboard with a lot of force—say with a sledgehammer—the sound would be louder because there would be more energy in the vibrations.

Sound can also vary in *pitch*, which is the speed of the vibrations in the air. Some materials, such as metal, tend to vibrate very quickly and will produce a high-pitched noise when hit with something. Other materials vibrate at different rates and produce different pitches.

Most sounds are a complex mixture of variations in both pitch and volume. If I were to drop a glass onto a stone floor, the initial impact would create a loud noise followed by a variety of sounds from the shards as they vibrate and fall back to the ground. The combination of all these sounds produces a noise that we would recognize as a glass smashing.

Sound can also be altered before it reaches the ears of the listener. We are all familiar with how a wall between you and someone talking *muffles* the sound and makes it difficult to understand. This is because sound can travel through walls as well as air, but it reduces the volume and changes the vibrations on the way. Sound may also *bounce* off some surfaces and create effects such as echoes. Replicating such physical effects in games is a great way to enhance the illusion of the visuals. If the game character enters a large cavern, it will be much more convincing if the sound of his footsteps echoes as he walks. But like with most aspects of game design, a little artistic license is allowed. There is no sound in space because there is no atmosphere for it to travel through, but I would still expect my laser cannons to produce a satisfying zap noise!

Storing Sound

Early computer games used chips that created simple tones to produce electronic bleeps and whistles, but were incapable of producing complex sounds. These days, gaming hardware can store and reproduce real-life sounds to create a rich extra dimension to the gameplay. The sound card on your computer can both record and play back high-quality audio.

Sound can be represented as a *wave*. Figure 10-1 shows a sound wave that represents a brief portion of a sound (a fraction of a second)—a full sound would be much longer and more complex. The wave shows how the energy, or *amplitude*, of the sounds varies over time.

Sound waves form a number of peaks and troughs; the greater the difference in the amplitude of these peaks and troughs, the greater the *volume* of the sound. The pitch of the sound is determined by frequency of the waves (the distance in time between the peaks); the closer the peaks are together in time, the higher the sound will be.

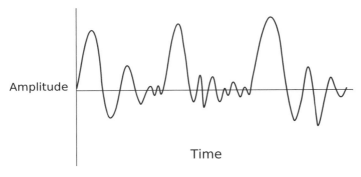

Figure 10-1. *A sound wave*

To store a sound on a computer, you must first convert it to digital form, which you can do using a microphone plugged into the *mic* socket of your sound card, or the USB port for newer microphones designed specifically for computer use. When a microphone picks up sound, the wave is converted into an electrical signal, which is *sampled* at regular intervals by the sound card to produce a sequence of numbers that can be saved to a file. Samples are values representing the amplitude of a wave at a particular moment in time, and are used to reconstruct the wave when it is played back. The more samples you have, the more accurately the sound card can play back the sound. Figure 10-2 shows a wave reconstructed from a low sample rate, overlaid over the original. You can see that the sampled wave generally follows the real wave, but much of the detail is lost, resulting in low-quality sound. A higher sample rate would produce a wave that followed the original more closely, and would sound better when played back.

Sample rates are measured in hertz (Hz), which means samples per second, or kilohertz (KHz), which means thousands of samples per second. Phone quality is about 6KHz and CD quality is 44KHz. Samples rates can go higher than CD quality, but only dogs and bats will be able to tell the difference!

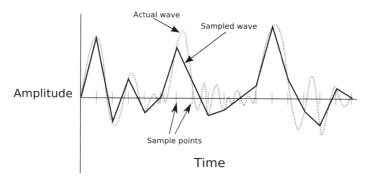

Figure 10-2. *Sample sound wave*

Sound Formats

Like images, there are a number of different file formats for digital audio that affect the quality and file size. Pygame supports two audio formats for sound effects: WAV (uncompressed only) and Ogg. Most, if not all, software that deals with sound will be able to read and write WAV files. Support for Ogg is not quite as universal but is still very common. If an application doesn't support Ogg directly, it may be possible to add it via an upgrade or plug-in.

There are a number of attributes for sound that can affect the quality and file size:

- *Sample format*—The size of a single sample, which is typically either 8-bit or 16-bit integers, although some formats do support float samples. Generally you should use 16-bit when storing sound files, because it can reproduce CD-quality sound and is best supported by sound cards.

- *Sample rate*—The number of samples stored per second. The most common values for sample rate are 11025Hz, 22050Hz, or 44100Hz, but there are a number of other potential values. Higher sample rates produce better-quality sound but will result in larger files.

- *Channels*—Sound files can be *mono* (a single channel of sound), or *stereo* (an individual channel for the left and right speakers). Stereo tends to sound better, but uses up to twice the amount of memory in uncompressed audio files.

- *Compression*—Sound can generate large files. For example, a one-minute-long, 44100Hz, 16-bit, stereo audio will create approximately 10MB of data. Fortunately, audio can be compressed so that it fits into a much smaller space. Pygame doesn't support compressed WAV files, but it does support the Ogg format, which has very good compression.

Deciding what combination of these attributes you need usually depends on how you will be distributing your game. If you will be distributing your game on a CD or DVD, you will probably have plenty of space to store high-quality sounds. However, if you want to distribute your game via e-mail or download, you may want to sacrifice a little quality for smaller files.

Creating Sound Effects

One way to create sound effects is to simply record your own. For instance, if you need an engine noise, the best way to create it is to record the sound of a real engine running. Other sounds are impractical or even impossible to capture, and a little creativity may be required to create an approximation—a good gunshot sound can be created by recording a balloon bursting and then using sound-editing software to extend and deepen the sound. Even phaser fire can be created by recording the sound of a pencil striking the grill of a metal desk fan and then increasing the pitch and adding a little echo.

■**Tip** If you want to record sounds outside, and don't want to drag a laptop around with you, buy a cheap dictaphone. The quality may suffer a little because you are not recording straight to high-quality digital, but you can always clean up the sound with Audacity (`http://audacity.sourceforge.net/`) or similar software.

To start recording sound effects, you will need a microphone. You can use either a standard microphone with a 2.5mm jack that plugs into the mic socket of your sound card, or a USB microphone that is specifically designed for computers. Both will give good results, but it is best to avoid headset microphones because they tend to be optimized for recording voice rather than general sound effects.

In addition to the microphone, you will need software to sample the sound and save it to your hard drive. Most operating systems come with a basic program that can record sound, but you will likely get better results from other sound software such as Audacity (Figure 10-3), which is an open source application for Windows, Mac OS X, and Linux. You can download Audacity (for free) from `http://audacity.sourceforge.net/`.

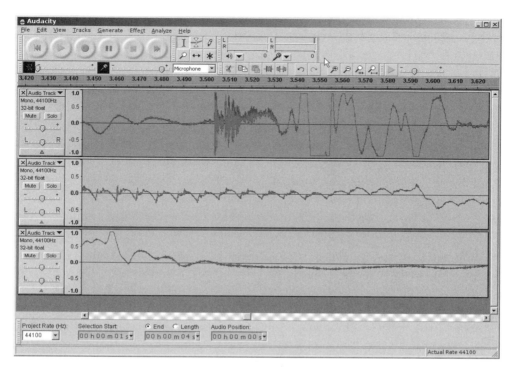

Figure 10-3. *Audacity*

To record sound with Audacity, click the record button (the red circle) to start recording, and then click the stop button (the yellow square) to finish. The waveform of the sound will then be displayed in the main window, which has a number of controls that you can use to examine the wave and select portions of it.

Audacity has many features that you can use to edit sound. Multiple sounds can be mixed together, and you can cut and paste between them. You can also apply various effects that can improve the quality of your sounds—or completely change them! To apply a sound with

Audacity, select a portion of audio you want to alter, then select one of the effects from the Effect menu. Here are a few of the effects you can use:

- *Amplify*—Makes a sound louder. Generally you should store your sounds as loud as possible, without *clipping*. Clipping occurs when the amplitude of a wave is greater than the range that can be stored, and tends to reduce the quality of the sound. If the top or bottom of the wave is a horizontal line, that means the sound has been clipped.

- *Change Pitch*—Makes the sound higher or lower. If you increase the pitch of a voice, it will sound like it is on helium, and if you lower the pitch it will sound deeper and *godlike*. Changing the pitch is a good way to turn one sound into another. If you were to record two metal spoons colliding and lower the pitch, it would sound something like a sword hitting armor.

- *Echo*—Adds an echo to the sound. Adding Echo can make your effects sound like they are in anything from an empty room to an enormous cave.

- *Noise Removal*—If you are not lucky enough to have access to a sound studio and professional equipment, your recordings may have a slight hissing noise, which is a result of background noise and imperfections in the microphone and sound card. The Noise Removal effect does a good job of *cleaning up* your sounds.

Once you have finished editing your sound effects, you can export them as a variety of other formats, including WAV and Ogg. It is a good idea to keep the original files so you can export them to a different format if you need to.

■**Caution** Recording sounds from a movie may seem like a good way to get interesting effects for your game, but you will likely break copyright laws—so it is best avoided.

Stock Sound Effects

You can also buy sound effects on CD or download them from the Web. These tend to be very high quality because they were produced in sound studios and professionally edited. A popular web site I have used personally is Sounddogs (www.sounddogs.com/). Their CDs tend to be expensive, but you can also purchase effects individually and pay by the second. If you just need a dozen or so short sound effects for your game, the price is reasonable.

There are also a number of sources on the Web for *free* sound effects. The Pygame wiki contains a page that lists some good sites (www.pygame.org/wiki/resources). You may also be able to find more good sites by searching the Web.

Playing Sounds with Pygame

You can play sound effects with Pygame through the pygame.mixer interface. Before you can use the *mixer*, it must first be initialized with a number of parameters that define what kind of sound you will be playing. This can be done with the pygame.mixer.init function, but on some platforms the mixer is initialized automatically by `pygame.init`. Pygame provides a `pyame.mixer.pre_init` function that you can use to set the parameters for this automatic initialization. Both of the initialization functions take the following four parameters:

- `frequency`—This is the sample rate of the audio playback and has the same meaning as the sample rate of sound files. A high sample rate can potentially reduce performance, but even old sound cards can easily handle a frequency setting of 44100, which is CD quality. Another common setting for frequency is 22050, which doesn't sound quite as good.

- `size`—This is the size, in *bits*, of the audio samples for the playback. The sample size can be either 8 or 16. A value of 16 is best because the sound quality is much higher than 8, with the same performance. This value can also be negative, which indicates that the mixer should use *signed* samples (required by some platforms). There is no difference in sound quality between signed or unsigned samples.

- `stereo`—This parameter should be set to 1 for mono sound or 2 for stereo sound. Stereo is recommended because it can be used to create the illusion that sound is coming from a particular point on the screen.

- `buffer`—This is the number of samples that are buffered for playback. Lower values results in lower *latency*, which is the time between asking Pygame to play a sound and the time you actually hear it. Higher values increase latency but may be necessary to avoid sound *dropout*, which can cause annoying pops and clicks over the sound. I have found that a value of 4096 works best for 44100, 16-bit stereo sound. This value must always be a power of 2.

Here's how you would initialize the mixer for 16-bit, 44100Hz stereo sound:

```
pygame.mixer.pre_init(44100, 16, 2, 4096)
pygame.init()
```

The call to `pygame.mixer.pre_init` sets the parameters for the mixer, which is initialized in the call to `pygame.init`. If you need to change any of the parameters after Pygame has been initialized, you must first quit the mixer with a call to `pygame.mixer.quit` before calling `pygame.mixer.init` to reinitialize.

Sound Objects

Sounds objects are used to store and play audio data, read from either WAV or Ogg files. You can construct a `Sound` object with `pygame.mixer.Sound`, which takes the file name of the sound file, or a Python `file` object containing the data. Here's how to load a sound file called `phaser.ogg` from the hard drive:

```
phaser_sound = Pygame.mixer.Sound("phaser.ogg")
```

You can play a `Sound` object with the `play` method, which takes two optional parameters: `loop` and `maxtime`. Setting a value for `loop` will make the sound repeat after it is initially played. For instance, if `loop` is set to 5, the sound will play through and then repeat five times (six times in total). You may also set `loop` to the special value of –1, which causes the sound to play continuously, until you call the `stop` method.

The maxtime parameter is used to stop playback after a given number of milliseconds, which is useful for sounds that are designed to loop (play continuously) because you can specify exactly how long they will play for.

If the call to play was successful, it will return a Channel object (see the next section); otherwise, it will return None. Here's how to play the phaser sound a single time:

```
channel = phaser_sound.play()
```

This line would play a five-second-long burst of phaser fire:

```
channel = phaser_sound.play(-1, 5000)
```

See Table 10-1 for a full list of the methods of Sound objects.

Table 10-1. *Methods of Sound Objects*

Method	Purpose
fadeout	Gradually reduces the volume of the sound on all channels. fadeout takes a single parameter, which is the length of the fade in milliseconds.
get_length	Returns the length of the sound, in seconds.
get_num_channels	Counts how many times the sound is playing.
get_volume	Returns the volume of the sound, as a float between 0.0 and 1.0, where 0.0 is silent and 1.0 is full volume.
play	Plays the sound. See the section "Sound Objects" for a description of the parameters. The return value is a Channel object, or None if Pygame was unable to play the sound.
set_volume	Sets the volume of the sound when it is played back. The parameter is a float between 0.0 and 1.0, where 0.0 is silent and 1.0 is full volume.
stop	Immediately stops any playback of the sound.

Sound Channels

A channel is one of several sound sources that are mixed together by the sound card, and are represented in Pygame by Channel objects. The play method of Sound objects returns a Channel object for the channel that will play the sound, or None if all channels are busy playing. You can retrieve the number of available channels by calling the pygame.mixer.get_num_channels function. If you find that you don't have enough channels to play all the sounds you need to, you can create more by calling the pygame.mixer.set_num_channels function.

If you just want the sound to play all the way through at full volume, you can safely ignore the return value of Sound.play. Otherwise, there are some useful effects you can create with the methods of Channel objects. One of the most useful is the ability to set the volume of the left and right speakers independently, which can be used to create the illusion that a sound is coming from a particular point on the screen—an effect known as *stereo panning*. The set_volume method of Channel objects can take two parameters: the volume of the left speaker and the volume of the right speaker, both as a value between 0 and 1. Listing 10-1 shows a function that calculates the volume of the speakers given the x coordinate of the sound-producing event and the width of the screen. The further away the x coordinate is from the speaker, the lower the volume will be, so as a point moves across the screen from left to right, the left speaker will *decrease* in volume, while the right speaker will *increase* in volume.

Listing 10-1. *Function That Calculates Stereo Panning*

```
def stereo_pan(x_coord, screen_width):

    right_volume = float(x_coord) / screen_width
    left_volume = 1.0 - right_volume

    return (left_volume, right_volume)
```

Listing 10-2 shows how you might use the stereo_pan function to play a sound effect for an exploding tank. Figure 10-4 shows how the position of the explosion relates to the values for the left and right channels.

■**Tip** If you update the stereo panning every frame for a moving sprite, it will enhance the stereo effect.

Listing 10-2. *Using the stereo_pan Function*

```
tank.explode() # Do explosion visual
explosion_channel = explosion_sound.play()
if explosion_channel is not None:
    left, right = stereo_pan(tank.position.x, SCREEN_SIZE[0])
    explosion_channel.set_volume(left, right)
```

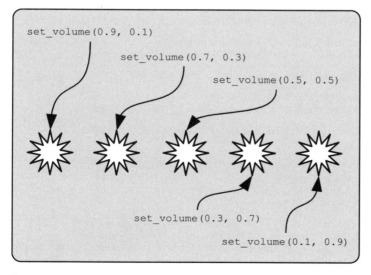

Figure 10-4. *Setting the stereo panning of an explosion*

Generally it is best to leave the task of selecting a channel to Pygame, but it is possible to force a Sound object to play through a particular channel by calling the play method of the Channel object, which takes the sound you want to play followed by the number of times you want it to repeat and the maximum time you want it to play. One reason to do this is to reserve one or more channels for high-priority sounds. For instance, you might not want background ambient noise to block the player's gunfire. To reserve a number of channels, call the pygame.mixer.set_reserved function, which prevents a number of channels from being considered by the Sound.play method. For instance, if you call pygame.mixer.set_serserved(2), Pygame will not select channel 0 or 1 when calling play from a Sound object. Listing 10-3 shows how to reserve the first two channels.

Listing 10-3. *Reserving Channels*

```
pygame.mixer.set_reserved(2)
reserved_channel_0 = pygame.mixer.Channel(0)
reserved_channel_1 = pygame.mixer.Channel(1)
```

Here's how you would force a sound to be played through one of the reserved channels:

```
reserved_channel_1.play(gunfire_sound)
```

See Table 10-2 for a complete list of the methods of Channel objects.

Table 10-2. *Methods of Channel Objects*

Method	Purpose
fadeout	Fades out (reduces volume) a sound over a period of time, given in milliseconds.
get_busy	Returns True if a sound is currently playing on the channel.
get_endevent	Returns the event that will be sent when a sound finishes playing, or NOEVENT if there is no end event set.
get_queue	Returns any sound that is queued for playback, or None if there is no queued sound.
get_volume	Retrieves the current volume of the channel as a single value between 0.0 and 1.0 (does not take into account the stereo volume set by set_volume).
pause	Temporarily pauses playback of any sound on this channel.
play	Plays a sound on a specific channel. Takes a Sound object and optional values for looping and max time, which have the same meaning as Sound.play.
queue	Plays a given sound when the current sound has finished. Takes the Sound object to be queued.
set_endevent	Requests an event when the current sound has finished playing. Takes the id of the event to be sent, which should be above USEREVENT (a constant in pygame.locals), to avoid conflict with existing events. If no parameter is given, Pygame will stop sending end events.
set_volume	Sets the volume of this channel. If one value is given, it is used for both speakers. If two values are given, the left and right speaker volume is set independently. Both methods take the volume as a value between 0.0 and 1.0, where 0.0 is silent and 1.0 is the maximum volume.

Method	Purpose
stop	Instantly stops playback of any sound on the channel.
unpause	Resumes playback of a channel that has been paused.

Mixer Functions

We've covered a number of functions in the pygame.mixer module. Table 10-3 presents a complete list of them.

Table 10-3. *Functions in pygame.mixer*

Function	Purpose
pygame.mixer.Channel	Creates a Channel object for a given channel index.
pygame.mixer.fadeout	Gradually reduces the volume of all channels to 0. Takes the fade time (in milliseconds).
pygame.mixer.find_channel	Finds a currently unused channel and returns its index.
pygame.mixer.get_busy	Returns True if sound is being played (on any channel).
pygame.mixer.get_init	Returns True if the mixer has been initialized.
pygame.mixer.get_num_channels	Retrieves the number of available channels.
pygame.mixer.init	Initializes the mixer module. See the beginning of the section for an explanation of the parameters.
pygame.mixer.pause	Temporarily stops playback of sound on all channels.
pygame.mixer.pre_init	Sets the parameters for the mixer when it is automatically initialized by the call to pygame.init.
pygame.mixer.quit	Quits the mixer. This is done automatically when the Python script ends, but you may need to call it if you want to reinitialize the mixer with different parameters.
pygame.mixer.set_num_channels	Sets the number of available channels.
pygame.mixer.Sound	Creates a Sound object. Takes a file name or a Python file object containing the sound data.
pygame.mixer.stop	Stops all playback of sound on all channels.
pygame.mixer.unpause	Resumes playback of paused sound (see pygame.mixer.pause).

Hearing the Mixer in Action

Let's write a script to experiment with sound effects in Pygame. If you run Listing 10-4 you will see a white screen with a mouse cursor. Click anywhere on the screen to throw out a silver ball that falls under gravity and plays a sound effect when it bounces off the edge or bottom of the screen (see Figure 10-5).

When the update method of the Ball class detects that the sprite has hit the edge or bottom of the screen, it reverses the direction of the sprite and calls the play method of the Sound object. The sprite's x coordinate is used to calculate the volume of the left and right speakers, so that the sound appears to be emitted from the point where the sprite has hit the screen boundary. The effect is quite convincing—if you close your eyes, you should still be able to tell where the ball bounces!

If you create a lot of sprites by clicking the mouse quickly, you will probably be able to detect that some bounces stop producing the sound effect. This happens because all available channels are used up playing the same sound effect, and new sounds can only play when a channel becomes free.

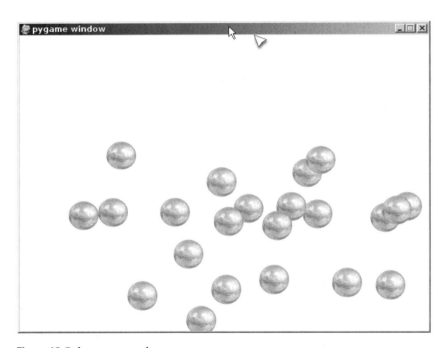

Figure 10-5. *bouncesound.py*

Listing 10-4. *Mixer in Action (bouncesound.py)*

```
SCREEN_SIZE = (640, 480)

# In pixels per second, per second
GRAVITY = 250.0
# Increase for more bounciness, but don't go over 1!
BOUNCINESS = 0.7
```

```
import pygame
from pygame.locals import *
from random import randint
from gameobjects.vector2 import Vector2


def stereo_pan(x_coord, screen_width):

    right_volume = float(x_coord) / screen_width
    left_volume = 1.0 - right_volume

    return (left_volume, right_volume)


class Ball(object):

    def __init__(self, position, speed, image, bounce_sound):

        self.position = Vector2(position)
        self.speed = Vector2(speed)
        self.image = image
        self.bounce_sound = bounce_sound
        self.age = 0.0

    def update(self, time_passed):

        w, h = self.image.get_size()

        screen_width, screen_height = SCREEN_SIZE

        x, y = self.position
        x -= w/2
        y -= h/2

        # Has the ball bounced?
        bounce = False

        # Has the ball hit the bottom of the screen?
        if y + h >= screen_height:
            self.speed.y = -self.speed.y * BOUNCINESS
            self.position.y = screen_height - h / 2.0 - 1.0
            bounce = True
```

```python
        # Has the ball hit the left of the screen?
        if x <= 0:
            self.speed.x = -self.speed.x * BOUNCINESS
            self.position.x = w / 2.0 + 1
            bounce = True

        # Has the ball hit the right of the screen?
        elif x + w >= screen_width:
            self.speed.x = -self.speed.x * BOUNCINESS
            self.position.x = screen_width - w / 2.0 - 1
            bounce = True

        # Do time based movement
        self.position += self.speed * time_passed
        # Add gravity
        self.speed.y += time_passed * GRAVITY

        if bounce:
            self.play_bounce_sound()

        self.age += time_passed


    def play_bounce_sound(self):

        channel = self.bounce_sound.play()

        if channel is not None:
            # Get the left and right volumes
            left, right = stereo_pan(self.position.x, SCREEN_SIZE[0])
            channel.set_volume(left, right)


    def render(self, surface):

        # Draw the sprite center at self.position
        w, h = self.image.get_size()
        x, y = self.position
        x -= w/2
        y -= h/2
        surface.blit(self.image, (x, y))
```

```python
def run():

    # Initialize 44KHz 16-bit stereo sound
    pygame.mixer.pre_init(44100, -16, 2, 1024*4)
    pygame.init()

    screen = pygame.display.set_mode(SCREEN_SIZE, 0)

    pygame.mouse.set_visible(False)

    clock = pygame.time.Clock()

    ball_image = pygame.image.load("ball.png").convert_alpha()
    mouse_image = pygame.image.load("mousecursor.png").convert_alpha()

    # Load the sound file
    bounce_sound = pygame.mixer.Sound("bounce.wav")

    balls = []

    while True:

        for event in pygame.event.get():

            if event.type == QUIT:
                return

            if event.type == MOUSEBUTTONDOWN:

                # Create a new ball at the mouse position
                random_speed = ( randint(-400, 400), randint(-300, 0) )
                new_ball = Ball( event.pos,
                                 random_speed,
                                 ball_image,
                                 bounce_sound )
                balls.append(new_ball)

        time_passed_seconds = clock.tick() / 1000.

        screen.fill((255, 255, 255))

        dead_balls = []
```

```
        for ball in balls:

            ball.update(time_passed_seconds)
            ball.render(screen)

            # Make a note of any balls that are older than 10 seconds
            if ball.age > 10.0:
                dead_balls.append(ball)

        # remove any 'dead' balls from the main list
        for ball in dead_balls:

            balls.remove(ball)

        # Draw the mouse cursor
        mouse_pos = pygame.mouse.get_pos()
        screen.blit(mouse_image, mouse_pos)

        pygame.display.update()

if __name__ == "__main__":

    run()
```

Playing Music with Pygame

Although the pygame.mixer module can play any kind of audio, it is usually not a good idea to use it for music, because music files tend to be large and will put a strain on the computer's resources. Pygame provides a submodule of pygame.mixer called pygame.mixer.music that can read (and play) music files a piece at a time rather than all at once, which is known as *streaming* the audio.

■**Note** Music may be the most common use of pygame.mixer.music, but you can use it to stream *any* large audio file, such as a voiceover track.

Obtaining Music

If you are not lucky enough to be blessed with musical talent, you may have to use music that someone else has created. There are a number of stock music web sites where you can purchase music files for use in games or download them for free. You can find a selection of both commercial and free music sites on the Pygame wiki (www.pygame.org/wiki/resources).

■**Caution** It may be tempting to select a few tracks from your music collection and have your favorite band as the soundtrack for your game, but this breaks copyright laws and should be avoided!

Playing Music

The pygame.mixer.music module can play MP3 and Ogg music files. The MP3 support varies from platform to platform, so it is probably best to use the Ogg format, which is well supported across platforms. You can convert MP3 to Ogg with Audacity or another sound-editing application.

To play a music file, first call the pygame.mixer.music.load function with the file name of the music track you want to play, and then call pygame.mixer.music.play to begin the playback (see Listing 10-5). Everything you may want to do with the module can be done with the pygame.mixer.music module (there is no Music object because only a single music file can be streamed at once). There are functions to stop, rewind, pause, set volume, and so forth. See Table 10-4 for a complete list.

Listing 10-5. *Playing a Music File*

```
pygame.mixer.music.load("techno.ogg")
pygame.mixer.music.play()
```

Table 10-4. *The pygame.mixer.music Functions*

Function	Purpose
pygame.mixer.get_busy	Returns True if music is currently playing.
pygame.mixer.music.fadeout	Reduces the volume over a period of time. Takes the fade time as milliseconds.
pygame.mixer.music.get_endevent	Returns the end event to be sent, or 0 if there is no event.
pygame.mixer.music.get_volume	Returns the volume of the music; see set_volume.
pygame.mixer.music.load	Loads a music file for playback. Takes the file name of the audio file.
pygame.mixer.music.play	Starts playing a loaded music file. Takes the number of times you want the music to repeat after it is initially played through, followed by the point you want to begin playback (in seconds). If you set the first value to –1, it will repeat until you call pygame.mixer.stop.
pygame.mixer.music.rewind	Restarts the music file at the beginning.
pygame.mixer.music.set_endevent	Requests an event to be sent when the music has finished playing. Takes the id of the event to be sent, which should be above USEREVENT (a constant in pygame.locals) to avoid conflict with existing events. If no parameter is given, Pygame will stop sending end events.

Continued

Table 10-4. *Continued*

Function	Purpose
pygame.mixer.music.set_volume	Sets the volume of the music. Takes the volume as a value between 0.0 and 1.0, where 0.0 is silence and 1.0 is full volume. When new music is loaded, the volume will be reset to 1.0.
pygame.mixer.music.stop	Stops playback of the music.
pygame.mixer.music.unpause	Resumes playback of music that has been paused.
pygame.muxer.music.get_pos	Returns the time that the music has been playing for, in milliseconds.
pygame.muxer.music.pause	Temporarily pauses playback of the music.
pygame.muxer.music.queue	Sets a track that will be played when the current music has finished. Takes a single parameter that is the file name of the file you want to play.

Hearing Music in Action

Let's use the pygame.mixer.music module to create a simple jukebox. Listing 10-6 reads in a list of Ogg files from a path on your hard drive and displays a number of familiar hi-fi-like buttons that you can use to play, pause, or stop the music and move through the list of tracks (see Figure 10-6). If you change the MUSIC_PATH value at the top of the listing, you can make it play from your own collection.

The jukebox uses the pygame.mixer.set_endevent function to request an event to be sent when a track finished playing. Pygame doesn't provide an event for this, but you can easily create one of your own by using an id value that is greater than USEREVENT (a constant in pygame.locals). Listing 10-6 uses the id TRACK_END, which has the value of USEREVENT + 1. When the TRACK_END event is detected in the main event loop, it starts streaming the next music file so that the tracks are played sequentially.

Figure 10-6. *The jukebox script*

Listing 10-6. *A Pygame Jukebox (jukebox.py)*

```python
SCREEN_SIZE = (800, 600)

# Location of music on your computer
MUSIC_PATH = "./MUSIC"

import pygame
from pygame.locals import *

from math import sqrt
import os
import os.path

def get_music(path):

    # Get the filenames in a folder
    raw_filenames = os.listdir(path)

    music_files = []
    for filename in raw_filenames:

        # We only want ogg files
        if filename.endswith('.ogg'):
            music_files.append(os.path.join(MUSIC_PATH, filename))

    return sorted(music_files)


class Button(object):

    def __init__(self, image_filename, position):

        self.position = position
        self.image = pygame.image.load(image_filename)

    def render(self, surface):

        # Render at the center
        x, y = self.position
        w, h = self.image.get_size()
        x -= w /2
        y -= h / 2

        surface.blit(self.image, (x, y))
```

```python
    def is_over(self, point):

        # Return True if a point is over the button
        point_x, point_y = point
        x, y = self.position
        w, h = self.image.get_size()
        x -= w /2
        y -= h / 2

        in_x = point_x >= x and point_x < x + w
        in_y = point_y >= y and point_y < y + h

        return in_x and in_y

def run():

    pygame.mixer.pre_init(44100, -16, 2, 1024*4)
    pygame.init()
    screen = pygame.display.set_mode(SCREEN_SIZE, 0)

    default_font = pygame.font.get_default_font()
    font = pygame.font.SysFont("default_font", 50, False)

    # Create our buttons
    x = 100
    y = 240
    button_width = 150

    # Store the buttons in a dictionary, so we can assign them names
    buttons = {}
    buttons["prev"] = Button("prev.png", (x, y))
    buttons["pause"] = Button("pause.png", (x+button_width*1, y))
    buttons["stop"] = Button("stop.png", (x+button_width*2, y))
    buttons["play"] = Button("play.png", (x+button_width*3, y))
    buttons["next"] = Button("next.png", (x+button_width*4, y))

    # Get a list of files in MUSIC_PATH
    music_filenames = get_music(MUSIC_PATH)

    if len(music_filenames) == 0:
        print "No OGG files found in ", MUSIC_PATH
        return

    white = (255, 255, 255)
    label_surfaces = []
```

```python
# Render the track names
for filename in music_filenames:

    txt = os.path.split(filename)[-1]

    print "Track:", txt

    txt = txt.split('.')[0]
    surface = font.render(txt, True, (100, 0, 100))
    label_surfaces.append(surface)

current_track = 0
max_tracks = len(music_filenames)

# Load the first track
pygame.mixer.music.load( music_filenames[current_track] )

clock = pygame.time.Clock()

playing = False
paused = False

# This event is sent when a music track ends
TRACK_END = USEREVENT + 1
pygame.mixer.music.set_endevent(TRACK_END)

while True:

    button_pressed = None

    for event in pygame.event.get():

        if event.type == QUIT:
            return

        if event.type == MOUSEBUTTONDOWN:

            # Find the pressed button
            for button_name, button in buttons.iteritems():
                if button.is_over(event.pos):
                    print button_name, "pressed"
                    button_pressed = button_name
                    break
```

```
            if event.type == TRACK_END:
                # If the track has ended, simulate pressing the next button
                button_pressed = "next"

    if button_pressed is not None:

        # If 'next' is pressed advance to next track
        if button_pressed == "next":
            current_track = (current_track + 1) % max_tracks
            pygame.mixer.music.load( music_filenames[current_track] )
            if playing:
                pygame.mixer.music.play()

        # If 'prev' is pressed, rewind or go to previous track
        elif button_pressed == "prev":

            # If the track has been playing for more than 3 seconds,
            # rewind it, otherwise select the previous track
            if pygame.mixer.music.get_pos() > 3000:
                pygame.mixer.music.stop()
                pygame.mixer.music.play()
            else:
                current_track = (current_track - 1) % max_tracks
                pygame.mixer.music.load( music_filenames[current_track] )
                if playing:
                    pygame.mixer.music.play()

        elif button_pressed == "pause":
            if paused:
                pygame.mixer.music.unpause()
                paused = False
            else:
                pygame.mixer.music.pause()
                paused = True

        elif button_pressed == "stop":
            pygame.mixer.music.stop()
            playing = False

        elif button_pressed == "play":
            if paused:
                pygame.mixer.music.unpause()
                paused = False
```

```
            else:
                if not playing:
                    pygame.mixer.music.play()
                    playing = True


        screen.fill(white)


        # Render the name of the current track
        label = label_surfaces[current_track]
        w, h = label.get_size()
        screen_w = SCREEN_SIZE[0]
        screen.blit(label, ((screen_w - w)/2, 450))

        # Render all the buttons
        for button in buttons.values():
            button.render(screen)

        # No animation, 5 frames per second is fine!
        clock.tick(5)
        pygame.display.update()


if __name__ == "__main__":

    run()
```

Summary

Sound is a very creative medium and it may require a lot of experimentation to perfect the audio in a game. Selecting good sound effects is essential because the player will likely hear them many times—and bad or annoying audio will quickly discourage further play. The same is true for the soundtrack, which has equal potential to either enhance or annoy.

The pygame.mixer module provides Pygame's sound effects capabilities, which allow you to load and play sound files on one of a number of *channels*. When sound is played through a Sound object, Pygame will automatically allocate a free channel. This is the simplest approach, but you have the option of managing channels yourself by playing the sound on a specific channel. I recommend this only if you will be playing many sounds and want to prioritize them.

Although you can play any audio with Sound objects, it is best to play music with the pygame.mixer.music module because it can *stream* the audio, rather than loading the entire file into memory. The music module provides a number of simple functions that you can use to manage the music in your game.

The next chapter covers more techniques that you can use to create convincing 3D visuals in a game.

CHAPTER 11

■■■

Lights, Camera, Action!

In Chapters 8 and 9, you learned how to manipulate 3D information and use OpenGL to display simple models. In this chapter we will cover how to work with images to create more visually appealing scenes. We will also discuss how to read a 3D model from a file, which is an important step in creating a polished game.

Working with Textures

In Chapter 9 you learned how to create a 3D model from shaded polygons, but in order to make an object look really convincing you need to use *textures*, which are images that have been stretched into the shape of a polygon. Vertices and polygons create the shape of a model, but textures define the final look of any 3D object. You could transform a model of a futuristic solider to a zombie, or even a statue, simply by changing which images are used for its textures.

OpenGL has excellent support for textures and can be used to create highly detailed models and scenery in a game.

Uploading Textures with OpenGL

Before you can use an image as a texture with OpenGL, you first have to *upload* it. This takes the raw image information and sends it to the high-speed *video memory* of your graphics card. Images used as textures must be at least 64×64 pixels in size, and both the width and height must be a power of 2 (64, 128, 256, etc.). If your image isn't a power of 2, you should scale it to fit in the next power of 2 up. Listing 11-1 is a function that can calculate the next power of 2, given one of the dimensions.

■**Note** Some graphics cards do have the capability to use textures that aren't a power of 2, but it is best to stick to power of 2 for maximum compatibility.

Listing 11-1. *Calculating the Next Power of 2*

```
from math import log, ceil
def next_power_of_2(size):
    return 2 ** ceil(log(size, 2))
```

The upper limit for the size of textures varies across graphics cards. You can ask OpenGL for the maximum supported texture size by calling glGetIntegerv(GL_MAX_TEXTURE_SIZE). On my computer this returns 4096, which is a very large texture indeed!

The following list outlines the steps required to upload image data and create a texture in OpenGL:

1. Load the image with pygame.image.load.

2. Use the pygame.image.tostring function to retrieve a string containing the raw image data.

3. Generate an id with glGenTextures that you can use to identify the texture.

4. Set any parameters that affect how the texture will be used when rendering polygons.

5. Upload the raw image data with the glTexImage2D function.

Loading the image is done in the same way as you would load an image in a 2D game—just call pygame.image.load with the image file name. For example, the following line loads an image called sushitex.png and returns a surface:

```
texture_surface = pygame.image.load("sushitex.png")
```

Once you have a Pygame surface containing your image, call pygame.image.tostring to retrieve a string with the raw image data. The first parameter to pygame.image.tostring is the surface; the second should be RGB for opaque images, or RGBA if the image has an alpha channel. The last parameter should be set to True, which tells Pygame to *flip* the rows in the returned data (otherwise, the texture would be upside down). The following line retrieves the raw image data for the surface that we loaded earlier:

```
texture_data = pygame.image.tostring(texture_surface, 'RGB', True)
```

Every texture in OpenGL must be assigned an id value (a number) with the glGenTextures function. These ids are used to select the texture to use when drawing OpenGL primitives. The glGenTextures function takes the number of ids you want to generate and returns a list of ID values, or a single value if you asked for just one. Texture ids are generally allocated sequentially (so the first three textures will probably be named 1, 2, and 3), but this may not always be the case.

■**Caution** Textures ids are integer values, and not objects. Deleting a texture id, or letting it go out of scope, will not clean up the texture. You should manually delete textures that you no longer want to use (see the "Deleting Textures" section a bit later).

Once you have assigned a texture id, call glBindTexture to tell OpenGL that all subsequent texture-related functions should use that texture. The glBindTexture function takes two parameters; the first should be GL_TEXTURE_2D for standard 2D textures, and the second parameter is the id that you want to bind. The following two lines create a single id for the sushitex.png texture and *bind* it for use:

```
texture_id = glGenTextures(1)
glBindTexture(GL_TEXTURE_2D, texture_id)
```

Before uploading the image data, we need to set a few *texture parameters*, which are values that affect how OpenGL will use the texture when rendering. To set a texture parameter call glTexParameteri for integer parameters, or glTexParameterf for float parameters. Both functions take the same three parameters; the texture type (GL_TEXTURE_2D for standard 2D textures) followed by the name of the parameter you want to set and the value you want to set it to. Most parameters are optional and will use default values if you don't change them.

Two parameters that we need to set for all textures are GL_TEXTURE_MIN_FILTER and GL_TEXTURE_MAX_FILTER, which tell OpenGL what method it should use to scale textures up or down. The GL_TEXTURE_MIN_FILTER parameter is used when the pixels of the texture (often called *texels*) are smaller than the pixels on the screen. The GL_TEXTURE_MAX_FILTER parameter is used when texels become *larger* than pixels. The following two lines set both parameters to GL_LINEAR, which makes scaled textures appear smooth and not so pixelated. We will cover other possible values later.

```
glTexParameteri(GL_TEXTURE_2D, GL_TEXTURE_MAG_FILTER, GL_LINEAR)
glTexParameteri(GL_TEXTURE_2D, GL_TEXTURE_MIN_FILTER, GL_LINEAR)
```

Next we need to call glPixelStorei(GL_UNPACK_ALIGNMENT, 1), which tells OpenGL how the rows in the raw image data have been packed together, then call glTexImage2D to upload the image data. The following lines upload the texture_data we retrieved earlier. Once this step is complete, the texture can be used to draw triangles, quads, and any other OpenGL primitive.

```
glPixelStorei(GL_UNPACK_ALIGNMENT, 1)
width, height = texture_surface.get_rect().size
glTexImage2D( GL_TEXTURE_2D,
            0,      # First mip-level
            3,      # Bytes per pixel
            width,
            height,
            0,      # Texture border
            GL_RGB,
            GL_UNSIGNED_BYTE,
            texture_data)
```

There are a lot of parameters to glTexImage2D because OpenGL was designed to be very flexible in the image formats it supports. Fortunately we can generally stick with the parameters we described earlier when uploading texture data from a Pygame surface, although for surfaces with an alpha channel you should change the 3 to a 4, and the GL_RGB to GL_RGBA. See Table 11-1 for a more detailed explanation of the parameters to glTexImage2D.

Table 11-1. *Parameters for glTexImage2D (in Function Call Order)*

Parameter	Explanation
target	Will typically be GL_TEXTURE_2D for image textures. OpenGL supports one-dimensional and three-dimensional textures, but these are less commonly used in games.
level	The mip map level, where 0 is the first (largest) level and 1 is the next size down. I'll explain mip maps in a bit.
internalFormat	Indicates how the data will be stored in video memory. Generally this will be 3 for opaque images and 4 for images with an alpha channel, but it will also accept a number of constants for other formats.
width	Width of the image, in pixels.
height	Height of the image, in pixels.
border	Sets a border for the textures. Can be either 0 for a border, or 1 for a single-pixel border.
format	The format of the image data that is to be uploaded. This will generally be either GL_RGB for opaque images, or GL_RGBA for images with an alpha channel.
type	Specifies how the components of the image are stored; typically this will be GL_UNSIGNED_BYTE, for image data retrieved from a Pygame surface.
data	A string containing raw image data.

Once the texture has been uploaded, the original Pygame surface object is no longer needed because OpenGL has a copy of it. You can either let it go out of scope and let Python clean it up for you, or call del to delete the reference.

Texture Coordinates

When textures are enabled in OpenGL, every vertex can be assigned a *texture coordinate* that defines a position within the texture. When a textured polygon is rendered to the screen, the texture will be *stretched* between these coordinates.

OpenGL uses *normalized* texture coordinates, which means that no matter how many pixels are in the texture image, the width and height of the texture are always 1.0 (see Figure 11-1). So a texture coordinate of (0.5, 0.5) will always be in the center of the texture. The bottom left of a texture is coordinate (0, 0) and the top right is (1, 1). The advantage of using normalized coordinates is that they will remain the same if you change the dimensions of the image.

Texture coordinates can be stored in the same way that you would store a two-dimensional vector: either a tuple or a Vector2 object. Components of a texture coordinate are called s and t in OpenGL, but you can still use a Vector2 object for convenience and refer to the components as x and y. Generally, though, you rarely have to do anything with texture coordinates other than store them and send them to OpenGL as needed, so a tuple is usually the best choice.

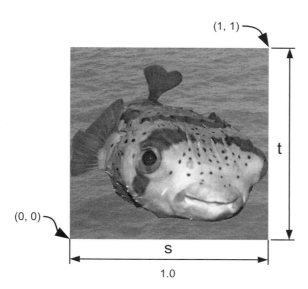

Figure 11-1. *Texture coordinates*

Rendering Textures

To use a texture when rendering a polygon, or any other OpenGL primitive, you must supply a texture coordinate for each vertex with the glTexCoord2f function, which takes the s and t components as parameters. The primitive will be drawn with the last texture that was bound with the glBindTexture function.

The following code draws a single quad aligned with the x and y axes. It uses texture coordinates for the four corners so that the entire image will be drawn in the quad.

```
# Draw a quad (4 vertices, 4 texture coords)
glBegin(GL_QUADS)

# Top left corner
glTexCoord2f(0, 1)
glVertex3f(-100, 100, 0)

# Top right corner
glTexCoord2f(1, 1)
glVertex3f(100, 100, 0)
```

```
# Bottom right corner
glTexCoord2f(1, 0)
glVertex3f(100, -100, 0)

# Bottom left corner
glTexCoord2f(0, 0)
glVertex3f(-100, -100, 0)

glEnd()
```

Deleting Textures

Each texture uses up video memory, which is a limited resource. When you have finished with a texture (switching levels, exiting the game, etc.), you should delete it with a call to glDeleteTextures, to free up its video memory. This function takes the id you want to delete, or a list of ids. Once the texture has been deleted, it is an error to bind it again, so you should discard the id value.

The following line deletes a single textured ID called texture_id:

```
glDeleteTextures(texture_id)
```

Seeing Textures in Action

Let's write a script to demonstrate uploading a texture and using it when rendering an OpenGL primitive. We are going to draw a single textured quad, and to show that it isn't simply a sprite we will rotate it around the x axis.

In the init function of Listing 11-2 is a call to glEnable(GL_TEXTURE_2D), which enables OpenGL textures. If you ever have problems getting textures to work in OpenGL, check whether you have made this call.

Listing 11-2. *Textures in Action (opengltex.py)*

```
SCREEN_SIZE = (800, 600)

from math import radians

from OpenGL.GL import *
from OpenGL.GLU import *

import pygame
from pygame.locals import *
```

```python
def resize(width, height):

    glViewport(0, 0, width, height)
    glMatrixMode(GL_PROJECTION)
    glLoadIdentity()
    gluPerspective(60.0, float(width)/height, .1, 1000.)
    glMatrixMode(GL_MODELVIEW)
    glLoadIdentity()

def init():

    glEnable(GL_TEXTURE_2D)
    glClearColor(1, 1, 1, 1)

def run():

    pygame.init()
    screen = pygame.display.set_mode(SCREEN_SIZE, HWSURFACE|OPENGL|DOUBLEBUF)

    resize(*SCREEN_SIZE)
    init()

    # Load the textures
    texture_surface = pygame.image.load("sushitex.png")
    # Retrieve the texture data
    texture_data = pygame.image.tostring(texture_surface, 'RGB', True)

    # Generate a texture id
    texture_id = glGenTextures(1)
    # Tell OpenGL we will be using this texture id for texture operations
    glBindTexture(GL_TEXTURE_2D, texture_id)

    # Tell OpenGL how to scale images
    glTexParameteri( GL_TEXTURE_2D, GL_TEXTURE_MAG_FILTER, GL_LINEAR )
    glTexParameteri( GL_TEXTURE_2D, GL_TEXTURE_MIN_FILTER, GL_LINEAR )

    # Tell OpenGL that data is aligned to byte boundries
    glPixelStorei(GL_UNPACK_ALIGNMENT, 1)

    # Get the dimensions of the image
    width, height = texture_surface.get_rect().size
```

```
# Upload the image to OpenGL
glTexImage2D( GL_TEXTURE_2D,
              0,
              3,
              width,
              height,
              0,
              GL_RGB,
              GL_UNSIGNED_BYTE,
              texture_data)

clock = pygame.time.Clock()

tex_rotation = 0.0

while True:

    for event in pygame.event.get():
        if event.type == QUIT:
            return

    time_passed = clock.tick()
    time_passed_seconds = time_passed / 1000.
    tex_rotation += time_passed_seconds * 360.0 / 8.0

    # Clear the screen (similar to fill)
    glClear(GL_COLOR_BUFFER_BIT)

    # Clear the modelview matrix
    glLoadIdentity()

    # Set the modelview matrix
    glTranslatef(0.0, 0.0, -600.0)
    glRotate(tex_rotation, 1, 0, 0)

    # Draw a quad (4 vertices, 4 texture coords)
    glBegin(GL_QUADS)

    glTexCoord2f(0, 1)
    glVertex3f(-300, 300, 0)

    glTexCoord2f(1, 1)
    glVertex3f(300, 300, 0)

    glTexCoord2f(1, 0)
    glVertex3f(300, -300, 0)
```

```
glTexCoord2f(0, 0)
glVertex3f(-300, -300, 0)

glEnd()

pygame.display.flip()

# Delete the texture when we are finished with it
glDeleteTextures(texture_id)

if __name__ == "__main__":
    run()
```

The run function performs the five steps required to read in the sushitex.png image and upload the image data to OpenGL. It then draws a textured quad by sending OpenGL four texture coordinates and four vertices. Texture coordinates are sent with the glTexcoord2f function, which takes the s and t components as parameters. An alternative to glTexcoord2f is the glTexCoord2fv function, which takes a sequence (tuple, Vector2, etc.) rather than individual values.

The rotation is done with the glRotate function, which creates a rotation matrix about an axis and multiplies it by the current model-view matrix. It takes four parameters: the first parameter is the angle you want to rotate by (in degrees), followed by the x, y, and z component of the axis. For example, a call to glRotate(45, 1, 0, 0) would rotate 45 degrees around the x axis, and a call to glRotate(-30, 0, 1, 0) would rotate *negative* 30 degrees (i.e., 30 degrees *clockwise*) around the y axis. You can also use this function to rotate around any axis, and not just the three basic axes.

When you run Listing 11-2, you will see something like Figure 11-2, with a large textured quad rotating around the x axis. Try experimenting with the texture coordinate values to see the effect they have on the quad.

Figure 11-2. *opengltex.py*

Mip Mapping

When there are fewer pixels in a polygon than there are pixels from the texture it is drawn with, OpenGL has to *skip* some of the pixels from the texture in order to make it fit. This can result in a distortion effect in the rendered polygon, an effect that worsens the more the texture is scaled down. This distortion can be distracting in an animated 3D scene and reduces the overall quality of the visuals.

Mip mapping is a technique to minimize this effect. It works by precalculating progressively smaller versions of the texture, each with half the dimensions of the previous texture (see Figure 11-3). For instance, a texture with 256×256 pixels will also have a 128×128-pixel version followed by a 64×64-pixel version, and further smaller versions of the texture where each is half the size of the texture preceding it, down to the final texture (which is a single pixel that is an average of all the pixels in the original). When OpenGL renders a polygon with a mip mapped texture, it will use the *mip level* that is closest to the size of the polygon on screen, which reduces the number of skipped pixels and improves visual quality.

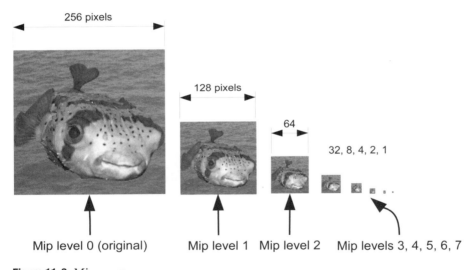

Figure 11-3. *Mip maps*

Note Mip is an acronym for *multum in parvo*, which is Latin for "much in a small space."

You can upload image data for each *mip level* by setting the second parameter to glTexImage2D. The original—and largest—texture is mip level 0. The first mip level is 1, which should be half the dimensions of the original, and the second mip level is 2, which should be one quarter of the size of the original.

Because calculating mip levels is a common task, there is a function from the OpenGL Utility library (OpenGL.GLU) that we can use to create and upload all the mip levels in one call. The gluBuild2DMipmaps function can replace a call to glTexImage2D, and takes the same parameters, with the exception of level and border (which are not needed). For example, the following call can replace the call to glTexImage2D in Listing 11-2:

```
gluBuild2DMipmaps( GL_TEXTURE_2D,
                   3,
                   width,
                   height,
                   GL_RGB,
                   GL_UNSIGNED_BYTE,
                   texture_data )
```

The only downside of using mip mapped textures is that they use a third more video memory than non–mip mapped textures, but the improvement in visual quality is well worth it. I recommend using mip mapping for all textures used in 3D scenes. You won't need to use mip maps for textures that aren't scaled, such as fonts or the heads-up display.

Texture Parameters

OpenGL is very flexible in the way it renders 3D scenes. There are a number of texture parameters that can be set to create visual effects and adjust how textures are used to render polygons. This section covers some commonly used texture parameters—the full list is beyond the scope of this book, but you can read the OpenGL documentation online (www.opengl.org/sdk/docs/man/) for all the details.

Min and Max Filters

In Listing 11-2 we set two texture parameters, GL_TEXTURE_MIN_FILTER and GL_TEXTURE_MAX_FILTER, which define the *minimizing* and *maximizing* filters for texture scaling. Both were set to GL_LINEAR, which gives good results in most cases, but there are other values that you can use to fine-tune the scaling.

When OpenGL renders a textured polygon to the screen, it *samples* the texture at regular intervals to calculate the color of pixels in the polygon. If the texture is mip mapped (see our earlier discussion), OpenGL also has to decide which mip level(s) it should sample. The method it uses to sample the textures and select a mip level is defined by the minimizing or maximizing filter parameter.

The only values you can set for the maximizing filter (GL_TEXTURE_MAX_FILTER) are GL_NEAREST and GL_LINEAR. Generally it is best to stick with GL_LINEAR, which makes OpenGL use *bilinear filtering* to smooth the texture when scaled, but textures can appear blurry at high scales. The alternative is GL_NEAREST, which looks sharper but blocky. These values are also supported by the minimizing filter (GL_TEXTURE_MIN_FILTER), in addition to four other constants that tell OpenGL how to include the mip level in the color calculation (see Table 11-2). The highest-quality setting for the minimizing filter is GL_LINEAR_MIPMAP_LINEAR, which softens the texture like GL_LINEAR but also blends between the two nearest mip levels (known as *trilinear filtering*). The following lines set the minimizing and maximizing filter methods to the highest-quality settings:

```
glTexParameteri(GL_TEXTURE_2D,  GL_TEXTURE_MAG_FILTER, GL_LINEAR)
glTexParameteri(GL_TEXTURE_2D,  GL_TEXTURE_MIN_FILTER, GL_LINEAR_MIPMAP_LINEAR)
```

Table 11-2. *Potential Values for Min and Max Filter Parameters*

Parameter Constant	Sample Effect
GL_NEAREST	Selects the texel nearest to the sample point. This keeps the texture looking sharp, but can appear low quality.
GL_LINEAR	Selects the four texels nearest to the sample point and blends between them. This smoothes the rendered texture and makes it appear less jagged when scaled.
GL_NEAREST_MIPMAP_NEAREST	Selects the texel nearest to the sample point, and the mip level that is closest to the size of the pixel being rendered. *Minimizing filter only.*
GL_LINEAR_MIPMAP_NEAREST	Blends between the four texels nearest to the sample point and selects the mip level that is closest to the size of the pixel being rendered. *Minimizing filter only.*
GL_NEAREST_MIPMAP_LINEAR	Selects the texel nearest to the sample point and blends between the two mip levels that most closely match the size of the pixel being rendered. *Minimizing filter only.*
GL_LINEAR_MIPMAP_LINEAR	Blends between the four texels nearest to the sample point and blends between the two mip levels that most closely match the size of the pixel being rendered. *Minimizing filter only.*

Texture Wrapping

A texture coordinate with components in the zero to one range will refer to a point inside the texture, but it is not an error to have a texture coordinate with components outside that range—in fact, it can be very useful. How OpenGL treats coordinates that are not in the zero to one range is defined by the GL_TEXTURE_WRAP_S and GL_TEXTURE_WRAP_T texture parameters. The default for these parameters is GL_REPEAT, which causes samples that go off one edge of the texture to appear on the opposite edge. This creates the effect of *tiling* the texture, so that multiple copies of it are placed edge to edge. You can see this in action by editing the calls to glTexCoord2f in Listing 11-2. Try replacing the lines between the calls to glBegin and glEnd with the following:

```
glTexCoord2f(0, 3)
glVertex3f(-300, 300, 0)

glTexCoord2f(3, 3)
glVertex3f(300, 300, 0)

glTexCoord2f(3, 0)
glVertex3f(300, -300, 0)

glTexCoord2f(0, 0)
glVertex3f(-300, -300, 0)
```

If you run the edited Listing 11-2, you should see something like Figure 11-4. Only a single quad is drawn, but the texture is repeated nine times because the texture components range from zero to three. Tiling textures like this is useful in games because you can texture very large polygons without having to break them up in to smaller pieces. For example, a long piece of fence could be created with a single elongated quad and a tiled texture, which is more efficient than small quads for each piece of fence.

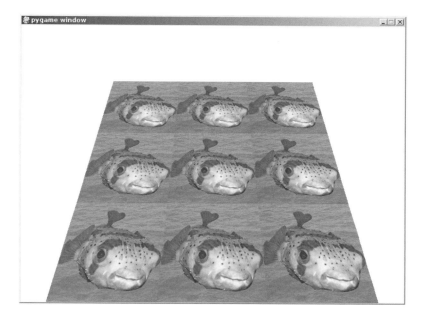

Figure 11-4. *Repeating texture coordinates*

Repeating textures has the same effect as transforming the components of every texture coordinate with the following Python function (although the wrapping is done by your graphics card and not Python). The % symbol is the modulus operator, which returns the remainder in a division, so % 1.0 would return the fractional part of a number.

```
def wrap_repeat(component):
    return component % 1.0
```

■**Tip** Tiling works best with textures that have been designed to be seamless—that is, if you place them side by side you can't see where one ends and the other begins.

An alternative setting for the wrap parameter is GL_MIRRORED_REPEAT, which is similar to GL_REPEAT but *mirrors* the sample point when it goes over the texture edge. To see this in action, insert the following two lines before the while True: line in the run function of Listing 11-2:

```
glTexParameteri(GL_TEXTURE_2D, GL_TEXTURE_WRAP_S, GL_MIRRORED_REPEAT)
glTexParameteri(GL_TEXTURE_2D, GL_TEXTURE_WRAP_T, GL_MIRRORED_REPEAT)
```

Now when you run Listing 11-2 you should see that the repeated images are mirrored around the s and t axes of the texture. The mirrored repeat setting is a good way of making textures appear seamless, even if they weren't designed to be. The Python equivalent of GL_MIRRORED_REPEAT is as follows:

```
def wrap_mirrored_repeat(component):
    if int(component) % 2:
        return 1.0 - (component % 1.0)
    else:
        return component % 1.0
```

The final texture wrap setting we will look at is GL_CLAMP_TO_EDGE, which *saturates* the texture components to a range of zero to one. If a texture component goes outside of that range, it is set to zero or one, depending on which is closest to the original value. The visual effect of saturating the texture components is that the outside edge of the texture is repeated indefinitely when OpenGL samples outside the texture borders. This setting is useful when you have texture coordinates that are very near to the texture edges but you want to make sure that OpenGL doesn't sample a point over the texture edge (which can happen if you have the GL_LINEAR filter setting enabled). To see the effect of this setting, change the calls to glTexParameteri to the following:

```
glTexParameteri(GL_TEXTURE_2D, GL_TEXTURE_WRAP_S, GL_CLAMP_TO_EDGE)
glTexParameteri(GL_TEXTURE_2D, GL_TEXTURE_WRAP_T, GL_CLAMP_TO_EDGE)
```

The following function is the Python equivalent of GL_CAMP_TO_EDGE:

```
def wrap_clamp_to_edge(component):
    if component > 1.0:
        return 1.0
    elif component < 0.0:
        return 0.0
    return component
```

We have been setting the values of GL_TEXTURE_WRAP_S and GL_TEXTURE_WRAP_T to the same value, but they can be set independently if you need to. To create a fence quad, for example, we might want the texture to repeat horizontally (on the s component), but not vertically (t component).

Try experimenting with Listing 11-2 to see the effects of combining texture wrap parameters.

Working with Models

Three-dimensional models are rarely defined directly in code. Generally they are read in from files produced with 3D applications such as 3D Studio or Blender. This section covers how 3D models are stored in files, and how to read and display them in the game.

Storing Models

As with images, there are a variety of file formats that can be used to store a 3D model, each produced by a different manufacturer with a different set of features in mind. Unlike images, there are no clear winners when it comes to storing models for a game, and there are many to choose from.

Models can be stored either as binary or text. Binary formats pack the information very efficiently and tend to produce smaller files, whereas text formats store the information as lines of text, which produces files that are larger but easier to work with.

Files for storing 3D information will contain at least a list of vertices, and will probably also contain a list of texture coordinates and normals. Many also contain additional information regarding textures and lighting. You don't have to use all the information in a 3D model, but the more features of the format you implement, the more closely it will resemble the model that was created by the artist.

▪Tip Many game developers publish the 3D model format used in their games. You may be able to test your game with characters taken from a commercial game—but be careful about breaking copyright laws!

OBJ Format for 3D Models

To work with 3D models we are going to use the Wavefront OBJ format (extension `.obj`), which is a simple text format that has been in existence for many years. Most software that works with 3D models will be able to at least write OBJ files, and probably read them as well. They are text based, so you can open them in a text editor such as Windows Notepad, or the equivalent on other platforms.

OBJ files often come with a material library file (with the extension `.mtl`), which contains various settings that define how the polygons in the model should be rendered, including the file name of the texture.

Parsing OBJ Files

Each line in an OBJ file defines a single piece of information (vertex, texture coordinate, etc.) and consists of one or more *words*, separated by spaces. The first word indicates what the line contains, and the remaining words are the information itself. For example, the following line defines a single vertex at (–100, 50, –20):

```
v -100 50 -20
```

Python is very good at reading text files and has built-in support for reading one line at a time. If you iterate over an open file object, it will return a string containing each line. Here is how we might begin writing Python code to parse a 3D model stored in an OBJ file:

```
obj_file = file("tank.obj")
for line in obj_file:
    words = line.split() # Split line on spaces
    command = words[0]
    data = words[1:]
```

Each pass through the `for` loop returns the next line in the file. Inside the loop we split the line into words. The first word is named `command` and the remaining words are stored in a list called `data`. A complete parser would select an action based on the value of `command`, and use any information contained in the `data` list.

Table 11-3 contains some commonly used commands in an OBJ file. There are more possible commands, but these can be used to store the kind of 3D models that are used in a game. We will be using the information in Table 11-3 to read and display a 3D model of a tank.

Table 11-3. *Lines in a Wavefront OBJ File*

Line	Explanation
#	Indicates the line is a comment and should be ignored by the software.
f <vertex1> <vertex2> etc.	Defines a face in the model. Each word consists of three values separated by forward slashes: the vertex index, the texture coordinate index, and the normal index. There is a triplet of values for each point in the face (3 for a triangle, 4 for a quad, etc.).
mtllib <filename>	Specifies the material library for the OBJ file.
usemtl <material name>	Selects a material from the material library.
v <x> <y> <z>	Defines a vertex at x, y, z.
vt <s> <t>	Defines a texture coordinate.

Material Library Files

Wavefront OBJ files are often partnered with a material library file that contains the texture and lighting information. When you encounter a mtlib command in the OBJ file, it introduces a material library file that contains this extra information. The file name of the material library is given in the first word of the command data, and should be appended with the extension .mtl.

Material libraries are also text files, and can be parsed in the same way as the parent OBJ file. In the material library file, the newmtl command begins a new material, which contains a number of parameters. One of these parameters is the texture file name, which is introduced with the map_Kd command. For example, the following lines from a material file would define a texture called tankmaterial that has a texture with the file name tanktexture.png:

```
newmtl tankmaterial
map_Kd tanktexture.png
```

Seeing Models in Action

Let's write a class to load a Wavefront OBJ file and render it with OpenGL. I have created a model of a futuristic tank (see Figure 11-5), which was built with AC3D (www.inivis.com/) and exported it as mytank.obj and mytank.mtl. My artistic skills are limited; feel free to replace my model with your own 3D object. You can use any 3D modeler software that has the capability to export OBJ files.

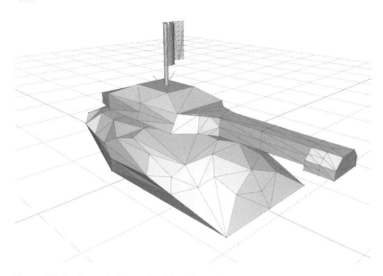

Figure 11-5. *Futuristic tank object in AC3D*

The class we will be building is called Model3D and will be responsible for reading the model and storing its *geometry* (vertices, texture coordinates, models, etc.). It will also be able to send the geometry to OpenGL to render the model. See Table 11-4 for the details of what Model3D needs to store.

Table 11-4. *Information Stored in the Model3D Class*

Name	Purpose
self.vertices	A list of vertices (3D points), stored as tuples of three values (for x, y, and z)
self.tex_coords	A list of texture coordinates, stored as tuples of two values (for s and t)
self.normals	A list of normals, stored as tuples of three values (for x, y, and z)
self.materials	A *dictionary* of Material objects, so we can look up the texture file name given the name of the material
self.face_groups	A list of FaceGroup objects that will store the faces for each material
self.display_list_id	A display list id that we will use to speed up OpenGL rendering

In addition to the Model3D class, we need to define a class to store materials and *face groups*, which are polygons that share the same material. Listing 11-3 is the beginning of the Model3D class.

Listing 11-3. *Class Definitions in model3d.py*

```python
# A few imports we will need later
from OpenGL.GL import *
from OpenGL.GLU import *

import pygame
import os.path

class Material(object):

    def __init__(self):

        self.name = ""
        self.texture_fname = None
        self.texture_id = None

class FaceGroup(object):

    def __init__(self):

        self.tri_indices = []
        self.material_name = ""

class Model3D(object):

    def __init__(self):

        self.vertices = []
        self.tex_coords = []
        self.normals = []
        self.materials = {}
        self.face_groups = []
        # Display list id for quick rendering
        self.display_list_id = None
```

Now that we have the basic class definitions, we can add a method to Model3D that will open an OBJ file and read the contents. Inside the read_obj method (see Listing 11-4), we go through each line of the file and parse it into a command string and a data list. A number of if statements decide what to do with the information store in data.

Listing 11-4. *Method to Parse OBJ Files*

```python
def read_obj(self, fname):

    current_face_group = None
    file_in = file(fname)

    for line in file_in:

        # Parse command and data from each line
        words = line.split()
        command = words[0]
        data = words[1:]

        if command == 'mtllib': # Material library

            # Find the file name of the texture
            model_path = os.path.split(fname)[0]
            mtllib_path = os.path.join( model_path, data[0] )
            self.read_mtllib(mtllib_path)

        elif command == 'v': # Vertex
            x, y, z = data
            vertex = (float(x), float(y), float(z))
            self.vertices.append(vertex)

        elif command == 'vt': # Texture coordinate

            s, t = data
            tex_coord = (float(s), float(t))
            self.tex_coords.append(tex_coord)

        elif command == 'vn': # Normal

            x, y, z = data
            normal = (float(x), float(y), float(z))
            self.normals.append(normal)

        elif command == 'usemtl' : # Use material

            current_face_group = FaceGroup()
            current_face_group.material_name = data[0]
            self.face_groups.append( current_face_group )
```

```
elif command == 'f':

    assert len(data) ==  3, "Sorry, only triangles are supported"

    # Parse indices from triples
    for word in data:
        vi, ti, ni = word.split('/')
        # Subtract 1 because Obj indexes start at one, rather than zero
        indices = (int(vi) - 1, int(ti) - 1, int(ni) - 1)
        current_face_group.tri_indices.append(indices)

# Read all the textures used in the model
for material in self.materials.itervalues():

    model_path = os.path.split(fname)[0]
    texture_path = os.path.join(model_path, material.texture_fname)
    texture_surface = pygame.image.load(texture_path)
    texture_data = pygame.image.tostring(texture_surface, 'RGB', True)

    # Create and bind a texture id
    material.texture = glGenTextures(1)
    glBindTexture(GL_TEXTURE_2D, material.texture)

    glTexParameteri( GL_TEXTURE_2D,
                     GL_TEXTURE_MAG_FILTER,
                     GL_LINEAR)
    glTexParameteri( GL_TEXTURE_2D,
                     GL_TEXTURE_MIN_FILTER,
                     GL_LINEAR_MIPMAP_LINEAR)

    glPixelStorei(GL_UNPACK_ALIGNMENT,1)

    # Upload texture and build map-maps
    width, height = texture_surface.get_rect().size
    gluBuild2DMipmaps( GL_TEXTURE_2D,
                       3,
                       width,
                       height,
                       GL_RGB,
                       GL_UNSIGNED_BYTE,
                       texture_data)
```

One of the first commands in an OBJ file is usually mtllib, which tells us the name of the material library file. When this command is encountered, we pass the file name of the material library to the read_mtllib method (which we will write later).

If the command consists of geometry (vertex, texture coordinate, or normal), it is converted to a tuple of float values and stored in the appropriate list. For instance, the line v 10 20 30 would be converted to the tuple (10, 20, 30) and appended to self.vertices.

Before each group of faces is a usemtl command, which tells us which material subsequent faces will use. When read_obj encounters this command, it creates a new FaceGroup object to store the material name and the face information that will follow.

Faces are defined with the f command, and consist of a word for each vertex in the face (3 for triangles, 4 for quads, etc.). Each word contains indices into the vertex, texture coordinate, and normal lists, separated by a forward slash character (/). For instance, the following line defines a triangle where the first point uses vertex 3, texture coordinate 8, and normal 10. These triplets of indices are stored in the current face group, and will be used to reconstruct the model shape when we come to render it.

```
f 3/8/10 4/9/15 5/12/20
```

Following the code to parse each line in the OBJ file we enter a loop that reads the textures in the material dictionary and uploads them to OpenGL. We will be using mip mapping and high-quality texture scaling.

■Note For simplicity, the Model3D class only works with OBJ files that contain triangles. If your model contains quads or other polygons, you will need to convert it to triangles with your 3D modeler.

The method to read the materials is similar to the read_obj method, but simpler because we are only interested in the texture name. There is other information stored in the material, but for the sake of simplicity we will ignore it for now.

In a material library file, the newmtl command begins a new material definition, and the map_Kd command sets the texture file name. The read_mtllib method (Listing 11-5) extracts this information and stores it in the self.materials dictionary.

Listing 11-5. *Parsing the Material Library*

```
def read_mtllib(self, mtl_fname):

    file_mtllib = file(mtl_fname)
    for line in file_mtllib:

        words = line.split()
        command = words[0]
        data = words[1:]

        if command == 'newmtl':
            material = Material()
            material.name = data[0]
            self.materials[data[0]] = material

        elif command == 'map_Kd':
            material.texture_fname = data[0]
```

These two functions (read_obj and read_mtllib) are enough to read all the information we need from OBJ files, and we can now write the code to send the geometry to OpenGL. The draw method (Listing 11-6) goes through each of the face groups, binds a texture, and sends OpenGL the data from the geometry lists.

Listing 11-6. *Sending the Geometry to OpenGL*

```
def draw(self):

    vertices = self.vertices
    tex_coords = self.tex_coords
    normals = self.normals

    for face_group in self.face_groups:

        # Bind the texture for this face group
        material = self.materials[face_group.material_name]
        glBindTexture(GL_TEXTURE_2D, material.texture)

        # Send the geometry to OpenGL
        glBegin(GL_TRIANGLES)
        for vi, ti, ni in face_group.tri_indices:
            glTexCoord2fv( tex_coords[ti] )
            glNormal3fv( normals[ni] )
            glVertex3fv( vertices[vi] )
        glEnd()


def draw_quick(self):

    if self.display_list_id is None:
        # Generate and compile a display list that renders the geometry
        self.display_list_id = glGenLists(1)
        glNewList(self.display_list_id, GL_COMPILE)
        self.draw()
        glEndList()

    glCallList(self.display_list_id)
```

Sending the geometry one vertex at a time can be slow, so there is also a draw_quick method that compiles a display list containing the model geometry, which can then be rendered with a single call to glCallList.

The Model3D class now contains everything we need to load and render a 3D model, but before we use it we should write the code to clean up the OpenGL resources we have used. Listing 11-7 adds a free_resources method to Model3D that deletes the display list and any texture that were created. This method can be called when you no longer need the model, or you can let it be called automatically by the __del__ method, which is called by Python when there are no more references left to the object.

■**Note** It is a good idea to manually call the `free_resources` function, because it may cause errors if Python cleans up your Model3D object after PyOpenGL has quit.

Listing 11-7. *Cleaning Up OpenGL Resources*

```
def __del__(self):

    #Called when the model is cleaned up by Python
    self.free_resources()

def free_resources(self):

    # Delete the display list
    if self.display_list_id is not None:
        glDeleteLists(self.display_list_id, 1)
        self.display_list_id = None

    # Delete any textures we used
    for material in self.materials.itervalues():
        if material.texture_id is not None:
            glDeleteTextures(material.texture_id)

    # Clear all the materials
    self.materials.clear()

    # Clear the geometry lists
    del self.vertices[:]
    del self.tex_coords[:]
    del self.normals[:]
    del self.face_groups[:]
```

Using the Model3D Class

Let's write a script that uses our Model3D class to load and render a model. Listing 11-8 creates a Model3D object and uses it to read mytank.obj (and materials).

Listing 11-8. *Rendering the Tank Model (tankdemo.py)*

```
SCREEN_SIZE = (800, 600)

from math import radians

from OpenGL.GL import *
from OpenGL.GLU import *
```

```python
import pygame
from pygame.locals import *

# Import the Model3D class
import model3d

def resize(width, height):

    glViewport(0, 0, width, height)
    glMatrixMode(GL_PROJECTION)
    glLoadIdentity()
    gluPerspective(60.0, float(width)/height, .1, 1000.)
    glMatrixMode(GL_MODELVIEW)
    glLoadIdentity()


def init():

    # Enable the GL features we will be using
    glEnable(GL_DEPTH_TEST)
    glEnable(GL_LIGHTING)
    glEnable(GL_COLOR_MATERIAL)
    glEnable(GL_TEXTURE_2D)
    glEnable(GL_CULL_FACE)

    glShadeModel(GL_SMOOTH)
    glClearColor(1.0, 1.0, 1.0, 0.0) # white

    # Set the material
    glMaterial(GL_FRONT, GL_AMBIENT, (0.0, 0.0, 0.0, 1.0))
    glMaterial(GL_FRONT, GL_DIFFUSE, (0.2, 0.2, 0.2, 1.0))
    glMaterial(GL_FRONT, GL_SPECULAR, (1.0, 1.0, 1.0, 1.0))
    glMaterial(GL_FRONT, GL_SHININESS, 10.0)

    # Set light parameters
    glLight(GL_LIGHT0, GL_AMBIENT, (0.0, 0.0, 0.0, 1.0))
    glLight(GL_LIGHT0, GL_DIFFUSE, (0.4, 0.4, 0.4, 1.0))
    glLight(GL_LIGHT0, GL_SPECULAR, (1.0, 1.0, 1.0, 1.0))

    # Enable light 1 and set position
    glEnable(GL_LIGHT0)
    glLight(GL_LIGHT0, GL_POSITION,  (0, .5, 1, 0))
```

```python
def run():

    pygame.init()
    screen = pygame.display.set_mode(SCREEN_SIZE, HWSURFACE|OPENGL|DOUBLEBUF)

    resize(*SCREEN_SIZE)
    init()

    clock = pygame.time.Clock()

    # Read the model
    tank_model = model3d.Model3D()
    tank_model.read_obj('mytank.obj')

    rotation = 0.0

    while True:

        for event in pygame.event.get():
            if event.type == QUIT:
                return

        glClear(GL_COLOR_BUFFER_BIT | GL_DEPTH_BUFFER_BIT)

        time_passed = clock.tick()
        time_passed_seconds = time_passed / 1000.0

        glLoadIdentity()
        glRotatef(15, 1, 0, 0)
        glTranslatef(0.0, -1.5, -3.5)

        rotation += time_passed_seconds * 45.0
        glRotatef(rotation, 0, 1, 0)

        tank_model.draw_quick()

        pygame.display.flip()

if __name__ == "__main__":
    run()
```

The init function in Listing 11-8 enables the OpenGL features we will be using. It also sets parameters for the material and light, which will give the tank a metallic look. We will cover material and lighting parameters in the next chapter.

Before the tank is drawn, the model-matrix is set so that the camera is slightly above the tank and looking down on it—this gives a slightly more interesting viewpoint than looking at it along the z axis.

The call to glRotatef(15, 1, 0, 0) creates a rotation matrix of 15 degrees around the x axis, which is the equivalent of looking down a little. This rotation matrix is multiplied by a translation matrix, with a call to glTranslatef(0.0, -1.5, -3.5), which effectively moves the tank down by 1.5 units and back by 3.5 units. The second call to glRotatef makes the tank rotate about the y axis so we can see it in motion.

When you run Listing 11-8, you should see a formidable-looking tank rotating about the y axis (see Figure 11-6). If you have a better model you would like to use in place of the tank, then replace mytank.obj with the file name of your model.

■**Note** Not all 3D modeler applications use the same scale. If you find that your model is extremely large or very small, you may have to scale it before exporting, or change the code to view the object at a different distance.

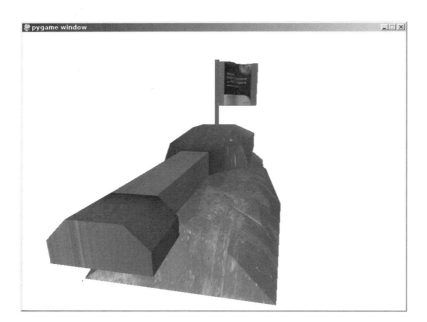

Figure 11-6. *tankdemo.py*

Summary

Textures are the primary way of making a 3D scene look convincing because you can apply images of the real world to objects in your game. Photographs are a great way of creating textures—a digital camera is a fantastic tool for game development! Or you can use images from other sources; the Pygame wiki (`www.pygame.org/wiki/resources`) has a great collection of links to sites with free textures.

Because OpenGL was created independently of Pygame, there is no one function that you can use to read and upload an image to be used as a texture; a few steps are required to get the image data from a file to high-speed video memory. If you use the steps outlined in this chapter, you should have no problem working with textures. Be sure to set the minimizing and maximizing texture parameters, as well as the wrapping functions.

You learned how to read a 3D model from a file and render it with OpenGL. The Wavefront OBJ format is well supported, and you may find the `Model3D` class adequate for any games you write. Or you may want to expand the `read_obj` method to cover more features (e.g., quads). If you want to support other formats in your game, you can probably find the documentation you need on the Web. Writing parsers can be challenging, but it's a great way to come to grips with the details of 3D model creation.

In the next chapter, you will learn how to work with OpenGL lighting and create impressive special effects that will add polish to your game.

CHAPTER 12

■■■

Setting the Scene with OpenGL

You've come quite far with OpenGL, having learned how to render and manipulate objects in a 3D scene. In this chapter, we will cover lighting in more detail and introduce you to other OpenGL features that will help you to add polish to your game.

Understanding Lighting

I introduced you to OpenGL's lighting capabilities in Chapter 7, but glossed over some of the details. In this section, we will explore how to work with lights and use them to add greater realism to a 3D scene.

OpenGL uses the *normals* that you assign to the vertices or faces of a model to calculate the color of light that will be seen by the player. These colors are used when rendering polygons in the scene, either by assigning a single color per face (flat shading), or by blending colors between the vertices (if smooth shading is enabled). The more detailed a model is, the more convincing the lighting will be, because colors are only calculated for entire faces or vertices and not for every pixel in the polygon.

OpenGL supports three types of lights:

- *Directional lights*: A directional light is a source of light where the rays are parallel to one another. The sun is generally treated as a directional light—even though it is technically a point light source—because it is so far away that by the time the light has reached the earth the rays are virtually parallel.

- *Point lights (also called positional lights)*: A point light is a light source that is emitted from a single point and is used to represent most close-by lights in a scene. Common uses for point light sources are bulbs, flames, and special effects.

- *Spotlights*: A spotlight is similar to a point light in that it is emitted from a single point but the rays are focused onto a circular area, creating a cone shape with the point as the tip. We won't cover OpenGL spotlights here, because they are not often used in games, but if you are interested, see the OpenGL documentation online at www.opengl.org/sdk/docs/man/. Spotlight-like effects can be achieved in other ways, usually with blending, which I cover later in this chapter.

Enabling Lighting

To enable lighting in OpenGL, simply call `glEnable(GL_LIGHTING)`. If you need to disable lighting temporarily—to render fonts, for example—call `glDisable(GL_LIGHTING)`. You will also need to enable the individual lights you want to use in a scene, which you can also do with `glEnable` by passing in one of the light constants (`GL_LIGHT0` to `GL_LIGHT7`).

Setting Light Parameters

There are a number of parameters for lights that can be set with the `glLight` function. This function takes a constant for the light you want to set (`GL_LIGHT0` through `GL_LIGHT7`), followed by a constant for the parameter you want to set and the value you want to set it to. See Table 12-1 for a list of the light parameters. (This table doesn't cover the parameters used in spotlights. See the OpenGL documentation for the full list.)

Table 12-1. *Light Parameters*

Parameter Name	Type	Explanation
GL_POSITION	Point	Sets the position of the light
GL_AMBIENT	Color	Sets the ambient intensity of the light
GL_DIFFUSE	Color	Sets the diffuse color of light
GL_SPECULAR	Color	Sets the color of the specular highlight the light will create
GL_CONSTANT_ATTENUATION	Number	Specifies the constant attenuation factor
GL_LINEAR_ATTENUATION	Number	Specifies the linear attenuation factor
GL_QUADRATIC_ATTENUATION	Number	Specifies the quadratic attenuation factor

The `GL_POSITION` parameter is used to set the position and type of light that will be created. It takes the x, y, and z coordinates of the position and an additional parameter called w. The light will be *directional* if w is set to 0.0, or *positional* (a point light), if w is set to 1.0. The following two lines create a directional light at (1.0, 1.0, 1.0), and a positional light at coordinate (50.0, 100.0, 0.0):

```
glLight(GL_LIGHT0, GL_POSITION, (1.0, 1.0, 1.0, 0.0))
glLight(GL_LIGHT1, GL_POSITION, (50.0, 100.0, 0.0, 1.0))
```

Directional lights send out parallel rays in the direction of the origin, so the positional light at (1.0, 1.0, 1.0) would simulate an infinitely faraway light source that is above-right and behind the current viewpoint. The positional light sends rays in all directions from coordinate (50.0, 100.0, 0.0).

There are also three-color values that can be set for lights: *ambient*, *diffuse*, and *specular*. Ambient color is used to simulate the effects of indirect light reflected from other objects in the scene. On a sunny day, the ambient color would be quite bright, because even in shade there would be enough light to see by. Conversely, in a cave illuminated with a single oil lamp, the ambient color would be dark, possibly even black, to create pitch-blackness in unlit areas.

The diffuse color of a light is the main color of the light that will illuminate the surrounding scene, and depends on the light source you are trying to simulate; sunlight will likely be bright white, but other light sources, such as candles, fireballs, and magic spells, may have different colors.

The final color value for light is the specular color, which is the color of highlights produced by reflective or polished surfaces. If you look at a shiny object, you will see bright points where the light is reflected directly into your eye. In OpenGL, the color of these bright spots is determined with the specular color parameter.

The following three calls to `glLight` would create a light that would work well as a fireball or rocket:

```
glLight(GL_LIGHT1, GL_AMBIENT, (0.05, 0.05, 0.05))
glLight(GL_LIGHT1, GL_DIFFUSE, (1.0, 0.2, 0.2))
glLight(GL_LIGHT1, GL_SPECULAR, (1.0, 1.0, 1.0))
```

The ambient is a dark gray because we want the effect to be localized and not contribute much light outside of a short distance. The diffuse is a bright flame red, and the specular is intense white to cause brilliant highlights in nearby surfaces.

Lights also have three *attenuation* factors, which define how the brightness of a point light source changes over distance. The three factors, *constant, linear,* and *quadratic,* are used by OpenGL to calculate a single number that is multiplied by the colors produced by the lighting calculations. The formula that OpenGL uses is equivalent to the `get_attenuation` function in Listing 12-1, which takes the distance of a point from the light source followed by the three attenuation factors. The return value of `get_attenuation` is a number that indicates the brightness of the light at a distance from the source.

■**Note** The maximum brightness level that OpenGL can use is 1.0—values greater than 1.0 will not have any additional effect.

Listing 12-1. *Function That Calculates the Attenuation Factor*

```
def get_attenuation(distance, constant, linear, quadratic):
    return 1.0 / (constant + linear * distance + quadratic * (distance ** 2))
```

For a fireball effect, we would probably want to make the emitted light intense in the immediate area surrounding the visual effect but fade away quickly. The following calls to `glLight` set the three attenuation factors so that the light is at full intensity in a one-unit radius but quickly drops off until it barely contributes any light a few units away:

```
glLight(GL_LIGHT1, GL_CONSTANT_ATTENUATION, 0.5)
glLight(GL_LIGHT1, GL_LINEAR_ATTENUATION, 0.3)
glLight(GL_LIGHT1, GL_QUADRATIC_ATTENUATION, 0.2)
```

> ■**Note** Attenuation requires OpenGL to do a little more work for each polygon rendered and can have a performance impact on your game—although it probably won't be noticeable unless you have an old graphics card.

Working with Materials

A *material* in OpenGL is a collection of parameters that define how polygons should interact with light sources. These parameters are set with the `glMaterial` function, and are combined with the light parameters to generate the final colors used when rendering. The first parameter to `glMaterial` is typically `GL_FRONT`, which sets the parameters for polygons facing the camera, but can also be `GL_BACK` for polygons facing away from the camera—or `GL_FRONT_AND_BACK` for both. For models that are completely enclosed—that is, you can't see inside them—you can stick with `GL_FRONT` because only the front faces will be visible (unless you are *inside* the model!). The second parameter to `glMaterial` is a constant for the material parameter you want to set, and the final parameter is the value you want to set it to. Table 12-2 lists the material parameters you can use.

Table 12-2. *Material Parameters*

Parameter Name	Type	Explanation
GL_AMBIENT	Color	Sets the *ambient* contribution of the material color
GL_DIFFUSE	Color	Sets the *diffuse* color of the material
GL_SPECULAR	Color	Sets the color of *specular* highlights on a material
GL_SHININESS	Number	Specifies a value, between 0 and 128, that defines the shininess of the material
GL_EMISSION	Color	Specifies the emissive color of the material

The ambient, diffuse, and specular color parameters have the same meaning as they do for lights, and are combined with the corresponding light parameter. The `GL_SHININESS` parameter defines the size of specular highlights on a material. Higher values produce small highlights, which make the material appear hard or polished. Lower values create more matte-looking materials. The `GL_EMISSION` parameter defines the emissive color of the material, which is the color of light emitted from the material itself. Materials can't be used as light sources in OpenGL, but setting the emissive color will make a model appear to have its own internal illumination.

Tweaking Parameters

Selecting parameters for the material and lights is more of an art than a science; experimentation is generally the best way of getting the look you are looking for. The material and light settings for the spinning tank in the previous chapter (Listing 11-8) were selected to make the tank appear metallic. Try experimenting with the material values for the tank to create a different look. You should be able to make it look like a plastic toy or a wooden model by changing some of the parameters.

■**Tip** Lighting parameters can be varied over time to produce some interesting effects.

Managing Lights

You have at least eight OpenGL lights at your disposal when rendering a scene, but it is easy to imagine a need for more than this. Consider a scene set in a church; there may moonlight from the windows, a few flickering lamps, and numerous candles on the altar. We can't have all those light sources active in one frame, so how do we manage them all? The first step is to combine close light sources into a single light. The candles on the altar are a perfect candidate for this; although there are many light sources, the player probably won't notice if they are replaced with a single point light source being emitted from somewhere in the center of a group of candles. The next step to reducing the number of lights used is to prioritize bright and/or close lights over lights that are further away or not very bright. If we perform these steps for every frame, we can keep the number of lights down without impacting the visual quality of the scene.

The number of lights in a scene can also affect the frame rate of your game because OpenGL has to do a set of calculations for each additional light. You may want to set the maximum number of lights used in your game to be *lower* than the maximum that OpenGL can handle, in order to improve performance.

Understanding Blending

So far when we have rendered polygons, the colors from the textures have completely replaced the pixels of the screen beneath them—which is what we need when rendering solid objects but won't help us render translucent objects. For this we need to make use of OpenGL's *blending* features, which combine the colors from the texture with the colors from the surface underneath it.

Blending is also essential for creating many of the effects that players take for granted in today's games as it can be used to create anything from a smudge on a car windshield to spectacular explosions. In this section, we will explore how to use blending in your game, and examine some of the effects that can be created with it.

Using Blending

When OpenGL performs blending, it samples a color from the source and destination (i.e., the texture and the screen), and then combines the two colors with a simple equation to produce the final color that is written to the screen. OpenGL does the math on the colors, but if it were written in Python it may look something like this:

```
src = texture.sample_color()
dst = screen.sample_color()
final_color = blend_equation(src * src_factor, dst * dst_factor)
screen.put_color(final_color)
```

The src and dst values are the two colors sampled from the texture and screen. These colors are each multiplied by a *blend factor* (src_factor and dst_factor), and combined with a `blend_equation` function that produces the final color written to the screen. Combining different blend factors and blend equations can produce a large number of visual effects.

In OpenGL terms, the blend factors are set with the `glBlendFunc` function, which takes two constants for the source and destination factors. For example, a call to `glBlendFunc(GL_SRC_ALPHA, GL_ONE_MINUS_SRC_ALPHA)` would multiply the source color by the source's alpha component and the destination color by one minus the source's alpha component. See Table 12-3 for a full list of possible blend factors.

Table 12-3. *Blend Factor Constants*

Blend Factor Constant	Explanation
GL_ZERO	Multiplies by zero
GL_ONE	Multiplies by one
GL_SRC_COLOR	Multiplies by source
GL_ONE_MINUS_SRC_COLOR	Multiplies by one minus the source color
GL_DST_COLOR	Multiplies by destination
GL_ONE_MINUS_DST_COLOR	Multiplies by one minus the destination color
GL_SRC_ALPHA	Multiplies by the source alpha component
GL_ONE_MINUS_SRC_ALPHA	Multiplies by the inverse of the source alpha component
GL_DST_ALPHA	Multiplies by the destination alpha
GL_ONE_MINUS_DST_ALPHA	Multiplies by the inverse of the destination alpha
GL_CONSTANT_COLOR	Multiplies by a constant color (set with `glBlendColor`)
GL_ONE_MINUS_CONSTANT_COLOR	Multiplies by the inverse of a constant color
GL_CONSTANT_ALPHA	Multiplies by the constant alpha
GL_ONE_MINUS_CONSTANT_ALPHA	Multiplies by the inverse of a constant alpha
GL_SRC_ALPHA_SATURATE	Specifies the minimum of the source alpha and one minus the source alpha

The blending equation is set with the `glBlendEquation` function, which takes one of a number of potential blending equation constants. The default is `GL_ADD`, which simply adds the source and destination colors together (after being multiplied by the blend factors). See Table 12-4 for a complete list of the blend equation constants.

Table 12-4. *Blending Equation Constants*

Blend Equation Constant	Explanation
GL_FUNC_ADD	Adds the source and destination colors
GL_FUNC_SUBTRACT	Subtracts the destination from the source color

Blend Equation Constant	Explanation
GL_FUNC_REVERSE_SUBTRACT	Subtracts the *source* from the destination color
GL_MIN	Calculates the minimum (darkest) of the source and destination colors
GL_MAX	Calculates the maximum (brightest) of the source and destination colors
GL_LOGIC_OP	Combines the source and destination colors with a *logic operation* (see the OpenGL documentation for information on logic operations)

Another OpenGL function involved in blending is glBlendColor, which sets a constant color that is used in some of the blending factors. This function takes the red, green, blue, and alpha components to be used as the constant color. For instance, glBlendColor(1.0, 0.0, 0.0, 0.5) would set a constant color of 50 percent translucent red.

The steps for enabling blending in your game are as follows:

1. Enable blending with a call to glEnable(GL_BLEND).

2. Call the glBlendFunc function to set the blending factors. See Table 12-3 for a complete list of blending factors.

3. Call the glBlendEquation function to set the blending equation. See Table 12-4 for a complete list of the blend equations.

4. If you have used one of the blending factors that refer to a constant color, you will also need to call the glBlendColor function, which takes the red, green, blue, and alpha color components as parameters.

OpenGL supports a great number of potential blending effects through the various blending options. The following sections cover some effects commonly used in games and the blend options needed to create them.

Alpha Blending

One of the most commonly used blending effects is alpha blending, which uses the alpha channel in an image to control the opacity of the pixels. Alpha blending can be used to create texture with holes or irregular edges, such as a torn flag.

We can set alpha blending with the following function calls:

```
glBlendFunc(GL_SRC_ALPHA, GL_ONE_MINUS_SRC_ALPHA)
glBlendEquation(GL_FUNC_ADD)
```

This tells OpenGL to multiply the source color with the source alpha, and multiply the destination color with 1.0 minus the source alpha. It then combines the two colors with the GL_FUNC_ADD blend equation—which simply adds them together to produce the final color that is written to the screen. The effect is to *interpolate* the colors based on the alpha component of the source color, and is equivalent to the alpha_blend function in Listing 12-2.

Listing 12-2. *Python Alpha Blend Function*

```
def alpha_blend(src, dst):
    return src * src.a + dst * (1.0–src.a)
```

This kind of alpha blending is useful for creating detail in places where many small polygons would otherwise be required. For instance, a tuft of weeds in an off-road racing game could be created with a single texture with translucent areas rather than a detailed model.

Blending can also be done with the constant alpha component instead of using the alpha channel in the textures. This is useful for varying the opacity of textures as a whole rather than for individual texels. Constant alpha blending can be used to render anything from windows to force fields. The following calls would make textures 50 percent transparent—or 50 percent opaque, if you prefer.

```
glBlendColor(1.0, 1.0, 1.0, 0.5)
glBlendFactor(GL_CONSTANT_ALPHA, GL_ONE_MINUS_CONSTANT_ALPHA)
glBlendEquation(GL_ADD)
```

Additive Blending

Another useful blending technique is *additive* blending, which is similar to basic alpha blending, with the exception that source color is added directly to the destination so that it brightens the underlying image. This creates a glowing effect, which is why additive blending is often used to render flame, electricity, or similar crowd-pleasing special effects. The following function calls select additive blending:

```
glBlendFunc(GL_SRC_ALPHA, GL_ONE)
glBlendEquation(GL_FUNC_ADD)
```

The only difference between this and regular alpha blending is that the destination blend factor is set to GL_ONE, which multiplies the color by 1.0—in effect, not changing it at all. Additive blending is equivalent to the additive_blend function in Listing 12-3.

Listing 12-3. *Python Additive Blend Function*

```
def additive_blend(src, dst):
    return src * src.a + dst
```

Subtractive Blending

The reverse of additive blending is *subtractive* blending, where the source color is subtracted from the underlying image, making it darker. The following function calls set the blend options for subtractive blending:

```
glBlendFunc(GL_SRC_ALPHA, GL_ONE)
glBlendEquation(GL_FUNC_REVERSE_SUBTRACT)
```

The blend equation is set to GL_FUNC_REVERSE_SUBTRACT rather than GL_FUNC_SUBTRACT because we want to subtract the source from the destination and not the other way around.

There is no reverse version of GL_ADD because A+B is always the same as B+A (the same is not true for subtraction; A–B is not always the same as B–A).

Subtractive blending is great for rendering smoke because several layers result in solid black. The subtractive_blend function in Listing 12-4 is the Python equivalent of subtractive blending.

Listing 12-4. *Python Subtractive Blend Function*

```
def subtractive_blend(src, dst):
    return dst—src * src.a
```

Seeing Blending in Action

Let's write some code to help us visualize some commonly used blending effects. When you execute Listing 12-5, you will see a background image and another smaller image—of our friend fugu—that can be moved around with the mouse. The fugu image contains alpha information, but because no blending options have been set, you will see parts of the image that would normally be invisible. If you hit the 1 key on your keyboard, it will enable alpha blending and the background pixels of the fugu image will become invisible (see Figure 12-1). Pressing 2 selects additive blending, which will give the fugu a ghostly glow, and pressing 3 selects subtractive blending, which creates a dark shadow fugu.

Try changing the constants in the glBlendFunc and glBlendEquation to produce some more interesting effects. If there is a particular effect you want to implement that isn't covered here, you will likely be able to find the parameters on the Web.

 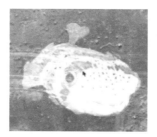 

Alpha blending   Additive blending   Subtractive blending

Figure 12-1. *Blending effects*

Listing 12-5. *Demonstrating Blending Effects (blenddemo.py)*

```
SCREEN_SIZE = (800, 600)

from OpenGL.GL import *
from OpenGL.GLU import *
```

```python
import pygame
from pygame.locals import *


def resize(width, height):

    glViewport(0, 0, width, height)
    glMatrixMode(GL_PROJECTION)
    glLoadIdentity()
    gluPerspective(45.0, float(width)/height, .1, 1000.)
    glMatrixMode(GL_MODELVIEW)
    glLoadIdentity()


def init():

    glEnable(GL_TEXTURE_2D)
    glEnable(GL_BLEND)
    glClearColor(1.0, 1.0, 1.0, 0.0)


def upload_texture(filename, use_alpha=False):

    # Read an image file and upload a texture
    if use_alpha:
        format, gl_format, bits_per_pixel = 'RGBA', GL_RGBA, 4
    else:
        format, gl_format, bits_per_pixel = 'RGB', GL_RGB, 3

    # Load texture and extract the raw data
    img_surface = pygame.image.load(filename)
    data = pygame.image.tostring(img_surface, format, True)

    # Generate and bind a texture id
    texture_id = glGenTextures(1)
    glBindTexture(GL_TEXTURE_2D, texture_id)

    # Set texture parameters and alignment
    glTexParameteri( GL_TEXTURE_2D, GL_TEXTURE_MAG_FILTER, GL_LINEAR )
    glTexParameteri( GL_TEXTURE_2D, GL_TEXTURE_MIN_FILTER, GL_LINEAR )
    glPixelStorei(GL_UNPACK_ALIGNMENT, 1)
```

```python
    # Upload texture data
    width, height =  img_surface.get_rect().size
    glTexImage2D(    GL_TEXTURE_2D,
                     0,
                     bits_per_pixel,
                     width,
                     height,
                     0,
                     gl_format,
                     GL_UNSIGNED_BYTE,
                     data )

    # Return the texture id, so we can use glBindTexture
    return texture_id


def draw_quad(x, y, z, w, h):

    # Send four vertices to draw a quad
    glBegin(GL_QUADS)

    glTexCoord2f(0, 0)
    glVertex3f(x-w/2, y-h/2, z)

    glTexCoord2f(1, 0)
    glVertex3f(x+w/2, y-h/2, z)

    glTexCoord2f(1, 1)
    glVertex3f(x+w/2, y+h/2, z)

    glTexCoord2f(0, 1)
    glVertex3f(x-w/2, y+h/2, z)

    glEnd()


def run():

    pygame.init()
    screen = pygame.display.set_mode(SCREEN_SIZE, HWSURFACE|OPENGL|DOUBLEBUF)
```

```
    resize(*SCREEN_SIZE)
    init()

    # Upload the background and fugu texture
    background_tex = upload_texture('background.png')
    fugu_tex = upload_texture('fugu.png', True)

    while True:

        for event in pygame.event.get():
            if event.type == QUIT:
                return
            if event.type == KEYDOWN:
                if event.key == K_1:
                    # Simple alpha blending
                    glBlendFunc(GL_SRC_ALPHA, GL_ONE_MINUS_SRC_ALPHA)
                    glBlendEquation(GL_FUNC_ADD)
                elif event.key == K_2:
                    # Additive alpha blending
                    glBlendFunc(GL_SRC_ALPHA, GL_ONE)
                    glBlendEquation(GL_FUNC_ADD)
                elif event.key == K_3:
                    # Subtractive blending
                    glBlendFunc(GL_SRC_ALPHA, GL_ONE)
                    glBlendEquation(GL_FUNC_REVERSE_SUBTRACT)

        glClear(GL_COLOR_BUFFER_BIT | GL_DEPTH_BUFFER_BIT)

        # Draw the background
        glBindTexture(GL_TEXTURE_2D, background_tex)

        # Draw the background texture to the screen
        glDisable(GL_BLEND)
        draw_quad(0, 0, -SCREEN_SIZE[1], 600, 600)
        glEnable(GL_BLEND)

        # Draw a texture at the mouse position
        glBindTexture(GL_TEXTURE_2D, fugu_tex)
        x, y = pygame.mouse.get_pos()
        x -= SCREEN_SIZE[0]/2
        y -= SCREEN_SIZE[1]/2
        draw_quad(x, -y, -SCREEN_SIZE[1], 256, 256)

        pygame.display.flip()
```

```
    # Free the textures we used
    glDeleteTextures(background_tex)
    glDeleteTextures(fugu_tex)

if __name__ == "__main__":
    run()
```

Blending Issues

There are a few potential problems with blending if you use it heavily in a scene. When you render a blended polygon, it will still write information to the depth buffer, which OpenGL uses to keep background objects from overlapping foreground objects. The problem with this is that once a translucent polygon has been drawn, no more polygons can be drawn behind it. A good solution is to draw all the opaque polygons, then draw the translucent polygons from back to front so that the farthest away polygon is drawn first.

Blended polygons also tend to take longer to render than opaque polygons, so if you find that your scene is rendering slowly, try reducing the number of translucent polygons.

Understanding Fog

Fog is an OpenGL feature that can be used to simulate the effects of the atmosphere on rendered objects. When the fog feature is enabled, OpenGL will blend polygons toward a solid color over distance, so that as an object moves from the foreground to the background it gradually takes on the fog color until it becomes a solid silhouette. Fog was often used in older games to hide the fact that objects could not be drawn very far into the distance. Rather than scenery suddenly appearing from nowhere, it would blend in from the background color over a few frames. Modern games suffer less from this problem because they can render scenery much farther into the distance, but fog is still often used to subtly blend in faraway objects as they come into range of the camera.

Fog is also useful for creating visual effects in its own right; the most obvious use is to simulate real fog, but you can also use the feature to enhance a gloomy indoor scene by fogging to black or to simulate red haze on Mars.

Fog Parameters

Call glEnable(GL_FOG) to have OpenGL apply fog to all polygons that are rendered. There are a number of fog parameters you can set with the glFog range of functions, which take a constant for the value you want to set followed by the value itself.

The color of the fog can be set with a call to glFogfv with the GL_FOG_COLOR constant, followed by the color you want to use. For example, the following line sets the fog color to pure white (to simulate a snow blizzard, perhaps):

```
glFogfv(GL_FOG_COLOR, (1.0, 1.0, 1.0))
```

OpenGL has three different fog modes, which define how the fog varies over distance. These fog modes can be set with the glFogi function. For instance, the following line would set the fog to use GL_LINEAR mode:

```
glFogi(GL_FOG_MODE, GL_LINEAR)
```

The GL_LINEAR fog mode is most often used to mask the effect of distance scenery coming into view, because the start and end points can be set independently and the fog will fade in between them. For instance, if you have a racing game that can render 1,000 units into the distance, and you want distance track and trees to fade in over the final unit, you set the following fog parameters:

```
glFogi(GL_FOG_MODE, GL_LINEAR)
glFogf(GL_FOG_START, 999.0)
glFogf(GL_FOG_END, 1000.0)
```

The GL_FOG_START and GL_FOG_END parameters mark the distance from the camera where the fog should begin and end.

The other potential values for the GL_FOG_MODE parameters are GL_EXP and GL_EXP2. Both produce a more natural-looking fog and are better for simulating real fog or haze. The GL_EXP mode blends the fog in quickly for objects near the camera but more slowly for objects that are farther away. The GL_EXP2 is similar but starts off with less fog color in the foreground.

Both GL_EXP and GL_EXP2 use a single *density* value rather than a value for the start and stop point. Density can be set with the GL_FOG_DENSITY parameter, which is a value between 0.0 and 1.0—higher values create thicker fog. The following calls would create a convincing Martian haze with red GL_EXP2 fog of density of 0.2:

```
glFogfv(GL_FOG_COLOR, (1.0, 0.7, 0.7))
glFogi(GL_FOG_MODE, GL_EXP2)
glFogf(GL_FOG_DENSITY, 0.2)
```

Seeing Fog in Action

Rather than write an entire script to test fog, let's modify the spinning tank from the previous chapter (Listing 11-8). We will start by adding a few lines to the init function to enable fog and set the fog parameters. The following lines create a simple linear fog that fades to white:

```
glEnable(GL_FOG)
glFogfv(GL_FOG_COLOR, (1.0, 1.0, 1.0))
glFogi(GL_FOG_MODE, GL_LINEAR)
glFogf(GL_FOG_START, 1.5)
glFogf(GL_FOG_END, 3.5)
```

If you run the modified Listing 11-8 now, you will see something like Figure 12-2. The fog starts at 1.5 units from the camera and ends at 3.5 units from the camera, which makes part of the tank completely obscured by fog. It is not a very useful fog since it would obscure anything that isn't very close to the camera, but it does demonstrate the effect well.

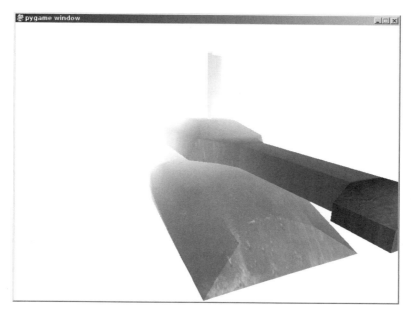

Figure 12-2. *A heavily fogged tank*

Another useful modification to the spinning tank demo is the ability to move the tank relative to the camera so that we can see how the fog changes over distance. Replace the call to glTranslate in the run function with the following lines, to move the tank with the mouse:

```
tank_distance = pygame.mouse.get_pos()[1] / 50.0
glTranslatef(0.0, -1.5, -tank_distance)
```

Now when you run the tank demo, you can control the tank's distance from the camera by moving the mouse up and down. Try replacing the calls to glFogi that we added to the init function with the settings for Martian haze, or experiment with your own values to come up with new effects. You might also want to change the clear color to be similar to the fog color so that a heavily fogged tank disappears completely into the background.

Rendering the Backdrop

A tank game would likely be set in an outdoors environment, possibly a desolate, postapocalyptic wasteland with mountains in the far distance. Naturally we would want to render the background scenery with as much detail as possible to provide a good backdrop for the game action, but even if we could model every mountain it would still be too slow to render 3D visuals all the way to the horizon. This is a common problem with any game where the player can potentially see the horizon (even games set indoors would be affected if they have a window).

Skyboxes

A common solution to the problem of rendering distant scenery is the *skybox,* which is simply a textured cube with scenery on each side. The front, back, left, and right sides of the cube show a view toward the horizon. The top of the cube is an image of the sky and the bottom of the cube is the ground. When the skybox is drawn around the camera, the player is surrounded on all sides with images of distance scenery, which creates a convincing illusion of being there.

Creating Skyboxes

A skybox is a model of a cube, and can be created in the modeler software of your choice—all 3D applications I have used offer the option of creating a cube primitive. The skybox should be created around the origin, so that the center of the cube is at (0, 0, 0). Each side of the cube should be assigned one of the six scenery textures from the skybox.

■**Note** You may have to *flip* the normals on the faces of the cube, which makes them point inward rather than outward. The reason for this is that the cube will be viewed from the inside rather than the outside, and you want the polygons to be facing the camera.

Generating the skybox textures may require a little more effort because each texture must seamlessly align with the four other textures it shares an edge with. If you are artistically inclined, you may be able to draw or paint these textures, but it is probably easier to use 3D modeling software to render six views of a scene for each face of the skybox. An excellent choice for rendering skyboxes is Terragen (`www.planetside.co.uk/terragen/`), which creates remarkably realistic-looking images of virtual landscapes. I used Terragen to create the skycube textures in Figure 12-3 that we will be using in the skybox sample code.

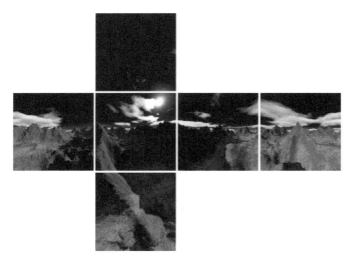

Figure 12-3. *The texture of a skybox*

Rendering Skyboxes

Rendering the skybox should be the first thing done in a new frame, and negates the need to clear the color buffer (although you will still need to clear the depth buffer).

Since a skybox is just a model of a cube, it can be stored as any other model, but there are a few additional steps required prior to rendering:

1. Set the wrap mode of all the textures in the skybox to GL_CLAMP_TO_EDGE. This is necessary to avoid seams in the skybox, where the cube faces meet. See the previous chapter for more information on wrapping modes. This step needs to be done only once.

2. Set the position of the skybox to be the same as the camera (i.e., the player). This is because the skybox represents very distant scenery that can never be reached by the player.

3. Disable lighting with glDisable(GL_LIGHTING). We don't need to use OpenGL's lighting features because the textures of the skybox have effectively been prelit. With lighting disabled, OpenGL will render the textures with the original brightness levels.

4. Disable the depth buffer with glDepthMask(False). Normally if the player was inside a cube he would not be able to see anything outside of the cube, which is obviously not want we want. Setting the *depth mask* to False with glDepthMask(False) tells OpenGL to ignore the depth information in the skybox, so that other models will be rendered on top of it.

Once the skybox has been rendered, be sure to reenable lighting and the depth mask, or the other models in the scene may not render correctly. The following two lines should follow the call to render the skybox:

```
glEnable(GL_LIGHTING)
glDepthMask(True)
```

Seeing Skyboxes in Action

Let's write code to render a skybox. Listing 12-6 uses the Model3D class from the previous chapter to load a skybox model and its associated textures. When you run it, you will see a scenic view of mountains, and if you adjust the viewpoint with the mouse you will be able to see the landscape from any direction.

Listing 12-6. *Rendering a Skybox (skybox.py)*

```
SCREEN_SIZE = (800, 600)

from OpenGL.GL import *
from OpenGL.GLU import *

import pygame
from pygame.locals import *
```

```python
# Import the Model3D class
import model3d

def resize(width, height):

    glViewport(0, 0, width, height)
    glMatrixMode(GL_PROJECTION)
    glLoadIdentity()
    gluPerspective(60.0, float(width)/height, .1, 1000.)
    glMatrixMode(GL_MODELVIEW)
    glLoadIdentity()


def init():

    # Enable the GL features we will be using
    glEnable(GL_LIGHTING)
    glEnable(GL_DEPTH_TEST)
    glEnable(GL_LIGHTING)
    glEnable(GL_TEXTURE_2D)
    glShadeModel(GL_SMOOTH)

    # Enable light 1 and set position
    glEnable(GL_LIGHT0)
    glLight(GL_LIGHT0, GL_POSITION,  (0, .5, 1, 0))


def run():

    pygame.init()
    screen = pygame.display.set_mode(SCREEN_SIZE, FULLSCREEN | HWSURFACE | ➥
OPENGL | DOUBLEBUF)

    resize(*SCREEN_SIZE)
    init()

    # Read the skybox model
    sky_box = model3d.Model3D()
    sky_box.read_obj('tanksky/skybox.obj')
```

```
# Set the wraping mode of all textures in the skybox to GL_CLAMP_TO_EDGE
for material in sky_box.materials.itervalues():

    glBindTexture(GL_TEXTURE_2D, material.texture)
    glTexParameteri(GL_TEXTURE_2D, GL_TEXTURE_WRAP_S, GL_CLAMP_TO_EDGE)
    glTexParameteri(GL_TEXTURE_2D, GL_TEXTURE_WRAP_T, GL_CLAMP_TO_EDGE)


# Used to rotate the world
mouse_x = 0.0
mouse_y = 0.0

#Don't display the mouse cursor
pygame.mouse.set_visible(False)

while True:

    for event in pygame.event.get():
        if event.type == QUIT:
            return
        if event.type == KEYDOWN:
            return

    # We don't need to clear the color buffer (GL_COLOR_BUFFER_BIT)
    # because the skybox covers the entire screen
    glClear(GL_DEPTH_BUFFER_BIT)

    glLoadIdentity()

    mouse_rel_x, mouse_rel_y = pygame.mouse.get_rel()
    mouse_x += float(mouse_rel_x) / 5.0
    mouse_y += float(mouse_rel_y) / 5.0

    # Rotate around the x and y axes to create a mouse-look camera
    glRotatef(mouse_y, 1, 0, 0)
    glRotatef(mouse_x, 0, 1, 0)

    # Disable lighting and depth test
    glDisable(GL_LIGHTING)
    glDepthMask(False)
```

```
        # Draw the skybox
        sky_box.draw_quick()

        # Reenable lighting and depth test before we redraw the world
        glEnable(GL_LIGHTING)
        glDepthMask(True)

        # Here is where we would draw the rest of the world in a game

        pygame.display.flip()

if __name__ == "__main__":
    run()
```

Skybox Enhancements

Although a skybox creates a convincing illusion of distance scenery, there are enhancements that can be used to add some more visual flare to the backdrop. One of the downsides of the skybox technique is that it doesn't change over time because the image has been prerendered. Animating parts of the skybox, or adding atmospheric effects on top of it, can add a little extra realism. For example, making the sun shimmer a little or rendering lightning in the distance can enhance a skybox. It is also possible to layer translucent skyboxes and animate one or more of them. For instance, there could be a skybox for distant mountains and another for clouds. Rotating the cloud skybox independently would create realistic-looking weather effects.

Skyboxes aren't the only method of rendering a backdrop in a game; a *skydome* is a similar technique that uses a sphere, or hemisphere, to display distant scenery. A dome may be a more obvious choice than a cube because the real sky is spherical in nature, but a sphere is not quite as easy to texture as a cube. A cylinder is another alternative, if the player will never look directly up.

Where to Go for Help

One of the joys of games programming is that it throws up many interesting problems that give a real sense of accomplishment when you finally solve them. Every time you figure out how to make something work, or fix a mistake you made, your game gets a little closer to how you imagined it. So facing problems and fixing bugs are part of the process of developing a game and not something to be afraid of. More often than not, all it takes is a short break from programming and a little bit of thought for the answer to come to you. Occasionally, though, even experienced game developers face problems they can't find the solution to. It's this point where you should seek assistance.

Chances are that another programmer has faced the same issue and has documented it on the Web, which is why the Internet is the programmer's best debugger tool. Try searching Google, or another search engine, for keywords that relate to the problem you are facing. If you don't come up with the answer, you could post a message about your problem to a mailing list or newsgroups. If the problem is Python related, the comp.lang.python newsgroup will probably be the best place to ask. Otherwise, if the problem is about Pygame, the Pygame mailing list would be a good place to ask. See `www.pygame.org/wiki/info` for more information on the Pygame mailing list.

Summary

In this chapter, we covered OpenGL's lighting features in some detail. OpenGL lighting is very powerful and can greatly enhance the realism of your games. Combinations of light and material parameters will help you create the kind of mood you are looking for in your game, whether it is a bright and cheerful cartoon world or a nightmarish landscape with unspeakable monsters lurking around every corner.

Blending is the key to creating a multitude of special effects but can also be used to simply render translucent objects. We covered only a few of the effects that can be created with OpenGL's blending features; combining blend factors and equations can create many more.

Fog is another OpenGL feature that can enhance your game by simulating atmospheric effects, or disguise the effects of distance scenery *popping in* as it comes into range of the camera. Fog is easy to add to a scene because it only takes a few lines to enable and set the parameters—so you can experiment with fog without changing your render code.

We also discussed skyboxes, which are a great way of adding a backdrop to your game. Skyboxes may be old technology, but they are still used in modern games—including cutting-edge console titles.

Game development is a constantly expanding field, which makes it a fascinating hobby or profession. Most developers—whether they are novices or industry veterans—are extremely enthusiastic about what they do, and are happy to share knowledge and code with others. Once you have built a game, you should consider submitting it to the Pygame web site (`www.pygame.org`) to share it with the Pygame community. You can also download projects from other programmers, and perhaps participate in one of the Pyweek challenges (`www.pyweek.org`), where programmers compete to produce the best game they can in a week.

I hope you enjoyed reading this book. If you have any questions about any of the topics we covered, I would be happy to answer them. You can find my contact details on my web site: `www.willmcgugan.com`.

Game Object Reference

This appendix documents some of the most fundamental classes in the Game Objects library that provide a toolbox for creating 2D and 3D games. For up-to-date information regarding Game Objects, see www.willmcgugan.com/game-objects/.

Importing

The Game Objects library consists of a number of submodules that can be imported separately. Generally it is best to import only the classes you need using the from <module> import <object> syntax. For example, this line imports the Color class:

```
from gameobjects.color import Color
```

Occasionally there are helper functions from the submodules that you may also want to use. In this case you can use from <module> import * to import everything into your namespace. For example, the following line will import everything in the gameobjects.vector3 class:

```
from gameobjects.vector3 import *
```

Contributing

The Game Objects library is an open source project, which means that any programmer may contribute. You are encouraged to submit any bug fixes you find, or classes that you think may be useful additions to the library.

gameobjects.color.Color

Color objects represent a color with an alpha value. The components are stored in the range zero to one, as used by OpenGL, but you can convert to integer RGBA format with the rgba8 attribute or as_tuple method. Color objects support the basic mathematical operators; multiply, divide, add, and subtract. You can also multiply or divide colors by a scalar value (e.g., an integer or float), but adding or subtracting a scalar will throw a TypeError exception.

Constructor

The gameobjects.color constructor takes the red, green, and blue components and an optional alpha component, in the range zero to one. The components can also be given as a sequence of three or four values. If a color is constructed without any parameters, it will default to black.

Attributes

The components can be retrieved and set with the r, g, b, and a attributes (see Table A-1). The rgba8 and rgb8 (read-only) attributes can be used to retrieve the component as a tuple of integers in the 0 to 255 range.

Table A-1. *gameobjects.color Attributes*

Attribute	Purpose
r	Red component in the zero to one range
g	Green component in the zero to one range
b	Blue component in the zero to one range
a	Alpha component in the zero to one range
rgba8	Tuple of (red, green, blue, alpha) components, in the 0 to 255 range (compatible with Pygame's draw functions)
rgb8	Tuple of (red, green, blue) components, in the 0 to 255 range

Methods

Color objects support the methods shown in Table A-2.

Table A-2. *Color Methods*

Method Name	Explanation
copy()	Returns a copy of the color
as_tuple()	Returns a copy of the color as a tuple of its components
as_tuple_rgb()	Returns a copy of the color as a tuple of its red, green, and blue components
as_tuple_rgba()	Identical to as_tuple
as_html()	Returns a string containing the color in HTML format
saturate()	Forces all components to be in the range zero to one
get_saturate()	Returns a copy of the color where all the components have been saturated to the range 0–1
invert()	Inverts the color (sets each component to one minus itself)
get_inverse()	Returns an inverted copy of the color
mul_alpha()	Multiplies the red, green, and blue components by the alpha component

Class Methods

The gameobjects.color class contains a number of class methods that offer alternative ways of creating new color objects (see Table A-3).

Table A-3. *Color Class Methods*

Method Name	Explanation
black()	Returns a color object representing black.
white()	Returns a color object representing full white.
from_rgba8(r, g, b, a)	Creates a color object from color components in the range 0–255.
from_html(col_str)	Creates a color object from a color encoded in HTML format.
gray (level)	Creates a gray color object; level is a value in the zero to one range.
from_palette(color_name)	Creates a named color from an internal palette, for example, red, ivory, aquamarine, etc. See the online documentation for a full list.

gameobjects.matrix44.Matrix44

The Matrix44 class stores a 4 × 4 matrix representing a 3D transform.

Constructor

If no parameters are given, the matrix is initialized to identity. If one parameter is given, it should be a sequence (e.g., a list) with the 16 components of the matrix. If four parameters are given, they should be four sequences of up to four values. Missing values in each row are padded out with values from the identity matrix (so you can use Vector3s or tuples of three values).

Attributes

The attributes of a matrix44 object (see Table A-4) represent the rows of the matrix. You can only retrieve or set the contents of these attributes as a whole—that is, you can't set parts of the row individually. If you need to access the components of the matrix as individual values, use the index ([ ]) operator of the matrix44 object.

Table A-4. *gameobjects.matrix44.Matrix44 Attributes*

Attribute	Explanation
x_axis	The x axis of the matrix
right	Alias for the x axis
y_axis	The y axis of the matrix
up	Alias for the y axis
z_axis	The z axis of the matrix

Attribute	Explanation
forward	Alias for the z axis
translate	The translation part of the matrix

Methods

Matrix objects contain a large number of methods to manipulate the components of the matrix and use it to transform points (see Table A-5).

Table A-5. *Matrix44 Attributes*

Method Name	Explanation
to_opengl()	Returns a list of the matrix components, compatible with OpenGL.
set(row1, row2, row3, row4)	Sets the four rows of the matrix.
get_row(row_no)	Retrieves a row of the matrix as a tuple of four values; row_no is the row index (0, 1, 2, or 3).
fast_mul(rhs)	Multiplies the matrix by another matrix. This is a little quicker than the *= operator, but can only be used with matrices that contain only rotate, scale, or translation.
copy()	Returns a copy of this matrix.
components()	Returns an iterator of the 16 matrix components.
transposed_components()	Returns an iterator of the 16 matrix components, in transposed order.
rows()	Returns an iterator of the matrix rows as tuples of four values.
columns()	Returns an iterator of the matrix columns as tuples of four values.
get_row_vec3(row_no)	Retrieves a row as a Vector3 object.
get_column(col_no)	Retrieves a column as a tuple of four values.
set_row(row_no, row)	Sets the contents of a row; row_no is the index of the row to set, and row is a sequence of up to four values to set it to.
set_column(col_no, col)	Sets the contents of a column; col_no is the index of the column and row is a sequence of up to four values to set it to.
transform_vec3(v)	Transforms a Vector3 object (v) with this matrix, and returns the result as another Vector3.
transform(v)	Transforms a vector and returns the result as a tuple.
transform_sequence(points)	Transforms a sequence of points and returns the result as a list of tuples.

Method Name	Explanation
`rotate(v)`	Transforms a point with the matrix, but ignores the translation part of the matrix.
`transpose()`	Swaps the rows and columns of the matrix.
`get_transpose()`	Returns a transposed copy of the matrix.
`get_inverse_rot_trans()`	Returns the inverse of a matrix with only rotation and translation.
`get_inverse()`	Returns the inverse of this matrix.
`invert()`	Inverts this matrix (in place).
`move(forward, right, up)`	Adds offsets to the translation based on its heading. The parameters are all optional and should be sequences of three values.

Class Methods

The `Matrix44` class contains a number of class methods to create basic transform matrices (see Table A-6).

Table A-6. *Matrix44 Class Methods*

Class Method Name	Explanation
`from_iter(iterable)`	Creates a matrix from an iterable (anything that can work in a for loop) of 16 values.
`clone(m)`	Creates a copy of matrix `m`.
`identity()`	Creates an identity matrix.
`scale(x, y, z)`	Creates a scale matrix. If the y and z scales are omitted, a uniform scale matrix of x is returned.
`translation(x, y, z)`	Creates a translation matrix to (x, y, z).
`x_rotation(angle)`	Creates a rotation matrix of `angle` radians about the x axis.
`y_rotation(angle)`	Creates a rotation matrix of `angle` radians about the y axis.
`z_rotation(angle)`	Creates a rotation matrix of `angle` radians about the z axis.
`rotation_about_axis(axis, angle)`	Creates a rotation matrix about an axis. The `axis` parameter can be any sequence of three values; the `angle` parameter should be in radians.
`xyz_rotation(x, y, z)`	Creates a matrix that has the combined effect of rotating around all three axes.

gameobjects.vector2.Vector2

The Vector2 class represents a two-dimensional vector and can be used to store headings and positions in a 2D game. The components of a Vector2 object can be accessed via the x and y attributes, or through the index operator ([ ]). Vector2 objects support the mathematical operators.

Constructor

The constructor for Vector2 objects takes either two values for the x and y components of the vector, or a sequence of two values. If no parameters are given, the vector will default to (0, 0).

Attributes

Table A-7 lists the attributes for Vector2 objects.

Table A-7. *Vector2 Attributes*

Attribute	Explanation
x	The x component of the vector.
y	The y component of the vector.
length	The length of the vector. This attribute can also be set to change the length of the vector.

Methods

Table A-8 lists the methods for Vector2 objects.

Table A-8. *Vector2 Methods*

Method Name	Explanation
copy()	Returns a copy of this vector.
get_length()	Returns the length of this vector.
get_magnitude()	Returns the magnitude (same as length) of this vector.
normalize()	Normalizes this vector, so that it has a length of 1. Also returns the vector.
get_normalized()	Returns a normalized copy of the vector.
get_distance_to()	Returns the distance from this vector to a point.

Class Methods

The Vector2 class has a number of methods to construct new Vector2 objects (see Table A-9).

Table A-9. *Vector2 Class Methods*

Class Method Name	Explanation
from_iter(iterable)	Creates a Vector2 object from an iterable of values.
from_points(p1, p2)	Creates a Vector2 object from two points.

gameobjects.vector3.Vector3

The Vector3 class represents a 3D vector, which can be used to store headings and position in three-dimensional space. Vector3 objects are very similar to Vector2 objects but contain an extra attribute, z.

Constructor

The constructor for Vector3 objects takes either three values for the x, y, and z components of the vector, or a sequence of three values. If no parameters are given, the vector will default to (0, 0, 0).

Attributes

Table A-10 lists the attributes for Vector3 objects.

Table A-10. *Vector2 Attributes*

Attribute	Explanation
x	The x component of the vector.
y	The y component of the vector.
z	The z component of the vector.
length	The length of the vector. This attribute can also be set to change the length of the vector.

Methods

Table A-11 lists the methods for Vector3 objects.

Table A-11. *Vector3 Methods*

Method Name	Explanation
set(x, y, z)	Sets the components of the vector to the float values.
as_tuple()	Returns the vector as a tuple of three values.
get_length()	Retrieves the length of the vector.
get_magnitude()	Retrieves the magnitude (same as length) of the vector.
set_length()	Sets the length of the vector.
get_distance_to(p)	Retrieves the distance from this vector to a point.
normalize()	Normalizes the vector, so that it has a length of 1. Also returns the vector.
get_normalized()	Returns a normalized copy of the vector.
dot(other)	Returns the dot-product of this vector with another vector.
cross(other)	Returns the cross-product of this vector with another vector.

Class Methods

Table A-12 lists the class methods that can be used to create new Vector3 objects.

Table A-12. *Vector3 Class Methods*

Class Method Name	Explanation
from_points(p1, p2)	Creates a Vector3 object between two points.
from_iter(iterable)	Creates a Vector3 object from an iterable of three values.

APPENDIX B

■■■

Packaging Your Game

If you have gone to the effort of writing a game with Pygame, you will likely want to share your masterpiece with others. The simplest way to distribute your game is to bundle your Python code and data as a compressed archive file, such as ZIP, TAR, or GZIP, and upload it to your web site or send it via e-mail. The problem with this approach is that Python and any external modules you use must be installed before your game can be played, which makes code distributions suitable only for other Python programmers. To distribute your game to a wider, nontechnical audience, you will need to package your game in a familiar way for your chosen platform(s). Microsoft Windows users, for instance, expect executable installer files that when double-clicked copy the game files to the Program Files directory and create icons in the Start menu and possibly the Desktop.

This appendix covers how to package your game into a format that will allow nontechnical users to install and play it.

Creating Windows Packages

Installing a game on Windows generally involves double-clicking an EXE file, which launches an installer application. The installer is typically in the form of a *wizard* with several pages that display the license agreement and ask the user where to copy the game files and what icons it should install. A Finish button on the final page begins copying the files and creating icons.

There are two steps required to create a user-friendly installer for your Pygame game on the Windows platform:

1. Use py2exe, or a similar solution, to turn your main Python file into an executable that will run without Python installed.

2. Use installer builder software to create a single EXE file that contains your game's files.

Creating the installer will make your game accessible to the widest audience, and is essential if your game is intended to be commercial. You can skip the second step if your intended audience is technical enough to uncompress a ZIP file and double-click an EXE file.

Using py2exe

To turn a Python file into an executable file, you can use py2exe, which is itself a Python module. py2exe isn't part of Python's standard library, but it can easily be installed with the following command:

```
easy_install py2exe
```

Before creating an executable for your Python code, you need to write setup.py, which contains information about your project and launches py2exe. Let's create a setup.py (Listing B-1) for the Ant state machine listing in Chapter 7.

Listing B-1. *Creating an Executable Python Project (setup.py)*

```
from distutils.core import setup
import py2exe

setup(
    windows = [{"script":"antsstatemachine.py"}],
    data_files = [ (".", ["ant.png", "leaf.png", "spider.png"]) ]
    )
```

The first line imports a function from distutils.core, which is part of the Python standard library and is used to distribute Python modules. The next line imports py2exe, which adds the ability to produce Windows executable files with distutils.

The call to setup contains the information about our project; the windows parameter tells py2exe which Python files to turn into executables, and the data_files parameter tells py2exe about any additional noncode files that are needed by the project—in this case, three image files. For more details on these and other parameters to setup, see the py2exe documentation online (www.py2exe.org/).

The setup.py script should be run with the following command:

```
python setup.py py2exe
```

This will search for and copy all the files used by the script to a folder called dist. Inside dist will be a antsstatemachine.exe file, which launches the Ant state machine simulation, as well as other files necessary for it to run without first installing Python. Sending the contents of this folder to another Windows user is enough to distribute your game, but for a professional touch you should also build an installer.

Building the Installer

After running our project through py2exe, we can now use any installer builder software to create installer executables. There are many to choose from; some are commercial (and very expensive), but there are some very good free options. We are going to use the free software, Inno Setup, which produces professional-looking installers. You can download Inno Setup from www.jrsoftware.org/isinfo.php.

Inno Setup *compiles* the executable from a script file (extension .iss), which is a simple text format that contains information about the files in your application and how you want the installer to look and behave. You can edit these ISS files by hand in any text editor, but I like to use ISTool (www.istool.org/default.aspx), which is an easy-to-use graphical front end for Inno Setup.

Listing B-2 is an ISS file produced with ISTool, which creates the installer executable setup.exe in a folder called Output.

Listing B-2. *Script for Inno Setup (ants.iss)*

```
[Setup]
SolidCompression=true
AppName=Ant State Machine
AppVerName=Ant State Machine 1.0
DefaultDirName={pf}\ant state machine
DefaultGroupName=ant state machine
ShowLanguageDialog=yes
[Files]
Source: dist\*.*; DestDir: {app}
[Icons]
Name: {group}\Launch Ants; Filename: {app}\antsstatemachine.exe; WorkingDir: {app}
Name: {group}\Uninstall Ants; Filename: {uninstallexe}
```

If you double-click setup.exe, it will display a simple wizard (Figure B-1) that will guide you through the installation process and then copy files and create icons in the Start menu. Listing B-2 is probably the simplest installer you can produce—see the Inno Setup documentation for more information on how to change the look and feel of the installer.

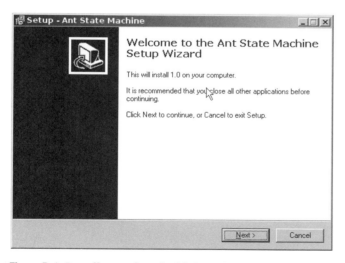

Figure B-1. *Installer produced with Inno Setup*

■Tip An alternative to Inno Setup is the Nullsoft Scriptable Install System (http://nsis.sourceforge.net/Main_Page), which is also free and produces high-quality installers. Another option is BitRock InstallBuilder (http://bitrock.com/products_installbuilder_overview.html), which is a commercial product that has a free license for open source projects.

Creating Packages for Linux

Creating packages for Linux is easier than for Windows, because most distributions come with Python installed by default and package managers can download the required version of Python, if it is not present. To create a Linux package, use the distutils module in the Python standard library, which can produce source archives (tarballs) or RPM files. It is also a good idea to include a description of the game's requirements, just in case the Linux distribution is unable to provide them.

For more information on the distutils module, see the documentation online at http://docs.python.org/dist/dist.html.

Creating Packages for the Mac

Packages for Mac operating systems can be created with py2app, which works in a similar way to py2exe on Windows. You can install py2app with the following command:

easy_install py2app

To build Mac applications from Python source code, you should create a setup.py file that contains information about your code and files and then call it with this command:

python setup.py py2app

This will create your stand-alone application in the dist folder. To wrap up your game for distribution, simply Control-click the application from the Finder and choose Create Archive.

For more information on the contents of setup.py and creating Mac applications, see the py2app documentation online at http://svn.pythonmac.org/py2app/py2app/trunk/doc/index.html.

Index

Find it faster at http://superindex.apress.com

Find it faster at http://superindex.apress.com

Find it faster at http://superindex.apress.com

Find it faster at http://superindex.apress.com

You Need the Companion eBook

Your purchase of this book entitles you to buy the companion PDF-version eBook for only $10. Take the weightless companion with you anywhere.

We believe this Apress title will prove so indispensable that you'll want to carry it with you everywhere, which is why we are offering the companion eBook (in PDF format) for $10 to customers who purchase this book now. Convenient and fully searchable, the PDF version of any content-rich, page-heavy Apress book makes a valuable addition to your programming library. You can easily find and copy code—or perform examples by quickly toggling between instructions and the application. Even simultaneously tackling a donut, diet soda, and complex code becomes simplified with hands-free eBooks!

Once you purchase your book, getting the $10 companion eBook is simple:

1. Visit www.apress.com/promo/tendollars/.

2. Complete a basic registration form to receive a randomly generated question about this title.

3. Answer the question correctly in 60 seconds, and you will receive a promotional code to redeem for the $10.00 eBook.

THE EXPERT'S VOICE™

2855 TELEGRAPH AVENUE | SUITE 600 | BERKELEY, CA 94705

Offer valid through 04/08.